THE SEARCH FOR A NEW CHINA

THE SEARCH
FOR A NEW CHINA

A Capsule History, Ideology, and Leadership

of the Chinese Communist Party,

1921–1974

with selected documents

by Winberg Chai

Capricorn Books, New York
G. P. PUTNAM'S SONS,
New York

To Carolyn, May-Lee and Jeffrey

PREFACE

My goal is simply to present a concise, readable, and yet thoroughly objective analysis of the People's Republic of China from the founding of the Chinese Communist Party in 1921 to the 1970's. I hope this small volume will enhance the knowledge of the general readership and college students and serve as a valuable introduction to the history of contemporary China.

In preparation of this work, my debts are many and they are acknowledged in the footnotes and suggested reading lists which have been included for those who may wish to make further studies on this subject. My special thanks are due to Walter C. Betkowski for his appreciation of the need of this work, and to my friend and colleague, T. K. Tong, for his constructive criticism and review of the draft manuscript.

My acknowledgments would indeed be incomplete if I did not record the personal debt I owe to my parents, Dr. and Mrs. Ch'u Chai, formerly of Nanking, Taipei, and now of New York City, for their love and devotion; and to my wife, Carolyn, and Fred Sawyer for reading and editing the manuscript.

WINBERG CHAI

New York City
December, 1974

CONTENTS

PREFACE   vii

INTRODUCTION   13

ONE: BIRTH OF THE CHINESE
COMMUNIST PARTY   23

   I   The Marxists   24
  II   Organizing the Party   29
 III   Party Programs   35
    Suggested Reading   38

TWO: THE COMMUNIST-NATIONALIST
COLLABORATION   39

   I   The First United Front   41
  II   The First Schism   44
 III   The Northern Expedition   49
    Suggested Reading   54

THREE: COMMUNIST PUTSCHISM   56

   I   Communist Uprisings   57
  II   The Li Li-san Line   60
 III   Factionalism   64
    Suggested Reading   71

Four: THE LONG MARCH   72
    I Growth of Soviet Bases   73
   II The Long March   77
  III The Rise of Mao Tse-tung   83
       Suggested Reading   88

Five: SINIFICATION OF COMMUNISM   89
    I The War Years   90
   II Yenan Legacy   93
  III The Birth of Maoism   97
       Suggested Reading   101

Six: THE PEOPLE'S REPUBLIC   103
    I Civil War Victories   105
   II Establishing the Government   110
  III Setting Priorities   114
       Suggested Reading   122

Seven: IDEOLOGY AND PERSONALITY   124
    I Ideological Campaigns   125
   II The Cultural Revolution   133
  III Personality and Factional Conflicts   138
       Suggested Reading   145

Eight: POST-CULTURAL REVOLUTION
POLITICS   147
    I The Rise and Fall of Lin Piao   148
   II The Uncertain Role of the Military   153
  III Politics of Political Succession   158
       Suggested Reading   164

DOCUMENTS ON POST-CULTURAL
REVOLUTION CHINA   167

APPENDIX 1:   The Constitution of the Communist
Party of China, April, 1969   169

APPENDIX 2:   Lin Piao: Report to the Ninth National
Congress of the Communist Party of China,
April, 1969   177

APPENDIX 3:   Secret Document on the "Lin Piao
Affair"   221
   A.   Mao Tse-tung's Private Letter to Chiang
Ching, July, 1966   222
   B.   Lin Piao's "Outline of the
Five-Seven-One Project," 1971   226
   C.   Chairman Mao's Talks with Responsible
Comrades, August-September, 1971   230
   D.   Evidence of the Lin Piao Anti-Party
Clique's Attempt to Launch a
Counterrevolutionary Coup, 1971   241

APPENDIX 4:   The "New" Constitution of the
Communist Party of China, August, 1973   250

APPENDIX 5:   Chou En-lai: Report to the Tenth
National Congress of the Communist Party
of China, August, 1973   258

APPENDIX 6:   Wang Hung-wen: Report on the
Revision of the Party Constitution, August, 1973   277

APPENDIX 7:   Yang Jung-kuo: Confucius—a Thinker
Who Stubbornly Upheld the Slave System,
August, 1973   286

APPENDIX 8:   Draft of the Revised Constitution of
the People's Republic of China (August, 1973)   299

INDEX   307

CHARTS, TABLES, AND MAPS

Growth of Party Membership, 1921–1973   34
Map of the Long March, 1934–1936   78
Chart of the Supreme State Organs   115
Development of the Cultural Revolution,
1966–1968   134
Map of Main Force Transfers between
Military Regions, 1967–1970   156

INTRODUCTION

ON the eve of the advent of Communism, China was in a period of foreign encroachments and witnessing the collapse of her traditional social order. This was also a time of economic difficulties, political chaos, and military conflicts.

Foreign Aggressions

The disintegration of Chinese society can be traced to the Opium War of 1839–1842. A treaty was signed in Nanking in 1842 which provided for the opening of five Chinese ports: Canton, Amoy, Foochow, Ningpo, and Shanghai to British traders. It imposed on China an indemnity of 21 million taels, and it provided that the island of Hong Kong, which controls the sea entrance to Canton, be ceded to England. Furthermore, in the supplementary Treaty of Bogus concluded with China in 1843, the British introduced the infamous "most-favored-nation" clause, guaranteeing the British any further concessions that China might subsequently grant to other nations. Thereafter, all foreign treaties with China contained this clause. These treaties set a pattern for China's relations with the West and Japan that lasted 100 years.

Finally, Japan's defeat of China in 1895 stripped China of any remaining prestige and precipitated a scramble for new concessions. The closing decades of the nineteenth century found foreign powers engaged in a battle of concessions, through which they leased territory from the Manchu government. Foreign troops were permitted to station in the concessions and foreign warships patrolled Chinese coasts and rivers.

In the continuing scramble for China, foreign powers negotiated the partition of China into spheres of influence. Russia, in Manchuria, occupied Dairen and Port Arthur; Britain occupied the port of Wei-hai-wei and made the Yangtze Valley its sphere of influence; Germany seized Kiao-chow Bay and placed Shantung Province under its control; France had its sphere of influence in Yunnan Province and in certain parts of Kwangtung and Kwangsi, and also leased Kwangchow Bay. Japan, after it had seized the Ryukyu Islands and Korea, made Taiwan a colony of the Japanese Empire.

Reform and Rebellion

China's display of weakness stirred many scholar-officials; and they began the organization of reform clubs throughout the country. In 1898, the eminent Cantonese scholar K'ang Yu-wei (1858–1927), convinced that to revive, China must follow the example of Meiji Japan, launched a reform movement with the support of the young emperor Kuang-hsü. The movement advocated a basic change from absolute monarchy to constitutional rule, but it resulted in precipitating the coup d'etat executed by the empress dowager. The emperor was imprisoned and the reforms abandoned.

The failure of the reform movement intensified the reaction of the conservative forces. They were convinced that even though China suffered many defeats in war, her culture could eventually dominate the world. They tried to incite the masses to xenophobia and were able to turn a fundamental anti-imperial peasant revolution, the Boxer Rebellion (I-ho Tuan), into an antiforeign uprising.

The Boxers burned churches, destroyed Westernized schools, dug out railroads, and cut telegraph lines. And in the imperial capital, Peking, they went on a rampage, destroying everything foreign; among their victims was the German diplomat, Minister von Ketteler. These antiforeign activities led to the invasion of the Chinese capital by an expeditionary force of the eight Allied Powers in 1900. China was forced to sign a devastating peace treaty in 1901, which included:

(1) the execution of Chinese officials responsible for these activities;

(2) the right of foreign powers to station troops in legation sites in Peking;

(3) the destruction of China's defenses from Taku to Peking;

(4) the establishment by China of an effective 5 percent tariff; and

(5) the payment of $333 million in reparations. A substantial share, $25 million, was later voluntarily returned to China by the United States for establishing scholarships for Chinese students in the United States.

Sun Yat-Sen's Revolution

During these years of political and economic disaster, Dr. Sun Yat-sen (1866–1925) began his revolutionary work. He was convinced that the Manchu dynasty was beyond hope of reforming. He founded the China Regeneration Society (Hsing-chung Hui) in Honolulu in 1894, and reorganized it in Japan into a new organization, the League of Common Alliance (T'ung-meng Hui) in 1905, which promoted the Three People's Principles as its program of action:

(1) the principle of nationalism;

(2) the principle of democracy and the establishment of a republic; and

(3) the principle of socialism, including equal distribution and nationalization of land.

Although there were many reverses, persecutions, and rebuffs, the revolutionary work led by Sun Yat-sen finally broke out in October, 1911, and culminated in the overthrow of the Manchu dynasty. The next year, Dr. Sun reorganized his League of Common Alliance into the Nationalist Party, or the Kuomintang, as a democratic party with open membership. The party's purpose was to promote Dr. Sun's political doctrine, the Three People's Principles, in the minds and lives of the Chinese people.

The success of Dr. Sun's revolution did not, however, free China from the economic difficulties, ideological conflicts, political chaos, and foreign intervention of the old empire. Governmental power was, in fact, soon to pass into the hands of political opportunists and militarists; and China was again torn by civil wars among the warlords for thirteen years.

Warlord Politics

Yuan Shih-k'ai succeeded Sun Yat-sen as the President of the new Republic in 1913. With the assistance of the United States, Japan, Britain, and Germany, Yuan became a dictator and by 1915, he restored himself as a new monarch. But Yuan's government was weaker than the Manchu and the real control soon was assumed by various warlords upon his death on June 6, 1916.

Warlords are military leaders who claimed to be acting for the people but in fact were dictators in their individual geographical areas. Under their control in each area were a number of civilians who formed the warlord bureaucracy. Some had certain capacities for administration. Many of the lesser warlords were military parvenus of lowly origins—bandits, coolies, peddlers, and army privates risen from the ranks.

As a rule, the lesser warlords attached themselves to more powerful warlords and the most powerful warlords were sometimes affiliated with and supported by foreign powers. A warlord was sovereign within the territory he controlled; he recruited his own bureaucratic and military personnel, levied taxes, and administered his own brand of justice. He was a man (no known woman was a warlord during this period) who fought for personal gain. His main objectives were usually to acquire his opponent's territories and wealth.

In the early 1920's, there were several major warlord factions contesting for national power. The first was the Anfu faction, led by Tuan Ch'i-jui and Hsu Shu-tseng. This faction consisted of Ni Ssu-ch'un of Anhwei, Yang Shan-te of Chekiang, Li Hou-chi of Fukien, and Lu Yun-hsiang of Shanghai.

The second faction was known as the Chih-li group, under the leadership of Feng Kuo-chang and Ts'ao K'un, of the Peiyang army system, as well as Wu P'ei-fu of Honan. A third faction was headed by Chang Tso-lin of Manchuria. Other minor factions included Sun Ch'uan-fang in the lower Yantzu provinces of Chekiang and Fukien; Yen Hsi-shan of Shansi; Feng Yu-hsiang of the northwest; and T'ang Sheng-chih in Hunan. Meanwhile, Nationalist forces under Sun Yat-sen and Chiang Kai-shek were in the process of being organized in Canton, southern China, waiting for their opportunity to strike against the northern warlords and to unify China into a single modern nation-state.

Japanese Aggressions

The young republic, weak, and divided by various warlords, was again subjected to intensified foreign aggression. Russia shifted its expansion into Outer Mongolia; Britain began her penetration into Tibet. Their aggressive moves were conducted under the pretense of supporting local autonomous movements against an inefficient, corrupt central authority.

Meanwhile, Japan made the Twenty-One Demands on Yuan Shih-kai's Peking government in 1915. The twenty-one demands were intended to make China a colony of Japan. Their contents were divided into five groups, stipulating:

Group I: The transfer of Shantung from German possession into a Japanese sphere of influence;

Group II: Japanese rights in southern Manchuria and eastern Inner Mongolia, plus extension of leases of Port Arthur and Dairen from twenty-five to ninety-nine years;

Group III: Japanese control of the Han-yeh-ping mining company in Hupeh;

Group IV: That China not grant any leases or rights to any other power except Japan;

Group V: That China be brought under Japanese political, economic, and military control, such as the employment of Japanese as political, financial, and military advisers in the Chinese government and the joint control of Chinese police forces.

Yuan Shih-kai accepted all the Japanese demands with the exception of Group V. Meanwhile, China launched a diplomatic offensive and declared war on Germany in the summer of 1917 in order to join the Allied Powers of Europe and Japan. The Chinese government expected that at the Paris Peace Conference her sovereign and territorial integrity would be preserved.

The May Fourth Movement

In 1919, when news arrived in China that the Chinese delegation to the Paris Peace Conference had failed to secure the return of Shantung from the Japanese, thousands of students began to protest in the streets of Peking to reflect their long-built-up patriotic indignation over Japanese aggressions in China. In fact, at the peace conference, England and France had already entered into the secret agreement with Japan in favor of Japan's control of territory in China leased by Germany.

On the afternoon of May 4, 1919, more than 3,000 students in Peking assembled at Tien-an Men (the Gate of Heavenly Peace) and issued an emotional manifesto before erupting into violence. The demonstrators burned the residence of Ts'ao Ju-lin, Minister of Communications of the Peking government, and beat up Chang Tsung-hsiang, the Chinese minister to Japan. More than thirty students were arrested, but the movement immediately spread throughout the country with similar demonstrations in other cities.

The students now declared a general strike to carry forward their protest. They were joined by workers and merchants. A movement to boycott Japanese goods and to oppose the decisions of the Paris Peace Conference swept the country. Merchants in several large cities temporarily suspended business. Between 60,000 and 70,000 workers in Shanghai walked out of their jobs in protest over governmental policy. Local student associations were set up one after another.

The immediate result was that the Chinese delegation at Versailles refused to sign the peace treaty. This at least preserved China's legal claim to the Shantung territory, seized by the Japanese. The students thus proved themselves to be a new force in Chinese politics, cloaked under the banner of nationalism. And at the same time, they aroused the intellectual class to a full realization of the fermenting state of their country.

Out of the political activity of the May Fourth Movement came China's new cultural awareness. Foreign scholars, including John Dewey and Rabindranath Tagore, were invited to lecture in China. From this movement, the Chinese mind, long confined by tradition, seemed to burst forth with new ideas and modern doctrines. With this liberation there arose a new type of Chinese intellectual, trained in the knowledge of the West and anxious to liberate the Chinese mentality from traditionalism.

With the translation of the works by Marx, Engels, and Kautsky, the introduction of Lenin's theories on revolution and imperialism, and the publication of the Bolshevik Party programs in Chinese, the study of Marxism became popular among the intellectual elite. The Chinese were impressed that the intervention of foreign power had failed to arrest the Russian Revolution. In addition, in July, 1918, the new Soviet government suggested to the Chinese that they would give up the privileged positions in China obtained under the czars. (The Russians never carried this out.) This new Soviet attitude further aroused widespread pro-Soviet enthusiasm among Chinese intellectuals and students, among whom were two men, who not only converted to Marxism but also played decisive roles in the organization of a Communist Party in China: Li Ta-chao and Ch'en Tu-hsiu.

On the eve of the victory of the Chinese Communist Party in 1948, a Communist historian wrote:

> In the May Fourth Movement, there emerged in the Chinese revolution a fresh and vigorous political force which refused to reconcile itself with imperialist rule in China. Before this movement, the "revolutionaries," with elements of the bourgeoisie and petty bourgeoisie as their core, in spite of the fact they did carry on a patriotic struggle to rid the country of imperialist oppression, harbored illusions about the imperialists and dared not take a firm stand against them. At the time of the May Fourth Movement, the newly born working class joined the revolution as an independent political force. Two years later, in 1921, the Communist Party of China—the Party of the Chinese working class—was founded. . . ."*

*Hu Sheng, *Imperialism and Chinese Politics, 1948* (Peking, Foreign Language Press, 1955), p. 248.

THE SEARCH FOR A NEW CHINA

CHAPTER ONE:

BIRTH OF THE CHINESE COMMUNIST PARTY

IN June, 1971, the Chinese Communist Party issued a position paper commemorating its fiftieth anniversary. This paper, according to an eyewitness account, became by early July "a Bible for China."[1] Its concluding portion stated: "A review of the fighting course traversed by our Party over the past 50 years confirms this truth: when our Party departs from Chairman Mao's leadership and goes against Mao Tse-tung Thought and Chairman Mao's line, it suffers setbacks and defeats; when our Party closely follows Chairman Mao, acts in accordance with Mao Tse-tung Thought and implements Chairman Mao's line, it advances and triumphs. Comrade Mao Tse-tung's works are the most comprehensive summary of the theory and practice of the Chinese Communist Party in leading the revolution and construction. . . ."[2]

The history of the Communist Party of China is clearly inseparable from the history of its contemporary leader, Chairman Mao Tse-tung. But to credit all its accomplishments to one individual is certainly an oversimplification of the movement and does a disservice to the fifty-year struggle of the Chinese people and the Communist Party in forging a new China.

[1] Ross Terrill, "The 800,000,000—Report from China," *Atlantic Monthly* (November, 1971), p. 92.

[2] From the joint editorial of *Jen-min Jih-pao*, *Jie-fan Jun-pao* and *Hungchi* (June 30, 1971), translation published in *Peking Review* (July 2, 1971), p. 17.

1.　The Marxists

The founding of the Chinese Communist Party can be traced to the formation of a society for the study of Marxism by Li Ta-chao and Ch'en Tu-hsiu in 1918, and various other Marxist study groups after the May Fourth Movement of 1919, which we have discussed in the Introduction.

Li Ta-chao was neither a proletarian worker nor a peasant. He was born into a well-to-do family in Hopeh province in 1888. Li's own parents died when he was two, and he was reared by his grandparents. Maurice Meisner, in his study of Li Ta-chao, suggested that the affectionate ties between Li and his grandparents were at least partly responsible both for the sympathy that he later showed for older people and for his generally warm and open temperament.[3] He became known as "a friend of everyone," and even as a Communist he maintained close personal relationships with many non-Communist intellectuals.

Like many other founders of the Chinese Communist Party, Li Ta-chao came from China's rural middle class and enjoyed a traditional classical education. In fact, Li was married at the age of eleven, by the order of his grandfather, to a young village girl with bound feet, who later would bear him six children.

Li grew devoted to his wife, who encouraged him to seek better educational opportunities away from the village. In 1907, he took the money left by his grandfather and went to the treaty port of Tientsin, where he took the entrance examination at the Peiyang College of Law and Political Science. He studied at Peiyang for six years, from 1907 to 1913, majoring in political economy. He also studied Japanese and English.

---

[3] See Maurice Meisner, *Li Ta-chao and the Origins of Chinese Marxism* (Cambridge, Harvard University Press, 1967).

It was at Tientsin that Li witnessed the 1911–1912 revolution led by Dr. Sun Yat-sen. Li was very disappointed when the revolution was perverted by tyranny, civil strife, and warlordism throughout China. He then went to Japan and enrolled in the department of political economy of the famous Waseda University in Tokyo. While in Japan he read the Western philosophers and political theorists, including Marxist works.

He lived in the YMCA Chinese students' dormitory at Waseda and worked closely with the Chinese Revolutionary Party, the secret organization established by Dr. Sun Yat-sen. After Sun yielded the Presidency to Yuan Shih-k'ai, a number of secret organizations were formed in Japan against the Yuan dictatorship. Li organized a China study society to mobilize Chinese students in Japan in support of Sun Yat-sen.

During Li's years in Japan, he had been stimulated to develop an intense nationalistic and antiforeign sentiment. He wrote many articles accusing the foreigners of being incapable of understanding China. However, his mind was not closed to the ideas of the West. He soon developed a transcendental philosophy of dialectical evolution and argued for China's rebirth. This philosophy provided him with a highly optimistic view at a time when political developments in China offered very little cause for optimism.

In the spring of 1916 he returned to China and associated himself for awhile with the Progressive Party (Chinputang) in order to participate in the movement against Yuan Shih-k'ai. Less than two months after Li had arrived in Shanghai from Tokyo, on June 6, 1916, Yuan died. Politicians and generals rushed to Peking to reconvene the parliament Yuan had dissolved in 1913; but the politicians were celebrating a victory that belonged to others. Soon it became clear that warlords had become the real beneficiaries of the fall of Yuan's dictatorship.

Li went to Peking and assumed a new position as chief

editor of the Peking *Ch'en-chung pao,* organ of the Progressive Party. He became disillusioned with petty politics in Peking. When the news of the Russian February Revolution reached China, he welcomed it and hoped for a similiar revolution in China. He published an important essay, *Violence and Politics,* on October 15, 1917, with the thesis that political reform in China could not be accomplished without revolution.

In January, 1918, he joined Ch'en Tu-hsiu and several young intellectuals as members of the board of editors of the influential periodical, *New Youth.* They began to proclaim their rejection of the entire Chinese intellectual and cultural tradition, and advocated the Western concepts of democracy and science as the foundation of a new culture and a new society for China. However, Li Ta-chao never subjected the Confucian tradition to the thoroughgoing criticism and sarcastic deprecation that chacterized the writings of Ch'en Tu-hsiu and other radical intellectuals.

Li Ta-chao was not fully converted to Marxism until he was appointed librarian of Peking University in February, 1918. There, he began to closely examine the Russian Revolution and publicly announced his support of Bolshevism:

> Whenever a disturbance in this worldwide social force occurs among the people, it will produce repercussions all over the earth, like storm clouds gathering before the wind and valleys echoing the mountains. In the course of such a world mass movement, emperors, nobles, warlords, bureaucrats, militarism, capitalism, will certainly be destroyed as though struck by a thunderbolt. Encountering this irresistible tide, these things will be swept away one by one. . . . Henceforth, all that one sees around him will be the triumphant banner of Bolshevism, and Bolshevism's song of victory. The bell is rung for humanitarianism. The

dawn of freedom has arrived. See the world of tomorrow; it assuredly will belong to the red flag. . . . Although the word "Bolshevism" was created by the Russians, the spirit it embodies can be regarded as that of a common awakening in the heart of each individual among mankind of the 20th century."[4]

Li's writings began to attract the interest of students at Peking University, and they began to organize themselves into Marxist study groups. From these groups emerged the future leader of Chinese Communism, Mao Tse-tung, among others. Mao was also appointed as an assistant in the library at the university. Soon Li Ta-chao's office in the library became known as the "Red chamber"—the secret meeting place for a variety of radical student organizations.[5]

Li developed a personal relationship with his students. He was not only a teacher and intellectual guide, but also assumed a father's role in personal matters and frequently gave his own money to needy students. At one time, his wife complained to the university chancellor that Li's generosity had left her insufficient funds for household necessities. Later, in fact, the chancellor withheld a large portion of Li's salary and turned it over directly to his wife.[6]

As Li Ta-chao's name became widely known, he was sought after by students in search of intellectual and political guidance. He became concerned with the problem of the isolation and political impotence of the Marxist study groups and urged that the students and youthful intellectuals leave the corrupting life of the cities and join the

[4]William Theodore de Barry, *et al.*, *Sources of Chinese Tradition* (New York, Columbia University Press, 1964), Vol. II, p. 203.

[5]Maurice Meisner, "Li Ta-chao and the Intellectual Prerequisities for the Maoist Strategy of Revolution," in Chun-tu Hsueh, ed., *Revolutionary Leaders of Modern China* (New York, Oxford University Press, 1971), p. 377.

[6]Maurice Meisner, *Li Ta-chao and the Origins of Chinese Marxism, op. cit.*, p. 118.

peasant masses in the villages. He was, in fact, advocating a sort of peasant revolution. For, in his view, "China is a rural nation and most of the laboring class is made up of peasants." [7]

In addition, Li adapted Marxism to Chinese conditions and produced a unique synthesis of militant nationalism and voluntaristic Marxist-Leninism. He perceived the road to socialism in China in a rather special way: First, he attributed a "latent socialist class consciousness to virtually all men"; and secondly, he proclaimed that the search for an immediate Chinese road to socialist revolution could be found in a "single, final world struggle."[8] Li viewed the Chinese Communist revolution as a populist revolution involving the whole nation, and people exploited and oppressed by foreign imperialism, with the central role to be played by the Chinese peasants. This is strikingly similar to the core of the philosophy of Mao Tse-tung.

The early Marxists in China were far less than disciplined Leninist revolutionaries. Li's group in Peking originally consisted of eight members, of whom six were said to be anarchists. One of the eight, Tai Chi-t'ao, later became a leader of the Kuomintang right wing and Chiang Kai-shek's chief ideologist. However, Li began actively recruiting members for the party after his Russian colleague, Sergei A. Polevoy, introduced him to the Comintern official representative to China, Gregori Voitinsky, in March, 1920. Many of the early members were his favorite students, including Teng Chung-hsia, Chang Kuo-t'ao, Lo Chang-lung, Ho Meng-hsiung, and Liu Jen-chin. Both Mao Tse-tung and Chou En-lai were also in contact with Li from their respective bases.

Li later directed Voitinsky to his friend Ch'en Tu-hsiu so

---

[7]Maurice Meisner, "Li Ta-chao and the Intellectual . . .,", p. 380.

[8]*Ibid.*, p. 387.

that they could work together in the organization of a Chinese Communist Party. Li and Ch'en did not attend the First Congress of the founding of the party in Shanghai, but Li was elected as the party regional secretary of northern China. At the Second Party Congress in July, 1922, he was named to the Central Committee and the party directed him to organize the labor movement in Manchuria, among other tasks. He also participated in negotiating alliances with the Nationalists under Sun Yat-sen. However, during the tragic student demonstration in Peking on March 18, 1926, Li was wounded during a fight with the police. He took refuge in the Russian Embassy compound in Peking and was arrested a year later and executed by warlord general Chang Tso-lin on April 28, 1927.

II. Organizing the Party

In the developing years of the Chinese Communist movement, there was a famous slogan: "Nan-ch'en, Pei-li," denoting two important aspects of the leadership of the party—Ch'en Tu-hsiu in the south and Li Ta-chao in the north. In fact, it was Ch'en Tu-hsiu who negotiated with the Comintern agent in organizing the Chinese Communist Party.

Ch'en was born October 8, 1879, at Huaining, Anhwei Province.[9] He, like Li, lost his father very early and was brought up by his paternal grandfather. He studied the Chinese classics in quiet seclusion in his native village. At the age of eighteen, he married a girl from his province. However, he left his family to engage in political activity, especially after the failure of the Reform Movement of 1898 and the Boxer Uprising of 1900.

He returned to his native district of Anching for a short

[9]Yu-ju Chih, "Ch'en Tu-hsiu: His Career and Political Ideas," in Chun-tu Hsueh, op. cit., p. 335.

while and initiated a private library as a center for disseminating radical ideas. When the local authorities closed the library, Ch'en fled to Nanking, then sailed to Tokyo and studied at the Kobun Gakuin (the Higher Normal School) in 1902. His stay in Japan offered him the opportunity to identify himself with other Chinese revolutionary intellectuals. He was one of the few Chinese students in Tokyo to establish a Chinese youth association with the aim of destroying the old political order of Imperial China.

He returned to China at the end of 1902 and joined the editorial staff of the *China National Gazette (Kuo-min jih-pao)*, a revolutionary journal published in Shanghai in 1903. A year later, he went back to his home province and organized his own *Anhwei Vernacular Daily (Anhwei-Su-hua-pao)*, while teaching at the Anhwei Academy in Wuhu. In 1905 he went back to Shanghai and participated in a secret experiment making high explosives to carry out assassination schemes. The next year, he sailed to Japan for a short visit, again to communicate with other revolutionaries in rebellion against the Manchu government.

In 1907 he went to France, where he stayed until 1910. There he was profoundly influenced by the French political thought of human rights, social Darwinism, and scientism. He returned to China in 1910 and participated in the Chinese Revolution of 1911. After his failure to overthrow Yuan Shih-k'ai in 1913, he again went to Japan where he remained until 1915.

When Ch'en Tu-hsiu received the news of Japan's Twenty-one Demands, he returned to China and published a magazine, *New Youth (Hsin Ch'ing-nien)* or *La Jeunese Nouvelle*, which was to play an extraordinary part in the May Fourth Movement. Warlordism and the lack of freedom of the press made it difficult for Ch'en to start his magazine. Therefore, to avoid direct political confrontation with the authorities, the magazine was declared to be dedicated to "reformation of thought and behavior of youth rather than the launching of political criticism."[10] Chinese youth were reminded of their mission to revitalize the nation and were urged to discard the old morality for a new code of ethics: to be independent, progressive, assertive, cosmopolitan, utilitarian, and scientific. The journal was eventually transformed into an official Communist Party organ in 1920.

From 1915 to the end of 1916, Ch'en's activities were centered around Shanghai. But at the beginning of 1917, Ch'en's influence widened as a result of his appointment to the prestigious post of dean of the School of Letters of Peking University. Peking University had already, in 1916, been placed under the new leadership of Chancellor Ts'ai Yuan-p'ei, one of the greatest educators and liberals of modern China. Ts'ai carried out many important reforms in the university, including his policy of permitting the coexistence of divergent opinions. The university was in the main governed by professors rather than administrators, and students were permitted to take part in political activities as individuals. A policy of freedom in education made the university a public forum for debates between conservative scholars and the new intelligentsia and made possible an alliance of the new intellectuals.

During the years at Peking University, Ch'en introduced two important concepts into Chinese political thought: democracy and science. He looked upon science as the most powerful instrument in the study of human society. Ch'en also personally led the open assault on China's sage, Confucius, and perhaps as a gesture of personal defiance of Confucian social convention, he lived for some time with a female companion, Miss Kao Chun-man, whom he subsequently married.

[10]Chow Tse-tsung, *The May Fourth Movement* (Stanford, Stanford University Press, 1967), p. 45.

Ch'en carried on his attack on Confucius with great enthusiasm. He was the first man to call the sage "feudal" and termed Confucius' teachings as incompatible with modern life. He wrote, for example, in December, 1916:

> Confucius lived in a feudal age. The ethics he promoted were the ethics of the feudal age. The social mores he taught, and even his own mode of living, were teachings and modes of a feudal age. The political institutions he advocated were those of a feudal age. The objectives, ethics, social norms, mode of living, and political institutions did not go beyond the privilege and prestige of a few rulers and aristocrats and had nothing to do with the happiness of the great masses. How can this be shown? In the teachings of Confucius, the most important element in social ethics and social life is the rules of decorum and the most serious thing in government is punishment. In chapter one of the *Book of Rites*, it is said that "The rule of decorum does not go down to the common people and the penal statutes do not go up to great officers." Is this not solid proof of the (true) spirit of the way of Confucius and the spirit of the feudal age? [11]

Meanwhile, Ch'en was engaged in the quest for a new philosophy, which led him eventually to Marxism. Because of his uncompromising attack on Chinese tradition, he was forced to resign from Peking University in 1919 and left the following year for Shanghai, where he continued to publish *The New Youth.* It was in Shanghai that he began a new chapter in his career. With the aid of Comintern agents from Moscow, he undertook the organization and leadership of the Chinese Communist Party.

At Ch'en's home in the French concession in Shanghai, the Comintern's Far Eastern representative, Gregori Voitinsky, urged the Chinese Marxists to organize themselves into a Communist Party. Finally, in May, 1920, a

[11]William Theodore de Barry, *op. cit.*, p. 56.

Provisional Central Bureau of the Chinese Communist Party was established at Ch'en's home at 2 Yu Yang Lane, Shanghai, to direct propanganda and organizational work.[12] Their major activities may be summarized as follows:[13]

1. Formation of Communist cells in the urban centers of Shanghai, Peking, and Canton; in Hupeh, Hunan, and Shantung provinces; plus overseas groups in Japan and Paris. Some of the leaders in these areas included:

Peking: Chang Kuo-t'ao, Li Ta-chao, Chang Shen-fu, Huang Ling-shuang, Ho Meng-hsiung, Yuan Ming-hsun, Chang T'ai-lei, Liu Jen-chin, and Teng Chung-hsia

Canton: Ch'en Kung-po, T'an P'ing-shan, T'an Chih-t'ang, and Pao Hui-tseng

Hupeh: Tung Pi-wu, Ch'en T'an-ch'iu, Yung Tai-ying

Hunan: Mao Tse-tung, Ho Shu-heng

Shantung: Wang Ching-wei

Japan: Chou Fu-hai

Paris: Ts'ai Ho-sen, Chou En-lai, Li Li-san, Lo Mai, Li Fu-ch'un, Wang Jo-fei, Hsiang Chin-yu, Ch'en Yen-nien, Chao Shih-yen, Ts'ai Ch'ang, and Nieh Jung-chen

2. Expansion of propaganda publications. In addition to Ch'en Tu-hsiu's *The New Youth*, which was now expanded to include news of workers' movement in foreign countries, the party cells in various localities published their own periodicals to promote Communism. There was the *Communist Party Monthly*, *Labor Circle*, and *Group Friendship*, of Shanghai; the *Laborers*, of Peking; and *Women*, of Canton.

3. Establishment of Socialist Youth Corps, or Young Socialists, in Shanghai in August, 1920, as a heterogeneous group of young Marxists, anarchists, guild socialists, and labor unionists.

[12]Warren Kuo, *Analytical History of the Chinese Communist Party*, I (Taipei, Institute of International Relations, 1966) p. 10.

[13]*Ibid.*, pp. 10–14.

TABLE 1:   *Growth of Party Membership**
(1921–1973)

	Members
First Party Congress, 1921	57
Second Party Congress, 1922	123
Third Party Congress, 1923	432
Fourth Party Congress, 1925	1,000
Fifth Party Congress, 1927	57,000
Sixth Party Congress, 1928	40,000
Seventh Party Congress, 1945	1,210,000
Eighth Party Congress, 1956	10,734,000
Ninth Party Congress, 1969	20,000,000 (est.)
Tenth Party Congress, 1973	22,000,000 (est.)

*from various sources.
See *Issues and Studies* (July, 1971), pp. 36–37.

4. Founding of the Foreign Language Society (or School) primarily for the purpose of providing Russian language lessons to the Youth Corps members with Yang Ming-chai as its principal. Yang was a Chinese immigrant to Russia from Shantung and returned to China in 1920 to act as Voitinsky's interpreter.

5. Promoting workers' movements in labor unions and incorporating the movements into the mainstream of the Communist Party. Two of the earliest Communist labor unions were founded in Shanghai in 1920—the Shanghai Mechanical Workers Union and the Printers Union. The party cell in Peking also started a workers' subsidiary school to advance ideological training of the Chinese proletarian class.

It must be remembered that the earlier Communist movement was a small radical movement led by China's intellectuals and some anarchists. At the time of the First National Party Congress in July, 1921, there were only fifty-seven members. There were several hundred activists affiliated with the Socialist Youth Corps. However, because of their anarchistic leanings, they were not permitted to join the party. In fact, the Youth Corps was disbanded in May, 1921, and was not reestablished until several months later. After almost a decade of intensive struggle, the party emerged from a small, loosely organized group as a militant mass party in several areas of China.

III. Party Programs

The first session of the First Party Congress assembled at the Po-ai Girls School in the French concession in Shanghai on July 1, 1921.[14] Later sessions were held in several other places in order to avoid the harassment of Shanghai police. In fact, during the fourth meeting at Li Han-chün's apartment, police arrived at the scene and the delegates fled. Later, they congregated again in a boat on the Nan-hu Lake in nearby Chiahsin.

Twelve Chinese, plus two Russians, allegedly attended the organizational session and they represented the Communist cells of seven areas:

Shanghai: Li Han-chün, Li Ta
Peking: Chang Kuo t'ao, Liu Jen-chin
Canton: Ch'en Kung-po, Pao Hui-tseng
Wuhan: Tung Pi-wu, Ch'en T'an-ch'iu
Changsha (Hunan): Mao Tse-tung
Tsinan: Wang Ching-wei, Teng En-ming
Japan: Chou Fu-hai
USSR: G. Maring, Nikonsky

The two founding fathers of the party could not attend. Ch'en Tu-hsiu was working in Canton and Li Ta-chao had to be in northern China to iron out some organizational problems in that area. The party congress, however,

---

[14] There are many historical problems concerning the First Party Congress. See James Pinckney Harrison, *The Long March to Power* (New York, Praeger Publishers, 1972), chapter 2.

adopted a first party constitution and outlined the basic tasks of the party. It elected Ch'en Tu-hsiu as Secretary-General, Chang Kuo-t'ao as head of the organizational department, and Li Ta as the head of the propaganda department. These men, plus three alternate members, Chou Fu-hai, Li Han-chün, and Liu Jen-chin, formed the powerful Central Bureau. Since the total party membership was small, the congress felt it was not necessary to formulate the larger Central Committee. Mao Tse-tung, who dominated the party after the Long March, was not given an important position at the First Party Congress. Instead, he went back to Hunan as secretary of the small party branch there.

The congress accepted the draft of Ch'en Tu-hsiu's program, which was sent from Canton as the basis for general discussion. There was considerable debate among various members at the congress, especially with respect to the question of the proper attitude for the party to take toward Sun Yat-sen's Nationalist Party. Several "Leftists" under the leadership of Liu Jen-ching demanded drastic action and opposed any attempt by the "Rightists" led by Li Han-chün for a more restrained approach to party programs. Finally, after many heated debates among the dozen delegates, the congress adopted two important resolutions:

(1) The First Program of the Communist Party of China, 1921; and

(2) The First Decision as to the Objectives of the Communist Party of China, 1921.[15]

Under the first resolution, the programs of the party included: (1) "overthrow of the capitalistic classes," (2) "implementing the dictatorship of the proletariat," (3) "overthrow of the private ownership of capital," and

---

[15] See Ch'en Kung-po, *The Communist Movement in China* (New York, Octagon Books, 1966), p. 102.

(4) "uniting with the Third Communist International."[16] The first resolution was in fact a propaganda paper outlining the basic philosophy of the party in order to gain sympathy from the Communist International.

The second resolution stressed the importance of organizing China's labor movement. The party resolution declared: "In any locality where there is more than one kind of industry, industrial unions shall be organized; if there is no great industry in a certain locality, but only one or two factories, a factory union can be organized suitable to conditions in that locality."[17] In addition, there shall be "labor supplementary schools" as well as "institutions for studying labor organization" in several areas.

At the conclusion of the congress, Ch'en Tu-hsiu came to Shanghai from Canton to organize a Labor Secretariat. Special efforts were made directing the labor movement against traditional gang lords who had been in control of Shanghai for several decades. Other branches of the Labor Secretariat were established in Wuhan, Tsinan, Canton, Changsha, and Peking. By 1922, the Communist Party organized the first effective Hong Kong-Canton strike, which involved some 100,000 workers. Hong Kong was virtually paralyzed by their activities.

Ch'en Tu-hsiu was arrested once in Shanghai, but he was soon released for lack of incriminating evidence. The party slowly expanded its propaganda, youth, and other organizational work under the personal leadership of Ch'en. The dissolved Socialist Youth Corps was reconstituted and expanded into seventeen areas with several thousand new members. Additional party cells were formed in some eighteen provinces throughout China with its core membership from the intellectual elite. However, during the first two years of its existence, the party was not able to make

[16]Ch'en Kung-po, *op. cit.*, pp. 103–10.
[17]*Ibid.*

much impact on Chinese society, and its existence, at least financially, was based on fundings from the Communist International in Moscow. Most party members held other jobs, and only professionals such as party-employed activists received a salary. In fact, the Comintern representative complained that "the spending of 200,000 rubles by the Third Communist International in China during the first year was not justified," because the party centered "too much on a limited number of students and workers and that it scarcely had any political significance."[18]

Suggested Reading

BRANDT, CONRAD, et al., eds., A Documentary History of Chinese Communism. Cambridge, Massachusetts, Harvard University Press, 1959, section one.

CHIH, YU-JU, The Political Thought of Ch'en Tu-hsiu. Unpublished PhD dissertation, Indiana University, 1965.

CHOW, TSE-TUNG, The May Fourth Movement. Stanford, California, Stanford University Press, 1967.

COLE, ALLAN B., Forty Years of Chinese Communism; Selected Reading with Commentary. Washington, D.C., American Historical Association, 1962.

HARRISON, JAMES PINCKNEY, The Long March to Power: A History of the Chinese Communist Party, 1921–1972. New York, Praeger Publishers, 1972, chapter 2.

HSUEH, CHUN-TU, ed., Revolutionary Leaders of Modern China. New York, Oxford University Press, 1971.

——, The Chinese Communist Movement, 1921–1937. Stanford, California, The Hoover Institution, 1960.

MEISNER, MAURICE, Li Ta-chao and the Origin of Chinese Communism. Cambridge, Massachusetts, Harvard University Press, 1967.

NORTH, ROBERT C., Moscow and the Chinese Communists. Stanford, California, Stanford University Press, 1963.

TENG, S.Y., and J. K. FAIRBANK, eds., China's Response to the West: A Documentary Survey, 1839–1923. Cambridge, Massachusetts, Harvard University Press, 1954.

[18]Warren Kuo, op. cit. , p. 55.

CHAPTER TWO:
THE COMMUNIST-NATIONALIST COLLABORATION

IN January and February, 1922, less than a year after the founding of the Chinese Communist Party, the Russian Communists organized in Moscow and Petrograd the Congress of the Toilers of the Far East.[1] The purpose of the congress was to acquaint the peoples of the Far East with Bolshevik views and at the same time to oppose the Washington Conference of 1921–1922 sponsored by the United States.

The Washington Conference was convened in November, 1921, and attended by nine countries —England, France, the United States, Italy, Japan, China, the Netherlands, Belgium, and Portugal. The purpose was to discuss naval disarmament and the consideration of the "Far Eastern question," especially with reference to China. The conference resulted in two major agreements:[2]

(1) The Five Power Naval Treaty, with provisions for a limitation of the tonnage of capital ships and aircraft carriers in a ratio of 5:5:3:1.75:1.75 for England, the United States, Japan, France, and Italy respectively;

(2) The Nine Power Open Door Treaty, which called on

---

[1] Robert C. North, *Moscow and Chinese Communists*, second edition (Stanford, Stanford University Press, 1963), p. 60.

[2] Ruhl J. Bartlett, ed., *The Record of American Diplomacy*, 4th ed. (New York, Alfred A. Knopf, 1964), pp. 486–491.

all signatories, other than China, to respect the sovereignty and territorial integrity of China. However, the treaty was worded in the most general and abstract terms so that each signatory could interpret it to advance its own interest.

The Russians took advantage of this situation and invited a delegation composed of members of the Chinese Communist Party as well as delegates from Dr. Sun Yat-sen's Kuomintang to attend their congress to consider the Far Eastern question. It was at this conference that the Russians argued for a common struggle against the Western Imperialists. G.E. Zinoviev, on behalf of the Communist International, opened the conference with these words:

> Our international brotherhood, since the first day of its existence, takes clear account of the fact that the complete victory of the proletariat over the bourgeoisie, under the circumstances, is possible only on a worldwide scale. . . . Remember that the process of history has placed the question thus: You either win your independence side by side with the proletariat or you do not win it at all. Either you receive your emancipation at the hands of the proletariat, in cooperation with it, under its guidance, or you are doomed to remain the slaves of an English, American, and Japanese camarilla. Either the hundreds and millions of toilers of China, Korea, Mongolia, and other countries understand that their ally and leader is the world proletariat and once and for all give up all hope in any kind of bourgeois and imperialist intrigue, or their national movement must be doomed to failure, and some imperialists will always ride on their backs, sow civil war, and crush and carve out their country.[3]

The congress did not resolve the problem of China; instead, the Soviets pursued a contradictory policy: On the one hand, it recognized the Chinese warlord government in

[3]Robert C. North, *op. cit.*, pp. 60–61.

Peking by accrediting it with a resident ambassador; on the other hand, this ambassador acted concurrently as an agent for the Third International, which was aiding Dr. Sun Yat-sen's Kuomintang in an effort to overthrow the warlord government in Peking. Meanwhile, the Third International also helped to finance the Communist Party of China.

I. The First United Front

Lenin had been observing Sun Yat-sen and his revolutionary movement for a long time, and the Bolshevik leaders decided almost from the beginning to use the Kuomintang as "a Trojan horse for gaining control of China."[4] The Comintern in Moscow decided that the Chinese Communist Party must approach Sun Yat-sen's party on two levels, making open overtures and agreements with one hand and secretly infiltrating and manipulating Nationalist groups with the other.[5] Therefore, the Chinese Communist Party at its Second National Congress modified previous radical demands for immediate social revolution and adopted a united front policy on July 10, 1922.[6] And the new party resolution urged Communist members to join the Kuomintang as individual members supporting Sun Yat-sen.

In his desire to unify China and fight against the warlords in the north, Sun Yat-sen welcomed Comintern support. He signed an agreement with A. Joffe in January, 1923, and sent Chiang Kai-shek to Russia to study political and military organization. The Soviets, in turn, sent Mikhail Borodin, an experienced revolutionary organizer, as an adviser to the Nationalists.

[4]Robert C. North, *op. cit.*, p. 66.

[5]*Ibid.*

[6]See "Manifesto of the Second National Congress of the CCP," in Conrad Brandt, *et al.*, *A Documentary History of Chinese Communism* (Cambridge, Harvard University Press, 1959) pp. 54–65.

Meanwhile, during the Communist Party's Third National Congress, June 10 to 20, 1923, the Comintern instructed the Chinese Communists to recognize the Nationalist Party as leader of this stage of revolution and to influence Nationalist policy toward a more leftist pro-Communist orientation.[7] Communists began actively supporting and working within the Nationalist Party. Li Ta-chao, for example, was appointed to the Presidium of the First Congress of the Nationalist Party on January 20, 1924. Other Communists such as T'an P'ing-shan and Yu Shu-te were also elected to the Central Executive Committee as regular members; and Chang Kuo-t'ao, Ch'ü Ch'iu-pai, Mao Tse-tung, Lin Tsu-han (Lin Po-ch'u), Han Lin-fu, and Yu Fang-chou were elected as alternate members. In fact, the Communists held twenty-six of twenty-nine key positions in the Nationalist organizational bureau in Canton.

On his return from the Soviet Union, Chiang Kai-shek founded the Whampoa Military Academy with the aid of many Communists including Chou En-lai as deputy head of political instruction and Lin Po-ch'u, Yeh Chien-ying, Nieh Jung-chen, and Ch'en Yi as instructors. More than eighty of the academy's first class of 460 were members of the Chinese Communist Party, and Lin Piao was graduated in the fourth class. By 1925, eight of the nine regimental political commissars of Chiang Kai-shek's First Army were Communists, headed by Chou En-lai.[8]

By the time the Fourth National Party Congress was held in January, 1925, the Chinese Communists were able to make a major shift in terms of membership policy. Instead of concentrating on China's intellectuals, the party congress now called for wider recruitment to draw in urban and rural workers. To further consolidate party control, an

[7]Conrad Brandt, op. cit., pp. 65–73.

[8]James Pinckney Harrison, op. cit., p. 56.

inner group of important members of the Central Committee, including party General-Secretary Ch'en Tu-hsiu, Chang Kuo-t'ao, Ts'ai Ho-sen, and Ch'ü Ch'iu-pai, met regularly at homes to discuss policy issues and organizational development.

Specialized departments, such as labor, peasant, and military affairs, as well as a women's league were established. Mao Tse-tung was at one time named head of the peasant department, while Chou En-lai headed the department of military affairs. Soon the party was able to develop nine levels of command organization: (1) central, (2) regional, (3) provincial, (4) sectional, (5) township, (6) district, (7) village, (8) branch, and (9) cell groups. Responsible party leaders were overseers of regional activities, such as in the southern region, under Chou En-lai in 1924 and under Ch'en Yen-nien (son of Ch'en Tu-hsiu), from 1925 to April, 1927; the northern region, under Li Ta-chao and Chang Kuo-t'ao; and Shanghai, under Lo Yi-nung.[9]

One of the major accomplishments of the party during this united front policy period included the promotion of Marxism among Chinese urban workers, especially in Shanghai. The party sponsored national labor congresses and established the National General Labor Union with ties to the Labor International. Li Li-san and Liu Shao-ch'i, among other Communist leaders, also became top officials of the union. In Shanghai alone, the union claimed to influence some 218,000 workers in 1925.

The successful labor movement culminated in the great anti-imperialist movement in 1925 when, on May 30, thousands of students demonstrated on the Nanking Road, the principal shopping area of Shanghai, on behalf of striking workers in that city. Fifteen days earlier, a factory guard in a Japanese-owned textile mill had killed one of the

[9]*Ibid.*, p. 61.

strikers. The Communist Party took this opportunity to call for coordinated demonstrations on May 30. The student demonstrators responded and subsequently clashed with Shanghai police. Eleven students were killed.

The party responded with calls for still greater demonstrations. A violent wave of xenophobia swept China from north to south and reached a climax in the greater Hong Kong-Canton strike. This new strike lasted a full sixteen months, until October, 1926, paralyzing the trade and life of that colony. Thus, the May Thirtieth Movement became a vast help to the revolutionary forces, both Nationalist and Communist. The issue became simple and clear—a Chinese had been killed by foreign-employed police for demonstrating against the exploitation of his fellow countrymen by foreign capitalists. It was a gross violation of China's sovereignty.

The much-needed ideology of Nationalism suddenly erupted in an immense, nationwide outpouring. For instance, foreign missionaries living in the interior were forced to withdraw in haste to the coastal cities, and more foreign troops and ships were sent to Shanghai to safeguard their nationals. Chinese Communists began a new propaganda offensive with such phrases as "running dog of the imperialists" and "thieves who sell the country." No one in authority seemed to be able to stand up to this strong emotional response, and the powerful warlord armies were derided as useless "running dogs" because of their inability to make war on the foreigners. The Chinese Communist leaders began for the first time to feel the power of mass movement and to assume their own role in shaping future revolutionary movements in China.

II. The First Schism

The Communist Party's success in preserving its independent organization and expanding its membership while affiliating with the Nationalist Party gave rise to the strong opposition of the conservative faction of the Nationalists. In July, 1924, the conservative right-wing leaders Chang Chi, Hsieh Ch'ih, and Feng Tzu-yu, who had not previously opposed the Communists, issued "A Proposal for the Impeachment of the Communist Party." They openly charged that the Communists were not acting as "individuals" within the Kuomintang, but were instead taking orders from the Central Committee of the Communist Party. The proposal went on to charge that Li Ta-chao's promise that the Communists would enter the Nationalist organization as individuals had not been kept and that the Communist Party was, instead, acting as a party within a party. Sun Yat-sen replied that "the experienced leaders of the Soviet Union are interested in working with our party and not with the inexperienced students of the Chinese Communists."[10]

After the sudden death from cancer of Sun in Peking on March 12, 1925, signs of discontent and factionalism began to reemerge within the Nationalist Party. Communists continued manipulating these divisions and supported the Kuomintang Left, led by Wang Ching-wei. At the Second National Congress of the Kuomintang in January, 1926, Wang Ching-wei was elected as the new leader, and seven Communists were elected to the Executive Committee. The Communists also dominated many key organizations. Mao Tse-tung was appointed secretary in the propaganda bureau.

At this time, the young commandant of the Whampoa Military Academy, Chiang Kai-shek, began to dominate Chinese politics. Chiang Kai-shek was born in 1887 in a village on the coast of Chekiang. His father died when he was only nine and he was raised by his mother. He was later accepted by the Pao-ting Military Academy in Chihli

[10]Quoted in Benjamin I. Schwartz, *Chinese Communism and the Rise of Mao*, 2nd ed. (Cambridge, Massachusetts, Harvard University Press 1958), pp. 51–52.

province, and on graduation went to Japan for additional training. There Chiang Kai-shek joined the Nationalists and was introduced to Sun Yat-sen shortly afterward.

As already noted, Chiang Kai-shek went to the Soviet Union under the direct order of Sun Yat-sen, and on his return he headed the Whampoa Military Academy. When Sun died in 1925, Chiang Kai-shek had already built a strong following among his student officers from the academy. Prior to the Second Nationalist Party Congress, the "Right-Left" split became a critical factor in the future of Nationalist-Communist collaboration. Since Chiang was politically left of center, the Soviet adviser to the Kuomintang, Borodin, maneuvered the appointment in Canton of a dictatorial triumvirate made up of Wang Ching-wei, Chiang Kai-shek, and Chiang's military superior, the Commander in Chief of the Nationalist forces, Hsu Chung-chih.[11] And in a subsequent coup, Chiang Kai-shek, with the aid of his Whampoa cadets, seized military power.

Meanwhile, Chiang displayed signs of growing discontent with the extent of Communist influence and the "brusque ways" of Soviet advisers in Canton. He was dismayed by the continuing opposition of the Russian advisers with respect to his proposal for the long-awaited northern expedition to defeat the warlords and unify China. In February, 1926, when Borodin left Canton to negotiate with Feng Yu-hsiang, a warlord who controlled the northwest of China, Chiang moved to restrict the operations of the Soviet advisers in Canton. And he also told Wang Ching-wei on March 8 that "we must draw a line somewhere. In no circumstances should we forfeit the freedom of making our own decisions."[12] He was also planning several actions against the Communists.

---

[11]Robert C. North, op. cit., p. 86. T.K. Tong considers North's statement questionable, however.

[12]Quoted in James Pinckney Harrison, op. cit., p. 77.

Apparently overreacting to Chiang's threats, the local Communists in Canton planned a complicated plot to kidnap Chiang and bring him to the Soviet Union. The accounts are still obscure, but this is what Chiang wrote:

> On March 18, Li Chih-lung, a Communist, who was acting/director of the Naval Forces Bureau, forged an order for the gunboat *Chung-shan* to move down the river from Canton to Whampoa. He told the dean of the Military Academy that he had the commandant's orders [Chiang's orders] to send the ship down to stand by. I was then in Canton and knew nothing about the move. . . . As a matter of fact, the ship was sent downriver to load up enough coal for a long voyage. . . . At the time, however, all that I suspected was that they [the Communists] intended to stage a revolt to harm me. I had no idea of the extent of their plans . . . to seize me on board . . . and then send me as a prisoner to Russia via Vladivostok.[13]

Chiang reacted immediately by declaring martial law. He placed his Russian advisers under house arrest, closed trade unions, disarmed the Canton headquarters of the Canton-Hong Kong strike committee, and arrested some fifty Communist leaders. He, in fact, had neutralized the Communists in Canton. Chiang Kai-shek also called the Central Executive Committee of the Nationalist Party into session and passed two resolutions—one laying down general principles governing the Nationalist-Communist relationship and the other limiting the status of Communists within the Nationalist Party.[14]

Meanwhile, the Soviet Union was more concerned with the potential threat of Japan and England than with Chiang Kai-shek's actions in Canton. The Comintern instructed Borodin to continue to cooperate with Chiang and to reject

[13]Chiang Kai-shek, *Soviet Russian in China* (New York, Farrar, Straus and Cudahy, 1958), p. 39.

[14]*Ibid.*, pp. 40–41.

more militant Chinese Communist efforts such as establishing independent armed forces. When Borodin finally returned from his trip to the northwest, he worked out an Eight-Point Compromise with Chiang as conditions for further collaboration between the two parties:

1. The Communist Party should order its members to modify their expressions and attitude toward Nationalists;

2. The Chinese Communist Party should provide the Nationalists with a complete list of its members in the party;

3. Only those without dual-party membership would be eligible for appointments as heads of departments;

4. Communists with Nationalist membership must not call any party caucus in the name of the Nationalists without the latter's specific permission;

5. Communists with Nationalist membership must not have separate organizations or take separate actions without permission from the Nationalists;

6. The Chinese Communist Party and the Third International should submit to a joint conference of Nationalists, and the Communists should submit any instructions or directives on strategy for its approval before sending them to Communists in the Nationalist Party;

7. Without first obtaining permission to resign from the Nationalist Party, no Nationalist member could acquire membership in any other party;

8. Party members violating these stipulations are subject to penalties.

As a direct result of this agreement, Communist membership in the higher executive committees of the Nationalist Party was limited to not more than one-third. Although Chinese Communist leadership found itself increasingly at the mercy of the Nationalists, especially Chiang Kai-shek, the Comintern in Moscow simply denied that anything unusual had taken place in China, and

Borodin's relations with Chiang Kai-shek became, to all appearances, more cordial than ever.[15]

III. The Northern Expedition

The continuing fighting intensified among northern Chinese warlords in mid-1926 and increased Kuomintang hopes of beginning their long-cherished drive against the warlords and to unify China. In July, 1926, after receiving support from progressive warlord-generals such as Li Tsung-jen, Li Chi-shen, and Pai Ch'ung-hsi, among others, Chiang Kai-shek was officially named Commander in Chief of the Nationalist forces in Canton and commenced his famous northern expedition.

The expedition forces in the western columns, allied with warlord T'ang Sheng-chih, and under Chiang's personal command, took Changsha, Hunan, on July 10, and the central Yangtze Valley by the end of August. Finally, the Wuhan metropolis, including Wuchang, Hanyang, and Hankow, were captured in early October. Chiang Kai-shek established his headquarters in Nanchang.

During the early days of the northern expedition, the Communists stepped up their efforts to strengthen the Kuomintang Leftists and to undermine Chiang Kai-shek's moderate policies. Then, Borodin, aware that the city of Wuhan was a perfect industrial center for Communist organization and agitation, took advantage of the fact that Chiang was in the field directing the war, and managed to persuade the Leftist leaders in Canton to move their government to Wuhan. They adopted radical policies and later welcomed Wang Ching-wei back from Europe as their leader. By 1927, the issues were multiplying between

---

[15]Tang Leang-li, *The Inner History of the Chinese Revolution* (London, Routledge and Sons, Ltd., 1930), p. 247.

Chiang Kai-shek in Nanchang and the Leftists in Wuhan; between Chiang and his chief adviser, Borodin; between Borodin and the Comintern representative H.N. Voitinsky; and among various factions of Communists.[16]

The reason for this is relatively simple. The Communists were more interested in converting the northern expedition from an anti-warlord campaign to a social and economic revolution. Ch'en Tu-hsiu, for example, wrote: "The northern expedition is merely a military move. . . . It does not necessarily mean Chinese national revolution. . . . It falls short of being a direct armed clash with the Imperialists. . . . So long as the cynical military men and politicians are actively seeking personal gains in their midst, the success of the northern expedition can be at the most a speculative military victory, not the victory of the revolution."[17]

With Wuhan now under their control, the Communists began to develop new strategies. Several Communist members held important governmental posts, including Tan P'ing-shan as Minister of Agriculture and Su Chao-cheng as Minister of Labor. Borodin's personal influence rose again to the point where he was once more in control of the state apparatus in Wuhan. By the end of the year, the Comintern sent another representative, M. N. Roy, who arrived in Wuhan to direct Communist activities. Meanwhile, the party sent Chou En-lai to Shanghai to overthrow local rulers in that city in order to gain control of Shanghai's financial empire. The Shanghai General Labor Union, under the auspices of the Communists, began with a workers' demonstration on October 24, which was called the first Shanghai insurrection; and additional mass demonstrations took place on November 28 and December 12.

[16]Robert C. North, *op. cit.*, pp. 92–93.

[17]Ch'en Tu-hsiu, "On the National Government's Northern Expedition," *The Guide Weekly*, No. 161 (July 7, 1926); quoted in Warren Kuo, *op. cit.*, p. 188.

On January 3, 1927, three days after the formal inauguration of the Nationalist's new government in Wuhan, the Chinese Communist Party led a crowd of workers to the British concession in Hankow, the first incursion of its kind in Chinese history since the Boxer Rebellion. Meahwhile, Chiang's army, after a short winter recess at Nanchang, advanced again and reached Hangchow and beyond in February, 1927. Shanghai's General Labor Union called for general strikes within the city in anticipation of Chiang Kai-shek's attack on that city. Finally, on March 21, after a previous failure, the workers, an estimated 600,000, left their jobs and joined in a massive demonstration of force. They began by taking over some key sections of the city.[18] Three days later, Chiang Kai-shek's troops captured the nearby city of Nanking. Immediately there were violent anti-foreign riots in Nanking, and several foreign residents were killed.

By now Chiang Kai-shek had become personally concerned with the possible adverse reactions of foreign powers against his northern campaign, because of the strong anti-foreign movements initiated by the Leftists and Communists. Shanghai became very tense. The city was divided into several sections: some controlled by the Communists; others by warlord garrison troops; the concessions were patrolled by foreign troops. Chiang withheld his anticipated attacks on the city and instead began to make political arrangements with several factional groups. On March 26, when Chiang Kai-shek finally arrived in Shanghai aboard a gunboat, he met no opposition from anyone; in fact, he found his support growing, from bankers and businessmen to the gang leaders of secret societies.[19]

Chiang brought 3,000 soldiers to Shanghai and on April

[18]James Pinckney Harrison, *op. cit.*, p. 93.

[19]Robert C. North, p. 97.

12, he carried out a bloody surpise coup against the Communists, who controlled some sections of the city. Chiang's soldiers rounded up all the Leftist radicals, seized what few weapons they had, and executed on the spot all those who resisted. Within a matter of days, the Communist movement in Shanghai was crushed. Many Communist and labor leaders were arrested, and only Chou En-lai was able to escape by his quick wits and luck. A similar coup ordered by Chiang Kai-shek was initiated in Canton two days later. On April 24, he proclaimed a new Nationalist government in Nanking.

The Communists could only appeal to the Wuhan Nationalist Leftists for support; the latter promptly dismissed Chiang (on paper) as the Commander in Chief of the northern expedition forces. The Communists then opened a Fifth Party Congress on April 27, 1927, in Hankow to consider this crisis. Ch'en Tu-hsiu reaffirmed the necessity and desirability of a united front policy with the Leftist leader, Wang Ching-wei. The new Central Committee reelected Ch'en as the secretary general and Chou En-lai as head of the military affairs committee, Li Li-san headed the labor department and Ch'ü Ch'iu-pai replaced Mao Tse-tung as supervisor of the peasant department.

But this time, the Wuhan Leftists were becoming increasingly alarmed with the Communist radical agrarian policies, since the Leftists in Wuhan were supported by some progressive warlord-generals such as T'ang Sheng-chih and other military men who were also large landholders. While Ch'en Tu-hsiu argued in favor of a compromise with the warlords affiliated with Wuhan Leftists, the Comintern representative, M. N. Roy, insisted that warlords and other militarists be demoralized and destroyed. During the ensuing debate that followed the Fifth Party Congress, Roy appealed to Moscow for new instructions. Finally, a telegram from Stalin arrived: IT IS

NECESSARY TO LIQUIDATE THE DEPENDENCE UPON UNRELIABLE GENERALS IMMEDIATELY. MOBILIZE ABOUT 20,000 COMMUNISTS AND ABOUT 50,000 REVOLUTIONARY WORKERS AND PEASANTS FROM HUNAN AND HUPEH, FORM SEVERAL NEW ARMY CORPS, UTILIZE THE STUDENTS OF THE SCHOOL FOR MILITARY COMMANDERS, AND ORGANIZE YOUR OWN RELIABLE ARMY BEFORE IT IS TOO LATE.[20]

Roy showed this telegram to Wang on June 1, 1927. Shocked by this new conspiracy, Wang secretly convened the Leftist Executive Committee of the Nationalist Party, not permitting Communist members from attending it. On July 15, 1927, the Communist Party was expelled from Wuhan and its militia disarmed. Mikhail Borodin, who came to China in 1923 to aid Sun Yat-sen, was now "escorted" along with other Russian advisers back to the Soviet Union. He survived the purges in Russia and held some minor positions. M. N. Roy, however, was made a scapegoat by the Comintern for the failure in China; he fled to Germany and later returned to his native country, India, where he died in 1954.

This action by Wang Ching-wei paved the way for a reconciliation with Chiang Kai-shek's government in Nanking. The Wuhan government dissolved and then amalgamated with the new Nanking government in September, 1927, from which Chiang Kai-shek had tactfully but temporarily stepped down and gone to Japan. Later, in Shanghai, he married Soong Mei-ling, sister of Madame Sun Yat-sen, in December, 1927.

Chiang returned to Nanking to resume the northern expedition in the early days of 1928 and was eventually to capture Peking. The warlord Chang Tso-lin was murdered by the Japanese while retreating to Manchuria, and his son, Chang Hsueh-liang, also known as "the young marshal,"

[20]Xenia J. Eudin and Robert C. North, *Soviet Russia and the East, 1920–1927* (Stanford, Stanford University Press, 1957), p. 304.

declared his allegiance to the Kuomintang government in December, 1928. Thus, the northern campaign came to an end, and, in name at least, China was unified.

Through this whole affair, Joseph Stalin maintained that his policy throughout the years 1923–1927 had been entirely correct; and he said that "only people who have no understanding of Marxism can demand that a correct policy must always lead to immediate victory over an opponent. The attainment of an immediate victory over opponents depends not only upon correct policy, but above all, on the relative strength of the class forces involved."[21] Soon, under his direction, the Comintern sent new agents, Besso Lominadze and Heinz Neumann, to reorganize the shattered Chinese Communist Party.

Suggested Reading

BRANDT, CONRAD, et al., A Documentary History of Chinese Communism. Cambridge, Massachusetts, Harvard University Press, 1959, Section II.

——, Stalin's Failure in China, 1924–1927. Cambridge, Massachusetts, Harvard University Press, 1958.

CH'EN, KUNG-PU, The Communist Movement in China. New York, Octagon Books, 1966.

CHIANG KAI-SHEK, Soviet Russia in China. New York, Farrar, Straus and Cudahy, 1958.

EUDIN, XENIA J. and ROBERT C. NORTH, Soviet Russia and the East, 1920–1927. Stanford, California, Stanford University Press, 1957.

HARRISON, JAMES PINCKNEY, The Long March to Power. New York, Praeger Publishers, 1972, chapter 3, 4, and 5.

ISSAC, HAROLD C., The Tragedy of the Chinese Revolution, rev. ed. Stanford, California, Stanford University Press, 1961.

KUO WARREN, Analytical History of the Chinese Communist Party. Taipei, Institute of International Relations, 1966, Book One.

LI CHIEN-NUNG, The Political History of Modern China, 1840–1928. Princeton, New Jersey, D. Van Nostrand, 1956.

[21] Quoted in Benjamin I. Schwartz, op. cit., p. 86.

LINEBARGER, PAUL, *The Political Doctrines of Sun Yat-sen*. Princeton, New Jersey, D. Van Nostrand, 1956.

NORTH, ROBERT C., *Moscow and Chinese Communists*, second ed. Stanford, California, Stanford University Press, 1963.

——, and XENIA EUDIN, *M. N. Roy's Mission to China*. Berkeley, California, University of California Press, 1952.

TANG, PETER S. H., *Russian and Soviet Policy in Manchuria and Outer Mongolia, 1911–1931*. Durham, North Carolina, Duke University Press, 1959.

WHITING, ALLEN S., *Soviet Policies in China, 1917–1924*. New York, Columbia University Press, 1954.

WILBUR, C. MARTIN and JULIE LIEN-YING HOWE, eds., *Documents on Communism, Nationalism and Soviet Advisors in China, 1918–1924*. New York, Columbia University Press, 1954.

WOO, T. C., *The Kuomintang and the Future of the Chinese Revolution*. London, G. Allen and Unwin, 1928.

CHAPTER THREE:

COMMUNIST PUTSCHISM

AS soon as the military phase of the northern expedition was completed, Chiang Kai-shek established firm control of the Nationalist Party. He was elected as its Chairman and as head of its standing committee, which was largely made up of experienced politicians but did not include any former members of the leftist Wuhan regime. The party was to implement Dr. Sun Yat-sen's Three People's Principles and to begin an era of political tutelage in order to facilitate the establishment of a constitutional government with five branches: executive, legislative, judicial, examination, and control.[1]

In operation, Chiang's government was a series of interlocking directorates dominated by a relatively small group of politicians and generals. When persuasion failed, he was known not to hesitate in the use of force to diminish the power of his opponents. During these same years, the Chinese Communist movement found itself fractured into scattered components and uncertain about a proper course. The party, in fact, convened its Sixth National Congress not in China, but in a village outside Moscow from June 18 to July 11, 1928.

The Chinese Communist Party's Sixth Congress declared

---

[1]For a study of Sun's Three People's Principles, see Paul Linebarger, *The Political Doctrines of Sun Yat-Sen* (Princeton, New Jersey, Van Nostrand and Co., 1956).

that the "danger of the party's alienation from the masses lies in putschism," and "putschism in theory, means a few individuals wishing to attack an obviously far superior enemy by continual military actions, blind and impetuous measures which forsake and ignore the masses."[2] The same party resolution continued: "A putsch in practical action is an insurrection by a few 'Party Men' without the necessary day-by-day economic and political preparation, a brutal struggle that relies entirely on military strength, in the nature of a military adventure. Naturally, such a putsch usually forces the masses into military insurrection, often resulting in unorganized, sporadic acts of terrorism. This will lower the party's prestige among the masses and end in the unrequited loss of the vanguard units of the workers and of Communism."[3]

I. Communist Uprisings

After the Communists were expelled by the Wuhan Nationalist Leftists, the Comintern ordered the Chinese Communist Party into a series of putschs in the cities in the fall of 1927. Under Comintern agent Lominadze's direction, the first uprising was staged at Nanchang, capital of Kiangsi province. On the night of August 1, more than 20,000 Nationalist troops under the command of two Communist military officers, Ho Lung and Yeh T'ing, revolted and captured Nanchang. They seized important business properties and demanded payments by local merchants. Both Ho Lung and Yeh T'ing had been officers of the Nationalist 11th Army. Yeh joined the party in 1925 and commanded a vanguard unit on the northern

[2] "Political Resolution" (September, 1928), quoted in Conrad Brandt, Benjamin Schwartz, and John K. Fairbank, *A Documentary History of Chinese Communism* (Cambridge, Harvard University Press, 1959), p. 145.

[3] *Ibid.*

expedition; and Ho Lung joined the party after the Nanchang uprising. Both men became outstanding military leaders in the Chinese Communist revolutionary movement.[4] Other important Communists participating in the uprising included Chou En-lai, Chang Kuo-t'ao, and Chu Teh.

Nanchang was recaptured by Nationalist General Chang Fa-k'uei and the Red Army withdrew southward through Kiangsi, entered Kwangtung province and, in late September, 1927, attacked and occupied the important port city of Swatow. Meanwhile, at an emergency meeting of the Central Committee in Hankow on August 7, 1927, a resolution was passed and a circular letter was issued to all party members which stated: "The Chinese Communist Party has not only carried out an erroneous policy, resulting in the defeat of the revolution, voluntary cancellation of the revolutionary efforts and capitulation to the enemy, but has also failed to admit its errors and obey the instructions of the Communist International."[5] Ch'en Tu-hsiu, the party founder, was condemned for his "rightist opportunism" and he was replaced by Ch'ü Ch'iu-pai.

The emergency meeting produced three important policy documents dealing with the peasant struggle, the labor movement, and party organization. For example, the policy statement on the peasant struggle states: "The Party's general line should be to work for revolt in the provinces on the basis of the peasant movement. The revolt should take place during the present autumn harvest so that the peasants can refuse to pay taxes and rents. . . . The Chinese Communist Party should be prepared to frustrate all counter-revolutionary attempts and to wage fierce revolutionary war. . . . It should engineer the insurrection

[4]*Cf.* Donald W. Klein and Anne B. Clark, *Biographic Dictionary of Chinese Communism, 1921-1965,* 2 vols. (Cambridge, Harvard University Press, 1971).

[5]Quoted in Warren Kuo, *op. cit.,* p. 286. Several sources also gave Kiukiang, Kiangsi, as the site of the August 7 emergency conference.

of workers and peasants under the banner of the left wing of the Nationalist Party. . . ."[6]

Because of the uncompromising resolutions, in September, 1927, the Communist Party members staged new autumn harvest uprisings in four provinces: Hunan, Hupeh, Kiangsi, and Kwangtung. Troops for the autumn harvest uprisings included Wuhan Nationalist forces which had defected from the Nationalist Leftists and peasant-guard forces from villages. They became the backbone of the First Peasants and Workers Army of the Chinese Communists.

The autumn harvest uprisings failed miserably. The party leadership under Ch'ü Ch'iu-pai, which had ordered them, blamed other party members for their inability to carry out directives. Mao Tse-tung, who had been charged with the task of raising a Communist revolt in his native province of Hunan, also failed. He only narrowly escaped capture and execution. Subsequently, he was dismissed from both the Politburo and the Central Committee. From this debacle he fled with a handful of followers to the Chingkang Mountain in neighboring Kiangsi province, where he established a rural soviet base that was to be the basis for his own later rise to power.

In spite of these failures, the Chinese Communist Party called an enlarged session of the Central Committee on November 10 to 14, 1927, in which it adopted another radical resolution stating: "The Chinese revolution not only did not ebb, but rose to a new higher stage."[7] The resolution demanded a threefold strategy for the party: "(1) To have spontaneous revolutionary struggles of the masses; (2) to combine the sporadic and scattered peasant uprisings into a large-scale one; and (3) to coordinate the worker uprisings with peasant uprisings. . . ."[8]

[6]Ibid., pp. 293-294.

[7]Ibid., p. 301.

[8]Ibid., p. 302.

This sanguine estimation of the revolutionary situation led the party to stage an abortive uprising in Canton, known as the "Canton Commune," on December 11, 1927. The immediate cause was the struggle between two Nationalist generals: Chang Fa-k'uei and and Li Chi-shen for control of Canton. This seemed to offer an opportunity for the Communists to seize the city. The Soviet consulate in Canton was one of the centers of the uprising, although Moscow was uninformed of the exact timetable of the insurrection. The Communists created a Canton Soviet Council, freed political prisoners, and proclaimed a radical political program. However, this new uprising was ruthlessly crushed two days later. Most Communist members escaped to Hong Kong, but thousands were executed.

II. The Li Li-san Line

To cope with the urgent crisis in China, the party convened its Sixth National Congress, as already stated, in the Soviet Union from June 18 to July 11, 1928. Many important Chinese leaders, with the exceptions of Mao Tse-tung and Chu Teh, who were in rather inaccessible rural areas, attended the session. (After the defeat in the south, Chu Teh and the remnants of his small force made their way northward into Hunan and early in 1928 joined Mao Tse-tung on Chingkang Mountain.)

The party Sixth Congress elected twenty-three members as its Central Committee and named an illiterate former boatman, Hsiang Chung-fa, to replace Ch'ü Ch'iu-pai as the general secretary. But the real power fell into the hands of Li Li-san, who headed the propaganda department, and Chou En-lai, chief of the military affairs committee. While the party resolution strongly criticized Ch'en Tu-hsiu's "opportunism" and Ch'ü Ch'iu-pai's "putschism," it continued to stress the need to link peasant uprisings with urban insurrections.[9]

The congress adopted, among others, a six-point directive: "(1) Revive destroyed Party cells and Party headquarters on all levels. Special attention should be paid to the establishment and development of Party cells in big industrial establishments and factories. . . . (2) Actively recruit Party members among workers, continue to promote worker-comrades and 'actives' to the leading organs of the Party. . . . (3) Realize true democratic centralism; maximum democracy within the Party should be guaranteed within the limits of secrecy. . . . (4) Resolve all intra-Party disputes and liquidate tendencies towards regionalism and 'clique-ism.' . . . (5) Intensify the training of Party members and of the masses . . . , and (6) Intensify propaganda for correct concepts of armed insurrection, and for the general task of setting up the regime of councils of workers', peasants', and soldiers' deputies (Soviets)."[10]

The delegates seemed to have exaggerated their ability to generate revolution in China; they also were confused about Chinese politics in terms of the Marxian class analysis of the Soviet Union. As a result, on returning to China, party leaders such as Li Li-san again sought to centralize and "Bolshevize" top party leadership and insisted that the urban proletariat must lead the revolution, including acceleration of the revolution in the cities. This policy later was identified as the "Li Li-san line."

In order to carry out the directives of the congress, various Red armies were organized, including the following four important groups:[11]

[9]Robert C. North, *Moscow and Chinese Communists*, second ed. (Stanford, Stanford University Press, 1963), chapters VIII and IX.

[10]Conrad Brandt, *et al.*, *op. cit.*, p. 149.

[11]James Pinckney Harrison, *op. cit.*, p. 163.

(1) The First Corps in southern Kiangsi and western Fukien, under Mao Tse-tung and Chu Teh;

(2) The Second Corps in northern Hunan and southern Hupeh under Ho Lung, Chou Yi-ch'un, and Tuan Teh-ch'ang;

(3) The Third Corps in western Kiangsi, under P'eng Teh-huai and T'eng Tai-yuan; and finally,

(4) The Fourth Corps in the Hupeh-Honan-Anhwei border area, under Hsu Hsiang-ch'ien, and later, Chang Kuo-t'ao.

Li Li-san insisted that these Red armies must not just carry out local guerrilla actions, but rather, concentrate on large-scale military campaigns directed toward capturing the urban centers. Again taking advantage of Chiang Kai-shek's war against two Nationalist generals, Yen Hsi-shan and Feng Yu-hsiang, Li Li-san urged the Central Committee to adopt a directive on June 11, 1930, to begin a new revolutionary upsurge in preparation for nationwide uprisings. Li Li-san also spoke of total insurrection in Wuhan, in southern China, northern China, Manchuria, Korea, northwest China, Yunnan, and Kweichow, and in an all-out uprising. He was hoping to get the Soviet Union involved in the Communist revolutionary warfare in China.

Li Li-san began to centralize his control of power within the party apparatus. There was little overt opposition to his moves, especially after the departure of Chou En-lai for Moscow. Then, on August 1, 1930, Li proclaimed the formation of a general action committee to coordinate the revolutionary activities of all Communist groups in China. And he himself issued "daily orders," which were sent by couriers to various soviet areas in China.

In one instance, Li Li-san personally ordered the Third Corps under P'eng Teh-huai to attack Changsha, a provincial capital in Hunan. He also ordered the First Corps under Chu Teh and Mao Tse-tung to attack Nanchang and then to join forces with the uprisings at

Wuhan. Under Li's strategic planning, the Red forces took Changsha on July 27 for at least ten days, but they were unable to gain support from the working class in the city. The workers were simply insufficiently organized, and the expected proletarian upsurge failed to materialize. Meanwhile, the Kuomintang troops, backed by foreign gunboats, forced P'eng Teh-huai's soldiers to retreat from the city of Changsha, and attempts to attack Nanchang and other cities also failed.

Soon after the defeat of the Red forces in China, Moscow sent Chou En-lai, Ch'ü Ch'iu-pai, and a number of other Russian-trained Chinese students, known later as the "returned students faction," back to China. Because the Comintern's prestige was at stake, Moscow instructed Chou En-lai and Ch'ü Ch'iu-pai to censure Li Li-san. An important Third Plenum of the Central Committee at Lushan, Kiangsi, was held from September 24 to 28, 1930. Li Li-san was criticized, but the Third Plenum upheld Li's general policy.[12] Finally, the Comintern dispatched a letter in October, which was received by the Chinese on November 16, and formally condemned the "Li Li-san line." Li resigned from the Politburo on November 27 and was sent into exile to Moscow the following year. The leadership in the party soon passed into the hands of the Russian "returned students."

Pavel Mif, director of the Sun Yat-sen University in Moscow, was placed in charge of Chinese affairs. Ch'en Shao-yu was named acting secretary-general at the Fourth Plenum of the Sixth Central Committee held in January, 1931. Chang Wen-t'ien was named director of the organizational department, and Chou En-lai, director of the military department.

[12] James Pinckney Harrison, *op. cit.*, p. 182. For a detailed study of Comintern influence, see Richard C. Thornton, *The Comintern and Chinese Communist Party, 1928-1931* (Seattle, University of Washington Press, 1969).

III. Factionalism

Although it is generally assumed that the Chinese Communist Party follows strict ideological discipline based on Marxism-Leninism, factionalism has always been a critical problem since its inception. Bitter struggles among various factional blocs became a fact of life of Chinese Communism. Toward the end of the first decade, party leadership changed four times (Ch'en Tu-hsiu, Ch'ü Ch'iu-pai, Li Li-san, and Ch'en Shao-yu) and there were at least five major factional groups within the Chinese Communist movement.

The Central Committee Faction

First, there was the "Central Committee faction," originally led by Ch'ü Ch'iu-pai and later by Li Li-san. This group included other such important leaders as Chou En-lai and Li Wei-han.

Ch'ü will be long remembered for the part he played in the struggle against the founder of the party, Ch'en Tu-hsiu, in 1927, when Ch'en was condemned for his "rightist opportunism" as previously mentioned in this chapter. Ch'ü was born into an impoverished gentry family in Kiangsu province in 1899.[13] After his father abandoned his mother and four children, the burden of responsibility fell to his mother. But the financial strain proved too much for her and in despair she committed suicide when Ch'ü was sixteen. The children were shared out among various relatives as wards, and Ch'ü passed his early years in considerable uncertainty and misery. Finally, he moved to Peking and gained admission to the Russian Language Institute in the summer of 1917. It was in Peking that he joined the Marxist study group.

[13]Donald W. Klein and Anne B. Clark, op. cit., pp. 239–44.

Ch'ü began his career as a translator of Tolstoy and went to Moscow in 1920–1922 as a special correspondent for the Peking *Morning Post*. In January, 1922, at the Congress of the Toilers of the Far East, he was made an interpreter. A month later he joined the Communist Party. Next year, he returned to China and was soon elected a member of the Central Committee.

Ch'ü indicated a greater confidence in the proletariat and a lesser degree of trust in the bourgeoisie than did Ch'en Tu-hsiu. He also stressed the importance of the peasantry as a revolutionary force. In fact, he openly disagreed with Ch'en Tu-hsiu that the Chinese peasants tended toward conservatism. In May, 1926, on the eve of the northern expedition, Ch'ü called for the arming of the workers and peasants in preparation for "direct revolution."[14]

Early in 1926, Ch'ü demanded that the proletariat assume the leadership of the national revolution. The following year, he wrote the *Issue of the Chinese Revolution* and made a forcible indictment of the existing Communist leadership, including those close to Ch'en Tu-hsiu. Since he was also one of the few Chinese Communist leaders who had a firsthand knowledge of Soviet Russia, he was well liked by the Russians. In the emergency conference held on August 7, 1927, he became the leader of rallying forces against Ch'en Tu-hsiu. And as Ch'en's successor, he established new party lines for a series of uprisings in the latter part of 1927.

After his own failure and replacement by Li Li-san, he returned to work in Moscow for several years, under the name Strakhow, and gained some prestige in the International Communist Movement. He was made chief of the Chinese delegation to the Comintern and delivered a co-report on the national and colonial question at the Sixth

[14]Quoted in Chester C. Tan, *Chinese Political Thought in the Twentieth Century* (Garden City, New York, Doubleday & Co., 1971), p. 317.

Comintern Congress in August, 1928. He also attended the Anti-imperialist Congress in Paris in the fall of 1929 and the Conference of the Unemployed in Berlin in the summer of 1930.

Subsequently, after the failure of the "Li Li-san line" in China, he again returned to China to help the party. However, his vacillating attitude antagonized the Comintern representative, Pavel Mif, and the man who succeeded Li Li-san, Ch'en Shao-yu. Ch'ü went to Shanghai in 1931 and together with Lu Hsün, the famous Chinese writer, took a leading part in the League of Left-Wing Writers. After his final dismissal from the Politburo in 1933, he went to work for Mao Tse-tung as educational commissar for the Juichin Soviet government. When the Communist forces retreated during the Long March, he was left behind. While trying to escape to Shanghai by way of Swatow, he was captured in Fukien by the Kuomintang forces.

During the four months' imprisonment, he wrote *Superfluous Words*, a personal testament and revelation: "My basic nature, I believe, does not make for a Bolshevik fighter, or even a revolutionary novitiate. But because of pride, I did not have the courage, after joining the group, to recognize my own self and ask them to wash me out."[15] He was executed on June 18, 1935.

The Returned Students Faction

A second major faction within the party involved the "returned students" from Russia, also called the "twenty-eight Bolsheviks." They took over the party in 1931, merged with the "Central Committee faction," and also became known as the "Internationalists." With the Comintern's strong support, they dominated the party until after the Long March, when Mao Tse-tung emerged to key leadership.

[15]Quoted in Chester C. Tan, *op. cit.*, p. 322.

The "returned students" were under the leadership of Ch'en Shao-yu, often known as Wang Ming, who headed the Chinese Communist Party in 1931 and was the Chinese representative to the Comintern in Moscow from 1932 to 1937. Ch'en gained a worldwide reputation as the proponent of the "anti-Japanese united front," a sort of second united front strategy with the Kuomintang in China.

Ch'en came from a well-to-do family in Anhwei, where he was born in 1904.[16] He went to Shanghai as a youth and joined the Communist Party in 1925. Then he went to Moscow to attend Sun Yat-sen University together with some fifty Chinese students. They went through a two-year course in the social sciences and they also took field trips to factories, law courts, and other Soviet institutions. Ch'en learned Russian well and made many friends in the Soviet Union. During the party's Sixth National Congress in 1928, he was the chief interpreter for many Russian observers. He remained in Moscow until 1930 and then returned to China to engage in political struggle against Li Li-san.

At the Third Plenum of the party in September, 1930, he attacked both the "Li Li-san line" and the compromising attitude of Ch'ü Ch'iu-pai. Although Li Li-san placed Ch'en on probation for a short period, he was elected the acting secretary-general in June, 1931, with the help of Pavel Mif and the "returned students." But the party found itself in an increasingly dangerous situation as Chiang Kai-shek's campaign mounted against the Red Army's bases. Ch'en's role in party policies after mid-1931 remains unclear, since he left for Moscow to become Chinese representative to the Comintern about September, 1932. The party apparatus was under the control of his "returned student" colleagues, especially Ch'in Pang-hsien and Chang Wen-t'ien.

While Ch'en advocated a policy of united front with the Kuomintang, he felt the participation by the Chinese Communist Party must not interfere with its struggle for

[16]Klein and Clark, *op. cit.*, pp. 127–34.

proletarian hegemony, especially the mistakes committed by Ch'en Tu-hsiu during 1924–1927. Meanwhile, he developed some basic policy differences with Mao Tse-tung in that he felt that the urban workers were being neglected. In fact, later in 1942, during the rectification campaign initiated by Mao, Ch'en and other "returned students" were criticized for lacking practical revolutionary experience. Ch'en was stripped of his authority by the new party leadership during the early 1940's and held nominal posts into the 1950's. Then he went into exile in Moscow where he died in 1974.

The Real Work Faction

There were two additional minor splinter groups, one called the "real work faction," which opposed the "returned students," and another, under Jen Pi-shih, which supported the "returned students." The "real work faction" was made up of leaders from Li Ta-chao's original Peking Marxist Society under the leadership of Ho Meng-hsiung and Lo Chang-lung. Ho was involved in organizing the labor unions for the Chinese Communists and took part in various strikes from Peking to Shanghai in the 1920's. Ho later emerged as a powerful figure of the Kiangsu provincial party committee. They first attacked the "Li Li-san" line and later opposed the recently arrived "returned students." Ho was expelled from the party; however, he was praised by Mao Tse-tung at the Seventh Plenum of the Central Committee in April, 1945, and thus became a martyr.

Jen Pi-shih's faction grew out of the strength of the Communist Youth Corps. He was born in 1904 in Honan of a middle-class family and was influenced by the May Fourth Movement. He went to Shanghai and studied Russian at a foreign language school headed by Yang Ming-chai, the aide to Comintern representative Voitinsky. In the winter of 1920–1921, he was sent to Moscow and enrolled in the Communist University of the Toilers of the East, studying there until 1924. He became a member of the party in Moscow.

On returning to China in 1924, Jen was deeply involved in the affairs of the Communist Youth Corps (as the Socialist Youth League was now known). He was elected to the Central Committee, from the Youth League, at the age of twenty-three at the Fifth Party Congress in 1927. During the power struggle between Li Li-san and the "returned students," Jen strongly supported the newly arrived elite and thus was elected to the powerful membership in the new Politburo in 1931, together with such notables as Mao Tse-tung and Chou En-lai. He became one of the few leaders who was able to ride out the political storms in the 1930's. He was a key political officer in the Red Army from 1933 to 1938 and worked in close association with Chairman Mao from the 1940's until he died in 1950.

The Red Army Leaders Faction

Finally, there was the "Red Army leaders faction," under Mao Tse-tung, Chu Teh, Ho Lung, and others in the soviet rural areas. They were responsible for building up a powerful and efficient revolutionary force from a small struggling band of soldiers in the famed Kiangsi soviet.

One important leader in this faction is Chu Teh, who was born of humble origins in 1886 in a hilly and isolated village of northern Szechwan.[17] He studied physical education in his early youth, then enrolled in the newly established Yunnan Military Academy in 1909. It was there he came under the influence of Sun Yat-sen's revolutionary ideas. On graduation he was assigned as a platoon commander and took part in campaigns against Yuan Shih-k'ai, who was attempting to restore the monarchy. He became part of a warlord's army in Szechwan and for a short time led an unproductive and dissolute life.

[17]Donald W. Klein and Anne B. Clark, *op. cit.*, pp. 245–54.

In early 1922 he went to Shanghai to seek medical treatment to break the opium habit which he had acquired during his years of working in Yunnan. The following year he sailed for France and then to Germany. With Chou En-lai's sponsorship, he joined the Chinese Communist Party in Berlin. He began to study Marxist works and attended lectures in the social sciences at the University of Göttingen from 1923 to 1924. He went to the Soviet Union in 1925 and studied at the Communist University of the Toilers of the East. As the northern expedition campaign was getting under way, Chu returned to China and went back to Szechwan to convince the warlord general Yang Sen to join the northern expedition. For a short while, in late 1926, Chu headed the political department of Yang's army.

Chu participated in a number of Communist uprisings, first in Nanchang, later in Swatow and Canton. Defeated in the south, as already noted, Chu Teh and his forces made their way northward into Hunan, and early in 1928 joined Mao Tse-tung on Chingkang Mountain. This event has been hailed in Communist history as a great turning point, because Mao Tse-tung had been operating with great difficulty from his base. The Chu-Mao troops merged to form a single Fourth Red Army of about 10,000 men, although only a fifth were armed.

The Chu-Mao forces were temporarily strengthened in the fall of 1928 when P'eng Teh-huai arrived from the north. However, when the Nationalists pressed their attack against them, Chu and Mao moved eastward toward Fukien and then to Juichin in southeastern Kiangsi. There they established the well-known Kiangsi soviet and Chu was elected a member of the Central Executive Committee in November, 1931. Chu was also appointed People's Commissar for Military Affairs as well as the Chairman of the important Central Revolutionary Military Council. Finally, at the 1931 All-China Congress of Soviets, Chu's role as Commander of the entire Red Army was confirmed.

In 1928, there were less than 10,000 soldiers in the Red Armies, but the forces grew from 22,000 in 1929 to 60,000 in April, 1930. It is surely true that, but for the guerrilla movement inaugurated by Chu and Mao, the Communist movement would at this time have lost all momentum and probably have diminished to an ineffectual intellectual protest with minimum mass support.

Suggested Reading

BRANDT, CONRAD, et al., A Documentary History of Chinese Communism, Cambridge, Massachusetts, Harvard University Press, 1959, especially section III.

HARRISON, JAMES PINCKNEY, The Long March to Power, New York, Praeger Publishers, 1972, especially chapters 7 and 8.

HOFHEINZ, ROY, "The Autumn Harvest Insurrection." China Quarterly, No. 32, October–December, 1967.

HSIAO, TSO-LIANG, Chinese Communism in 1927: City vs. Countryside. Hong Kong, the Chinese University of Hong Kong, 1970.

——, Power Relations within the Chinese Communist Movement, 1930–1934. Seattle, Washington, University of Washington Press, 1961.

——, "Chinese Communism and the Canton Soviet of 1927." China Quarterly, No. 30, April–June, 1967.

KUO, WARREN, Analytical History of the Chinese Communist Party. 4 books, Taipei, Institute of International Relations, 1966, et seq. This is the official Nationalist interpretation of the Communist movement in China, with selected documents.

LASSWELL, HAROLD D., and DANIEL LERNER, eds., World Revolutionary Elites. Cambridge, Massachusetts, MIT Press, 1966.

MIF, P., Heroic China. New York, Workers' Library Publishers, 1937. This is the account written by the Comintern representative.

RUE, JOHN E., Mao Tse-tung in Opposition, 1927–1935. Stanford, California, Stanford University Press, 1966.

THORNTON, RICHARD C., The Comintern and the Chinese Communists, 1928–1931. Seattle, Washington, University of Washington Press, 1969.

CHAPTER FOUR:

THE LONG MARCH

IN the early 1930's there were two centers of Communist power in China: the officially recognized Politburo, which headquartered in Shanghai after the 1927 defeats; and the rural base of "Red Army leaders." The official headquarters had lost much of its power and carried on primarily clandestine organizational and agitational activities in the urban centers.

Meanwhile, the Nationalists under Chiang Kai-shek began consolidating their control of the country. Chiang himself was particularly concerned over the seriousness of the Communists' threat, especially after the various urban uprisings. He set up a special anti-Communist headquarters at Hankow in order to inaugurate a series of campaigns against the Communists in the provinces of Hupeh, Hunan, and Kiangsi.

Chiang Kai-shek designated his initial expedition as the "first bandit-extermination campaign." It was launched in November, 1930. But the attack was met by the famous guerrilla tactics of Mao Tse-tung, which he has immortalized: "When the enemy comes forward, we withdraw; when the enemy withdraws, we go forward. When the enemy settles down, we disturb him. When the enemy is exhausted, we fight him."[1] Or, as he explained later:

---

[1] See Edgar Snow, *Red Star Over China*, rev. ed. (New York, Grove Press, 1968), p. 177, translations modified by this author.

Following out the tactics of swift concentration and swift dispersal, we attacked each unit separately, using our main forces. Admitting the enemy troops deeply into soviet territory, we staged sudden concentrated attacks, in superior numbers, on isolated units of the Kuomintang troops, achieving positions of maneuver in which, momentarily, we could encircle them, thus reversing the general strategic advantage enjoyed by a numerically greatly superior enemy.[2]

The next year, undeterred but also uninstructed by this experience, Chiang Kai-shek tried again, twice, in the second and third extermination campaigns. The second and third campaigns were no more successful than the first, leaving the Communists stronger than before through captured supplies and prisoners. At the same time, the Japanese, through the September 18, 1931, Mukden incident, began to seize Manchuria. The Japanese also fought a two-month battle around Shanghai to break a Chinese boycott of Japanese goods. All these Japanese aggressive actions temporarily interrupted Chiang Kai-shek's further extermination campaigns against the Communists until the summer of 1932.

I. Growth of Soviet Bases

On the Communist side from 1927 to 1930, there was the creation of six principal soviet bases and the expansion of the Red Armies. For example, Mao Tse-tung himself was responsible for the formation of a central soviet base in southern Kiangsi in 1930, although Mao did not emerge as the party leader until 1935. The central soviet base included such regions as southern Kiangsi and western Fukien. In March, 1930, a worker-peasant-soldier government in the form of a council with a body of delegates was inaugurated.

[2]*Ibid.*, p. 183.

Other soviet areas included the Hunan-Hupeh-Kiangsi soviet; the Hupeh-Honan-Anhwei soviet; the Hung Hu, western Hunan, and Hupeh soviet; the Fukien-Chekiang-Kiangsi soviet; and finally, the Yu Kiang and Tso Kiang River soviet.

In fact, from 1931 to 1934, there were eight important soviet bases that enjoyed some degree of continuity:

1. The Central soviet in southern Kiangsi and western Fukien
2. the Northeast Kiangsi soviet (Kan-Min-Wan)
3. the Hunan-Kiangsi soviet (Hsiang-Kan)
4. the Hunan-Hupeh-Kiangsi soviet (Hsiang-O-Kan)
5. the Southwest Kiangsi soviet (Kan-Yueh)
6. the Hupeh-Honan-Anhwei soviet (Oyuwan)
7. the Western Hunan-Hupeh soviet (Hsiang-O-Hsi)
8. the Hung Hu soviet[3]

The population under these soviet areas was estimated to be 9 million, including more than 300,000 in the Red Army and 600,000 militia. At first these soviet areas were essentially local in character, and it was not until 1931 that a First National Congress of the Chinese Soviet Republic was organized on November 7 in Juichin, the capital of the Kiangsi soviet. Over 600 delegates attended this congress. The congress adopted a draft constitution, a land law, a labor law, and resolutions on economic policies and other matters. Mao Tse-tung was elected as Chairman of the Executive Committee; Chang Kuo-t'ao and Hsiang Ying were Vice-Chairmen.

The land law was quite radical in content, and included (1) confiscation without any compensation of lands from landlords, gentry, and militarists; (2) awarding land to Red Army soldiers; (3) confiscation of rich peasants' land; (4) confiscation of all properties and lands of the White Army

---

[3]James Pinckney Harrison, *op. cit.*, Chapter 9.

(counterrevolutionary organizations); and (5) disposition of lands belonging to religious institutions.[4]

The land policy was implemented in three stages: (1) land confiscation and distribution; (2) land classification; and (3) land improvement. The soviet government in each area coordinated with Red Army units to set up administrative units to carry out the land policy. Such administrative units included a land committee, a confiscation committee, and a workers' and peasants' inspection team, with the active participation of local peasants. In addition, in each soviet area, class warfare was initiated, according to the classification of the peasants: the poor, middle, and rich. The land policy was restricted to carrying out class warfare campaigns only against rich peasants who exploited others.[5] In actual practice, many landlords and rich peasants managed to retain political authority as well as their holdings by simply declaring themselves as revolutionists and pro-soviets.[6]

Within the soviet governmental structure, there were three major groups: (1) leading administrative and policy personnel; (2) auxiliary mass organizations that paralleled the soviet governments; and (3) subordinate administrative cadres who worked in lower levels and in local village units. One of the most important techniques adopted involved "the broadest possible mass participation in the revolutionary process of the Chinese Soviet Republic."[7] In fact, by emphasizing the central concept of mass participation, the Communists achieved great success in implementing some social and economic reform policies in

[4]Conrad Brandt, et al., op. cit., pp. 224–26.

[5]Ilpyong J. Kim, "Mass Mobilization Policies and Techniques Developed in the Period of Chinese Soviet Republic," in A. Doak Barnet, ed., Chinese Communist Politics in Action (Seattle, University of Washington Press, 1969), p. 84.

[6]Conrad Brandt, et. al., op cit., p. 219.

[7]Ilpyong J. Kim, op. cit., p. 75.

the soviet areas, including the establishment of poor-peasant corps and the farm union.

Another important achievement during the period involved the expansion of the Red Army.[8] In 1931, the army, under the command of Chu Teh and Mao Tse-tung, was the most important group. It had been designated as the Fourth Red Army between 1928 and 1930 and was reorganized in June, 1930, as the First Corps and then the First Front Army. It grew from 30,000 to 40,000 men in 1931 to more than 100,000 in 1933.

The second-strongest Red Army was first led by Hsu Hai-tung and Hsu Hsiang-ch'ien in the Hupeh-Honan-Anhwei (Oyuwan) border area and later by Chang Kuo-t'ao. This was called the First Red Army in 1928–1930, became the Fourth Corps, and by 1931 emerged as the Fourth Front Army. It supposedly had up to 60,000 men early in 1932.

The third group was led by Ho Lung in the Hsiang-O-Hsi area and was designated as the Second Front Army in 1934 with some 5,000 to 10,000 men. And a final group, which had been designed as the Fifth Red Army, was reorganized as the Third Corps in mid-1930 and led by P'eng Teh-huai, with some 10,000 men in 1931. This final group was placed under the command of Chu Teh and Mao Tse-tung's First Front Army. Thus, by 1932, these units of the Red Army were grouped into what became known as the First, Second, and Fourth Front Armies with a total of over 150,000 soldiers.

The Red Army soldiers were young, drafted from the party (28 percent were party members in 1934) and the Communist Youth League (16.6 percent), with only 4 percent of them over thirty-nine years of age. Most of them were from peasant background (68 percent) and were recruited from soviet bases (77 percent). Their social and political backgrounds were similar to those of the party as a

[8]James Pinckney Harrison, pp. 199–201.

whole. At least 70 percent of the more than 100,000 members were said to be peasants in the 1930's.[9]

II. The Long March

After several unsuccessful attempts to eliminate the Communists in the rural soviet areas from 1930 to 1933, Chiang Kai-shek invited a group of German military advisers, under General von Seeckt,[10] to reorganize the Nationalist forces. The Nationalists built a new system of blockhouses and fortified points to encircle the Communist rural soviet areas, to starve them by economic blockades, and finally to attack and destroy them. The Communist leadership in 1933 seemed to adopt the wrong tactics to meet the formidable menace of the fifth extermination campaign, for they fought from fixed positions and no longer used guerrilla tactics as expounded by Mao.

Therefore, the Long March was in fact the retreat of the Red Armies across the country, to escape the Nationalist pursuing forces and to stay alive.[11] In addition to the main retreat from Kiangsi, the other Soviet bases were also abandoned and their defenders undertook separate long marches toward Shensi. According to Edgar Snow's account,[12] the Communists covered a total of 6,000 miles on foot in 235 days and eighteen nights and crossed eighteen mountains and twenty-four rivers in eleven provinces. They started the March with some 100,000 men. When they finally arrived at northern Shensi, not more than 20,000 had survived, and most of these losses were due to hardship rather than enemy action.

[9] *Ibid.*, p. 201.

[10] General von Seeckt was later commander of the German Army in Belgium in the Second World War.

[11] For a complete study of the March, see Dick Wilson, *The Long March: 1935. The Epic of Chinese Communism's Survival.* (London, Hamish Hamilton, 1971).

[12] Edgar Snow, p. 194.

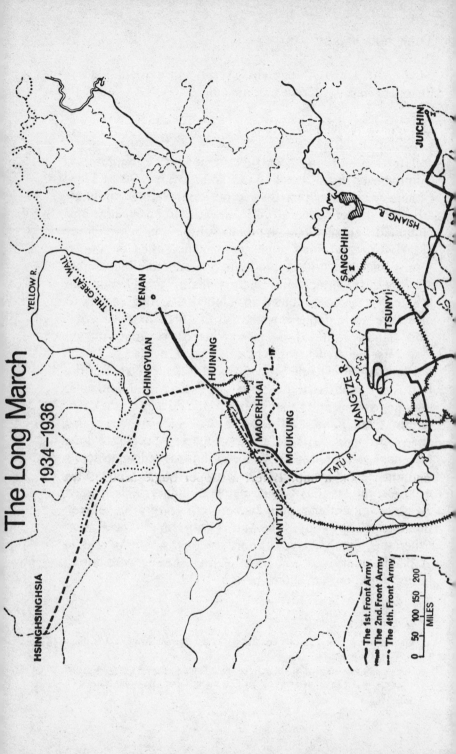

The Long March
1934-1936

HSINGHSINGHSIA

YELLOW R.

THE GREAT WALL

CHINGYUAN

YENAN

HUINING

MAOERHKAI

MOUKUNG

KANTZU

TATU R.

YANGTZE R.

SANGCHIH

TSUNYI

HSIANG R.

JUICHIN

— The 1st. Front Army
—₊— The 2nd. Front Army
–•–• The 4th. Front Army

0 50 100 150 200
MILES

The decision for the main columns of the First Front Army to break through the encirclement was allegedly made on October 2, 1934, by an ad hoc military council consisting of Mao Tse-tung, Chou En-lai, Wang Chia-hsiang, Liu Pao-ch'eng, and Otto Braun, among others. They made up the First, Third, Fifth, Eighth, and Ninth Corps; and most of the time, the First and Third Corps, under Lin Piao and P'eng Teh-huai, respectively, headed the line of march. The column of political workers was in the center, and the Fifth, Eight, and Ninth Corps guarded the flanks and rear.

The highest military authority was placed under the Central Soviet's Revolutionary Military Council, headed by Chu Teh, with Chou En-lai and Wang Chia-hsiang as vice-chairmen. Chou also served as director of the Central Committee's Military Affairs Committee; Liu Po-ch'eng was chief of staff, and Li Fu-ch'un directed the army's General Political Department.[13]

During the first week of the Long March, the First Front Army marched secretly and only at night to avoid Nationalist air attack. The soldiers bedded down each morning. In the afternoon, some of the soldiers plaited straw sandals (for walking shoes) and others cleaned rifles and then took a nap. Later, a supper bugle aroused the columns. Soldiers shouldered rifles, transport personnel carried boxes, cooks their kitchen utensils. All rushed to assemble for the march. The original objective of Mao's

---

[13] James Pinckney Harrison, *op. cit.*, p. 243. For an eyewitness account, see *On the Long March with Chairman Mao* (Peking, Foreign Language Press, 1959) and *The Long March: Eyewitness Accounts* (Peking, Foreign Language Press, 1963).

←
Reprinted with permission from Jerome Ch'en, *Mao and the Chinese Revolution*, New York, Oxford University Press, 1965.

Note: The First Front Army, the Second Front Army, and the Fourth Front Army indicate the three important routes of retreat by the Communist forces. Mao Tse-tung led the First Front Army from Juichin, Kiangsi province. Ho Lung commanded the Second Front Army from Sangchih; and Chang Kuo-t'ao headed the Fourth Front Army from Honan, Anhwei, and Hupeh provinces.

First Front Army was to join Ho Lung's Second Front Army in northwest Hunan. But Mao abandoned his plans after suffering severe losses in the process. Instead, he proceeded toward north-central Kweichow, where his troops captured Tsunyi on January 5, 1935.

At Tsunyi, Mao arose as the dominant figure at the important enlarged conference of the party Politburo.[14] Leading personalities of the party were all there, including the General Secretary Ch'in Pang-hsien, Chou En-lai, Ch'en Yun, Chu Teh, Liu Shao-ch'i, and Lin Piao. They reviewed their mistakes and demanded a new policy. Mao was most critical of the "returned students faction," which was then in control of the central leadership. Mao was given the key position to head the Military Affairs Committee[15] as well as being chairman of the government Executive Committee (not party Chairman, however). After the conference, Mao joined forces with Chang Kuo-t'ao's Fourth Front Army in northern Szechwan. By this time Chang's Fourth Front Army had decided to abandon his northern soviet base because of heavy pressure from the Nationalists.

The First Front Army was exhausted after many days of marching on foot into the frozen mountainous region. They had also met strong resistance during the crossing of the Tatu River in southwestern Szechwan, a narrow gorge spanned by a chain suspension bridge from which the planks had been removed. According to one account, "twenty volunteers, carrying with them swords and hand grenades, and covered by machine-gun fire, crawled along the chains to the other side, overawed and over-powered the guards, took the planks out of the warehouse, and placed them back on the bridge."[16] Finally, at Chiachin

[14]Famous as it is, the Tsunyi Conference is still shrouded in mystery. See Jerome Ch'en, *Mao and the Chinese Revolution* (New York, Oxford University Press, 1965), p. 188; also James Pinckney Harrison, pp. 245–48.

[15]Mao was replacing Chou En-lai.

Mountain south of Moukung, Mao's First Front Army at last met Chang's Fourth Front Army on June 12, 1935.

Mao immediately called a meeting at a small village in Liangkok'ou. The meeting turned into a stormy session between him and Chang Kuo-t'ao. Mao argued that the Red Army should continue to march northward and join the small soviet base set up by Liu Chih-tan and Kao Kang in northern Shensi. Chang, on the other hand, maintained that Mao's forces should join him in northwest Szechwan and continue to Sikang to build a new soviet base there and then, and contact the Soviet Union through Sinkiang.

Mao had known Chang early in the days of the Communist movement in Peking, where Mao was a library assistant at Peking University, and Chang, an undergraduate.[17] However, Chang's background and experiences differed considerably from Mao. Chang spent much of the interval between the First and Second Party Congresses in the Soviet Union, in connection with Comintern affairs. He had always had a closer relationship with Comintern representatives than with Mao; in fact, he was among the first Chinese to have close ties with the Comintern. Chang was also one of the moving forces behind the labor movement sponsored by the Communist Party, and believed that peasants took no interest in politics, while Mao had for the greater part worked among the peasants.

Although Mao was the party leader at the Liangkok'ou conference, and Chang had to obey him, Chang was the man who controlled 50,000 seasoned and well-rested troops, compared to Mao's tired and ragged troops. Consequently, a compromise was made. First, there was a reorganization of the two Front Armies and some of

[16] Nym Wales (Helen Snow), *Red Dust* (Stanford, Stanford University Press, 1952), pp. 71–72, quoted in Jerome Ch'en, *op. cit.*, p. 192.

[17] Donald W. Klein and Anne B. Clark, *op. cit.*, pp. 38–43.

Chang's men were sent to reinforce Mao's soldiers. Mao took his own First and Third Armies plus the Fourth and Thirtieth Armies from Chang. Mao's forces comprised the "east column" or the "right route." Chang was also joined by Chu Teh and Liu Po-ch'eng and became the "west column," or the "left route."

Mao and his "east column" crossed the vast grasslands of China and finally arrived in northern Shensi. Chang Kuo-t'ao, on the other hand, crossed and recrossed the grasslands, but nevertheless found no means of reaching his first objective, Sikiang. This "grassland" is in actuality a vast swamp in which a tough grass grows in stinking, treacherous black mud. There is always strong wind, often bringing with it rain or hailstones.

On route to Kantzu in June, 1936, Chang was joined by a third major group of Communists, the Second Front Army under Ho Lung and Jen Pi-shih. They joined forces, and now moved northward, after Ho and Jen convinced Chang to rejoin Mao. As they passed through Ninghsia province, the three commanding generals separated again. Chang led his remaining troops across the Yellow River into Kansu where his forces were all but annihilated by the local Moslem tribal army of Ma Pu-fang. He escaped to Ninghsia to rejoin Hsu Hsiang-ch'ien's forces and finally rejoined Mao Tse-tung in Shensi. Ho Lung was the last to arrive, nearly one year after Mao's army had reached Shensi.

In Yenan, Chang was given a post as vice-chairman of the Shensi-Kansu-Ninghsia border region government. However, his differences with Mao had not healed. In October or November, 1938, he had been expelled from the party at the Sixth Plenum, after his "defection" to the Kuomintang. Chang found refuge in Hankow, then the capital of the Nationalist government, and later moved on Chungking, the wartime capital. In 1945 he was elected to the Nationalist Party Central Executive Committee. When the Chinese Communists defeated the Nationalists in 1949, Chang lived in exile in Hong Kong. Mao Tse-tung, in his

1938 report, stated that the party had tried to save Chang but, because the latter "threw himself into the arms" of the Nationalists, the party "could not but resolutely expel him."[18]

The Chinese Communists regard the Long March as one of the greatest historic epics of victory.[19] But the fact is "a retreat is not a victory," as one historian put it. "The solid foundations for future success were laid less in the drama and agony of the March than in the less spectacular atmosphere of Yenan. The March salvaged the Chinese Communist Party from almost certain defeat, it gave Mao a precarious hold on Party leadership and it established an heroic myth of invincibility. But, without the slow work of consolidation during the Yenan period, it would have been an empty achievement: one of man's greatest feats of endurance would have been a Pyrrhic victory."[20]

III. The Rise of Mao Tse-tung

The road that led Mao Tse-tung to unchallenged predominance in the Chinese Communist Party, as we have seen, was a difficult one. This was in spite of the fact that he was identified with the earlier founders and had actively participated in the various phases of development of the party. Mao played a major role in the establishment of the Kiangsi Soviet base and the expansion of the Red Army in the early 1930's. He directed the Long March and later, as we shall see, directed the grand strategy during the Sino-Japanese War and the civil war against the Nationalists. He gained worldwide eminence after the founding of the People's Republic in 1949, and his thought became the instrument for analyzing problems of the

[18]*Selected Works of Mao Tse-Tung*, 11, *op. cit.*, p. 293.

[19]*On the Long March with Chairman Mao, op. cit.*

[20]Diana Lary's review on the Long March, *The China Quarterly*, 48 (October/December, 1971), p. 774.

present and a weapon for the consolidation of power in China.

Mao was born on December 26, 1893, in Shao-shan, a village in Hsiang-t'an, not far away from Changsha, the capital of Hunan.[21] He was constantly at odds with his father, who was a peasant. However, Mao did receive the traditional education in the classics before his father took him from school and put him to work. He then ran away from home and began studies at modern schools. In 1911, he went to Changsha where he was to spend most of the next decade. Mao's early life was certainly influenced by the trials and failures of Chinese politics, since he personally experienced the 1898 reform movement, the 1900 Boxer uprising, and the 1911 Sun Yat-sen revolution to establish a republic, and finally innumerable civil wars among warlords.

According to one historian and biographer, Mao has inherited some of the views of Wang Fu-chih through Yang Ch'ang-chi.[22] Wang was a prominent Hunanese scholar with a keen sense of history. He was against the restoration of ancient institutions and advocated a theory that "human nature had to adapt itself to the constantly changing environment."[23] Mao was also impressed with the leading Confucian scholars such as K'ang Yu-wei and Liang Ch'i-ch'ao of the reform movement. Mao Tse-tung related from memory:

> I began studying in a local primary school when I was eight and remained there until I was thirteen years old. . . . [Later] I went to the [new] school with my cousin. . . . I made good progress at this school. . . . I was reading two books sent to me by my cousin, telling me about the Reform

[21] See Edgar Snow, op. cit., also Donald W. Klein and Anne B. Clark, op. cit., pp. 676–88.

[22] Jerome Ch'en, op. cit., p. 12.

[23] Ibid.

Movement of K'ang Yu-wei. One book was edited by Liang Ch'i-ch'ao. I read and re-read these until I knew them by heart. I worshiped K'ang Yu-wei and Liang Ch'i-ch'ao. . . .[24]

It may be of interest to note that Mao is himself a classical scholar, well versed in the essays of Han Yu and Liu Tsung-yuan of the T'ang Dynasty (618–907 A.D.), poems of the Yuan Dynasty (1279–1368), and the *Precepts for Household Management* by Chu Pei-lu of the Ming Dynasty (1368–1644). In his *Selected Writings*,[25] he has quoted from the Confucian classics as such as *The Book of Rites*, *The Analects*, *The Golden Mean*, and the *Mencius*. He has also quoted from Taoist works such as *The Tao-teh Ching* and *Lieh-Tzu;* from the Han Dynasty (205 B.C.–220 A.D.), works such as Prince Liu An's *Huai-nan Tzu*, and Tung Chung-shu's *Discussions on the Spring and Autumn Annals;* from the great military work, *Sun Tzu*. Mao has also read many important Chinese historical works such as Tso Ch'iu-ming's *Commentary on the Spring and Autumn Annals*, Ssu-ma Ch'ien's *Chronicles*, Liu Hsiang's *Dialectics of the Warring States*, Pan Ku's *History of the Han Dynasty*, and Ssu-ma Kuang's general history, *Tzu-chih T'ung-chien*. Mao enjoys reading novels and often quotes from *The Water Margin*, the *Monkey*, *The Red Chamber Dream*, and *The Romance of the Three Kingdoms*. He is also fond of the contemporary writer Lu Hsün's satirical essays and stories.

On the other hand, Mao was not a scholar of Marxist writings. According to Edgar Snow, Mao cited only *The Communist Manifesto*, Kautsky's *Class Struggle*, and Kirkuppas' *A History of Socialism* as having made

[24]Edgar Snow, *op. cit.*, pp. 128–33.
[25] Jerome Ch'en, *op. cit.*, pp. 12–13.

important impressions on him in the early stages of his intellectual development.[26] And in a study published in 1964, in Mao's four-volume *Selected Works* only 4 percent of all references included are from Marx and Engels. Eighteen percent are from Lenin, and 24 percent from Stalin.[27] This does raise the question with respect to claims for Mao as a mighty contributor to the theory of dialectic materialism.

One cannot on the other hand deny Mao's contribution to Marxist-Leninist doctrine. In his report on the peasant movement in Hunan in 1927, for example, he outlined his rural strategy based on the peasantry, which he termed the "revolutionary vanguard."[28] In this sense he is a "Leninist in the best tradition; and the Report is a classic of Chinese Leninism."[29] But it must be remembered that Lenin, in spite of his reliance on the land hunger of the Russian peasant in the Russian revolution, regarded the peasantry as only an auxiliary force in the proletarian revolution. And Mao, by giving the peasant the main role in the Chinese revolution, diverged from Lenin and made a new contribution.

Another important contribution Mao made during this period of the Chinese Communist revolution involved his report on "the Struggle in the Chingkang Mountains" submitted to the Central Committee of the party in November, 1928.[30] As noted in the previous chapter, after the failure of the autumn-harvest uprising in Hunan in September, Mao retreated with his remaining forces into

[26] Edgar Snow, *op. cit.*, p. 153.

[27] V. Holnbnychy, "Mao Tse-Tung's Materialistic Dialectics," *China Quarterly*, 10 (July/September, 1964), p. 16.

[28] *Selected Works of Mao Tse-tung*, 1, *op. cit.*, p. 23.

[29] Conrad Brandt, *et al.*, *op. cit.*, p. 79.

[30] *Selected Works of Mao Tse-tung*, 1, *op. cit.*, pp. 73–78.

the Chingkang Mountains on the Hunan-Kiangsi border. There he and Chu Teh, among others, founded the revolutionary soviet base and consolidated the Red Army to turn away a series of initial attacks against them by the Nationalist troops.

To combat the pessimism of his fellow Communist officers, Mao stressed in this report his new policy of transferring the revolutionary force to the countryside to develop their strength in order to surround and eventually capture cities. Mao argued for two major organizational changes: (1) the development of a disciplined, trained and equipped Red Army, and (2) the organization of state power in the areas under Communist control in the form of a soviet following the example of the Russian revolution. What is unique in this and subsequent reports[31] is repeated moral exhortation and his stress on the importance of problem-solving, which filled a gap in the writings of Marx and Engels, widely regarded as being without any ethical criteria.[32]

Mao Tse-tung was instrumental in organizing and directing the Long March and had braved many dangers during and before the march. However, he spent almost all his time in the relative safety of Yenan and its environs making policy decisions and writing philosophical works. Other party leaders such as Chu Teh, P'eng Teh-huai, Lin Piao, Ho Lung, and Liu Pao-ch'eng did the front-line fighting. The day-to-day problem of Communist-Nationalist relations was left for Chou En-lai to handle: and internal

[31]Other writings include "Oppose Book Worship" (May, 1930), "In Memory of Norman Bethune" (December, 1939), "Serve the People" (September, 1944), "To be Attacked by the Enemy is not a Bad Thing but a Good Thing" (May, 1939), "The Foolish Old Man Who Removed the Mountains" (June, 1945).

[32]According to Sidney Hook, Marx and Engels were determined to get away from abstract moralizing about right and justice, and established an ethics firmly based in the real, class-divided world. See his *From Hegel to Marx* (Ann Arbor, University of Michigan Press, 1962), p. 51.

party management was also placed in the hands of lesser leaders such as Kao Kang, Lin Po-ch'u, and Liu Shao-ch'i. However, Mao was always the supreme leader, and whoever posed a threat to his leadership was driven out of the party.

Suggested Reading

BRANDT, CONRAD, BENJAMIN SCHWARTZ and JOHN K. FAIRBANK, *A Documentary History of Chinese Communism.* Cambridge, Massachusetts, Harvard University Press, 1959, section IV.

CH'EN JEROME, *Mao and the Chinese Revolution.* New York, Oxford University Press, 1967.

HARRISON, JAMES PINCKNEY, *The Long March to Power.* New York, Praeger Publishers, 1972, chapters 9, 10 & 11.

HSUEH, CHUN-TU and ROBERT NORTH, trans. "The Founding of the Chinese Red Army," in E. S. Kirby, ed. *Contemporary China, Vol. VI. Hong Kong, University of Hong Kong, 1962–1964.*

KIM, ILPYONG J., "Mass Mobilization Policies and Techniques Developed in the Period of Chinese Soviet Republic," in A. Doak Barnet, ed., *Chinese Communist Politics in Action.* Seattle, Washington, University of Washington Press, 1969.

NORTH, ROBERT C. *Moscow and Chinese Communists,* second ed. Stanford, California, Stanford University Press, 1963.

RUE, JOHN, *Mao Tse-tung in Opposition, 1927–35.* Stanford, California, Stanford University Press, 1966.

SCHWARTZ, BENJAMIN I., *Chinese Communism and the Rise of Mao.* Cambridge, Massachusetts, Harvard University Press, 1951.

SCHRAM, STUART, *Mao Tse-tung.* Baltimore, Maryland, Pelican Books, 1967.

SMEDLEY, AGNES, *The Great Road: The Life and Time of Chu Teh.* New York, Monthly Review Press, 1956.

SNOW, EDGAR, *Red Star Over China.* New York, Grove Press, 1968.

WILSON, DICK, *The Long March, 1935: The Epic of Chinese Communism's Survival.* London, Hamish Hamilton, 1971.

CHAPTER FIVE:

SINIFICATION OF COMMUNISM

AS we have noted in previous chapters, after the Chinese Communists had failed to capture cities by armed uprisings, the mainstream of the movement shifted from urban to rural areas. And then, they suffered devastating defeats during the Long March. However, during the War of Resistance Against Japanese Aggression from 1937 to 1945, the party began to recover from its early losses and gained tremendous strength in numbers.[1] It was also during this period that the nature of the party changed and the process of the sinification of Communism gelled.

The Red Army, which included the mere 20,000 survivors of the Long March, grew to more than 180,000 by late 1938 and to 500,000 in 1940. Party membership climbed in excess of 800,000 by 1940 and reached 1,210,000 by the Seventh Congress in April, 1945. The number of people under its control grew from 1.5 million in 1936 to 96 million by 1945. The militia expanded from 500,000 in the beginning of the War of Resistance to more than 2,000,000 by 1945 in a spectacular breakthrough. Because of the fact that most of the new recruits were from the peasant class, strenuous efforts were made to keep the party a disciplined, centrally controlled Leninist-Mao party, paving the way for the development of a new type of Communism, Maoism in China.[2]

[1] For their own story, see Hu Chiao-mu, *Thirty Years of the Communist Party* (Peking, Foreign Language Press, 1951).

[2] See Stuart Schram, *The Political Thought of Mao Tse-tung*, rev. ed. (New York, Praeger Publishers, 1969).

I. The War Years

After Mao Tse-tung had settled in Paoan, Chiang Kai-shek prepared a new extermination campaign against the Communists at the end of 1936 to destroy their final stronghold in Shensi. He might have succeeded except for the fact that Japan had begun its invasion of China. The Communists appealed to Chiang Kai-shek's soldiers to support them on patriotic grounds, and used the slogan "Chinese do not fight Chinese" to entice the Nationalists. The dramatic payoff came from the Nationalist Northeastern and Northwestern Armies, which had been assigned by Chiang Kai-shek to fight the Communists. They began to disobey Chiang Kai-shek's orders and reportedly negotiated with the Communists.[3]

To correct this challenge to his authority, Chiang Kai-shek, who had already become a national hero with his previous success in the northern expedition against the warlords, flew into the rebel soldiers' headquarters in Sian in late October and again on December 12, 1936. There he reaffirmed his determination to crush the Communists. Eight days after his second arrival, he was arrested by the rebellious troops under the command of Chang Hsueh-liang and Yang Hu-ch'eng. After extensive negotiations between Chiang and his captors, plus the intervention of the Soviet Union, which had concluded that the Communists must reunite with Chiang Kai-shek in order to fight the Japanese, Chiang was released on Christmas Day, 1936. He flew back to Nanking accompanied by the chief of the mutineers, Chang Hsueh-liang, who was promptly imprisoned on landing in Nanking, and remained under house arrest for the next thirty years, into the 1970's in Taiwan.[4]

Chiang had agreed, however, to give up his campaign

[3]See O. Edmund Clubb, *20th Century China*, 2nd ed. (New York, Columbia University Press, 1972), p. 276.

[4]For Chiang Kai-shek's personal account, see his *Soviet Russia in China, op. cit.*

against the Communists, and a second united front policy[5] was established to jointly resist Japanese aggression. The Communists acknowledged Chiang as the Supreme Commander of all Chinese armies, Nationalist as well as Communist. The Communists abolished their Red Army and renamed it the Eighth Route Army. Chu Teh and P'eng Teh-huai were appointed Commander and deputy commander, respectively, of the Eighth Route Army. Other important Communist military leaders such as Ho Lung, Lin Piao, and Liu Pao-ch'eng were designated as division commanders. The Eighth Route Army was linked into the Nationalist Military Command System, with Chu Teh assuming the post of Vice Commander in Chief of the Second War Zone under Nationalist General Wei Li-Huang.

Chiang Kai-shek furnished $100,000 (Chinese) per month for the operations of the Communist area, and another $500,000 (Chinese) monthly for the Eighth Route Army. The Nationalist government also invited Chu Teh and Chou En-lai to sit in on meetings of the Supreme National Defense Council in August, 1937. Chiang Kai-shek announced the creation of a People's Political Council in July, 1938, with seven Communist representatives, twenty-three representatives of third parties in China, twenty independents, and 150 members from the Nationalists.[6] In addition, the Nationalists authorized the publication of a Communist newspaper, the *New China Daily*, to be published in Nationalist-held areas. However, unlike the first united front policy of the 1920's, no Communist was permitted to join the Nationalist Party as an individual member.[7]

[5]For a detailed analysis, see Lyman P. Van Slyke, *Enemies and Friends: The United Front in Chinese Communist History* (Stanford, Stanford University Press, 1967).

[6]James Pinckney Harrison, *op. cit.*, p. 279.

[7]For a detailed analysis of Nationalist policy, see Milton J. T. Shieh, *The Kuomingtang: Selected Historical Documents: 1894–1969* (New York, St. John's University Press, 1970).

But the second united front did not endure. Nationalist leaders frequently declared the Communists had disobeyed Chiang Kai-shek's orders in attempts to fight the Nationalists and to gain territory for their own advantage.[8] The Communists' countercharge was that the Nationalists often rendered the position of Communist armies ineffectual. Clashes between the two contending forces began to occur again, such as the 1939–1940 conflict between the Eighth Route Army and the Nationalist Ninty-seventh Army under General Chu Huai-ping in southeastern Shansi. By 1940, clashes had increased, and expanded into Shangtung, Kiangsu, and Anhwei provinces. In January, 1941, a major confrontation between the two forces resulted in more than 2,000 Communist soldiers dead and 3,000 wounded. The Nationalists were reported to have suffered nearly 20,000 casualties in the incident later referred to as the "New Fourth Army incident."[9]

Meanwhile, as previously noted, Japan launched its large-scale offensive against the Nationalists on July 7, 1937. They had overrun all of Inner Mongolia by October and had invaded the provinces of Hopei, Shansi, and Shantung as well as central China. The Japanese used their concession in Shanghai to launch another invasion into China's industrial and population centers. With their naval forces on the Yangtze, the Japanese took the Nationalist capital, Nanking, in mid-December and advanced up the Yangtze to occupy Wuhan by 1938. The Japanese were also pushing the Chinese Nationalists back from the seacoast, and they occupied Canton on October 21, 1938. By the time the Japanese reached the eastern end of the Yangtzu gorges

[8] In the view of John King Fairbank, the Communists seemed to have done "less of the fighting against Japan than the Nationalist government." See his *The United States and China*, 3rd ed. (Cambridge, Harvard University Press, 1971), p. 282.

[9] James Pinckney Harrison, *op. cit.*, pp. 304–8.

above Yichang, they had occupied all of the eastern half of China.[10]

Although the Japanese had inflicted heavy casualties on some 800,000 Nationalist soldiers, Chiang Kai-shek would not seek peace, and set up a wartime capital in Chungking, in western China. The Japanese occupation of China was one of points and lines, and the invaders found that the countryside was turning hostile; the peasants were being organized into resistance by the Communists. The Japanese undertook no further major military operations in China for six years. Instead, they created a puppet Chinese government, with the former Nationalist Leftist leader Wang Ching-wei as its head. Venal politicians were placed to staff puppet governments, and local bullies and landlords were also induced to head local puppet police units to suppress peasant guerrilla forces. But these were the very people the peasants had hated for centuries. The Communists organized the peasants to fight with deadly hatred and cold courage and turned the war against the Japanese into a new ideological campaign based on resistance to imperialism and feudalism, as well as to the Japanese invasion.

II. Yenan Legacy

After reaching Shensi province in 1936, Mao Tse-tung first settled in Paoan. In December, the Communist forces captured Yenan, and they transferred their headquarters to that city. In Yenan, Mao consolidated his personal leadership over various factions of the Chinese Communist Party and expanded the Communist movement.

Adopting the tactics of guerrilla warfare, Communist forces, in 1937, infiltrated the mountainous regions of northern and eastern Shansi, southern Suiyuan and Chahar,

[10] O. Edmund Clubb, op. cit., chapter 7.

and central Hopei. They used captured weapons and equipment to arm the local peasants wherever they occupied an area, and they set up a border regional government with a "three-third" governing system: one-third Communists, one-third Leftist progressives, and one-third middle-of-the-roaders.

The party under Chairman Mao also strengthened its unity and discipline. In 1937 the party held a number of important conferences. For example, the National Conference of Party Delegates was held from May 3 to May 20, 1937, and attended by a hundred of the most important leaders. Another conference of the Politburo was held on August 25 in a village near Lochuan. Mao Tse-tung successfully defended his wartime expansion policy in spite of Chang Kuo-t'ao's challenge and emerged as the undisputed leader of the Politburo, a position that was reconfirmed at the Sixth Plenum of the Sixth Central Committee held in Yenan from September 28 to November 6, 1938.[11]

Under Chairman Mao's personal leadership, the party in Yenan began to reorganize its army, and to adopt the important policies of the mass line and the rectification movement.

The military forces were developed into four types: the central Red Army, district regional forces, local militia, and public security forces.[12] All these military units were closely linked with civilian organizations, such as labor associations, youth associations, and women's federations.[13] Probably the most important strategy adopted was the technique of "mass line," which is "the basic working

[11] James Pinckney Harrison, op. cit., pp. 282–89.

[12] See John Gittings, The Role of the Chinese Army (New York, Oxford University Press, 1967), and Samuel B. Griffith, The Chinese People's Liberation Army (New York, McGraw-Hill, 1967).

[13] James Pinckney Harrison, op. cit., p. 313.

method by which Communist cadres seek to initiate and promote a unified relationship between themselves and the Chinese population and thus to bring about the support and active participation of the people."[14] The mass line placed particular emphasis on the points of direct contact between the people and party cadres. This was illustrated in the technique of group study, which required participation by the entire population, under the leadership of a party propagandist. In this situation, everyone in the study group was expected to express an opinion, and a mere parroting of the official line was not considered sufficient. And often, after considerable discussion, a correct standard was adopted and the ideas of each individual member were criticized by others in the group.

As part of the overall policy of mass line, a rectification movement (*cheng-feng*) was initiated from 1942 to 1944. *Cheng-feng* can also be viewed as ideological remolding, directed especially toward those cadres accused of committing serious errors. They were subject to "struggle," under conditions of group psychological stress, with the goal "to reconstruct and reincorporate them within the movement,"[15] not to eliminate them as enemies. The rectification movement was quite extensive and was launched simultaneously by the party and government. It included:

(1) The campaign to consolidate and reduce organs and personnel in the bureaucracy of the government and army (*ching-ping chien-cheng*) from 1941 to 1943;

(2) The campaign to send intellectual cadres to the rural villages (*hsia-hsiang*, or *hsia-fang*) from 1941 to 1942;

---

[14]John Wilson Lewis, *Leadership in Communist China* (Ithaca, Cornell University Press, 1963), p. 70, See also Mark Selden, "The Yenan Legacy: The Mass Line," in A. Doak Barnett, ed., *Chinese Communist Politics in Action* (Seattle, University of Washington Press, 1969).

[15] Mark Selden, *op. cit.*, p. 105.

(3) The campaign for reduction of rent and interest paid by the peasantry from 1942 to 1944;

(4) The mutual-aid cooperative campaign to reorganize the village economy from 1942 to 1944;

(5) The production campaign to introduce a variety of new approaches to the political economy, such as increasing production with the creation of "labor heroes" in 1943; and finally,

(6) The educational campaign to spread literacy and to introduce new ideas to many villages in 1944. In this conjunction, there was an enormous production of illustrative art works: posters, cartoons, woodcuts, and picture storybooks, to serve a vast number of illiterate or barely literate persons. [16]

The final goal of Mao Tse-tung and the Chinese Communist Party in Yenan was more than just to consolidate military and political power, for they strove to create a new type of intellectual and emotional environment necessary for the development of a unified ideology in the Chinese Communist movement. This was clearly demonstrated in Mao Tse-tung's numerous speeches, including the "Talks at the Yenan Forum on Art and Literature" in May, 1942. Mao then stated, "There is in fact no such thing as art for art's sake, art that stands above classes or art that is detached from or independent of politics. Proletarian literature and art are part of the whole proletarian revolutionary cause. . . ." [17] Mao exhorted Chinese artists and writers to measure themselves against five yardsticks: standpoint, attitude, audience, work, and study. The five yardsticks would constitute control over ideological content in order to ensure the appearance of

[16] *Ibid.*, pp. 110–12.

[17] *Selected Works of Mao Tse-tung*, III, *op. cit.*, p. 80.

new revolutionary literature to advance the Chinese Communist revolutionary movement.[18]

III. The Birth of Maoism

During the Yenan period, Mao Tse-tung concentrated more on Marxist philosophy than he had previously been able to do, and established himself as a theoretician and interpreter of Marxism-Leninism in China. He wrote two basic theoretical works, *On Practice* and *On Contradiction*, which were based on his lectures delivered at the Anti-Japanese Military and Political College at Yenan in 1937. *On Contradiction* was not published until 1952.[19]

In *On Practice*, Mao perpetuates dialectical materialism and the neo-Confucian school of idealism. Mao stressed in this work that the process of knowledge has three stages: perception, conception, and verification. He also emphasized the relevancy of ideology to action; that is, the unity of theory and practice. On the basis of this analysis, Mao is said to have discovered the criterion of scientific truth which can be applied to the criticism of opposing policies as well as to the maintenance of leadership infallibility.

In the companion essay, *On Contradiction*, Mao insisted that contradictions are inherent in human relations and therefore govern politics. He stressed on the one hand the universality of contradictions, and on the other their particularity as determined by the needs of time and place. Mao's reasons in writing this essay related to the real contradictions which the Communists faced, as already discussed in earlier chapters, of their united front policy

[18]*Cf.*, Peter J. Seybolt, "The Yenan Revolution in Mass Education," *China Quarterly*, 48 (October/December, 1971).

[19]*Selected works of Mao Tse-tung*, I, *op. cit.*, pp. 295–308 and 311–46.

with the Nationalists. Mao stressed that contradictions are universal, absolute, existing in the process of development of all things, and from the beginning to the end in the process of development of each thing. As a result, day-to-day programs of orderly "resolution of contradictions" and periodical large-scale movement such as *cheng-feng* must be launched. Hence the theory of contradiction has been elevated to the level of supreme importance in the Communist Party to guide its future development.[20]

The formal Sinification of Communism began, however, in January, 1940, with the publication of the classic document *On New Democracy*.[21] In this important work, Mao aimed at, first of all, developing a new "democratic dictatorship" ruled by an alliance of several revolutionary classes made up of workers, peasants, the petty bourgeoisie, and the national bourgeoisie, a continuing concept which he first outlined in his 1935 *Report on Tactics of Fighting Japanese Imperialism*.[22] This was clearly distinct from the Soviet model based on Lenin's idea of political power for workers and peasants, which excluded the national bourgoisie class.[23]

In addition, in this major work, Mao Tse-tung envisioned that the Chinese revolution would be continued in two stages: the democratic and socialist. Though of different natures, the two stages could be homogenized into a continuous process if conducted by a coalition of all

[20]It has been suggested that Mao Tse-tung considers that contradictions will exist within Chinese society 100 years after his death, because "within the Communist Party, there had been a succession of renegades." See Frank Ching, "A Teasing, Chiding Mao Shown in Papers New to West." The New York *Times* (December 29, 1973).

[21]*Selected Works of Mao Tse-tung*, II, *op. cit.*, pp. 339–82.

[22]*Ibid.*, Vol. I, pp. 162–71.

[23]*Selected Works of Lenin*, I, Part 2, p. 56.

revolutionary classes.[24] Mao Tse-tung also proposed a "new democratic culture," or "a national, scientific and mass culture" for the Chinese state. He wrote:

New democratic culture is national. It opposes imperial oppression and upholds the dignity and independence of the Chinese nation. It belongs to our nation and bears our own national characteristics. It links up with the socialist and new-democratic cultures of all other nations and they are related in such a way that they can absorb something from each other and help each other to develop, together forming a new world culture; but as a revolutionary culture it can never link up with any reactionary imperialist culture of whatever nation. . . .

New democratic culture is scientific. Opposed as it is to all feudal and superstitious ideas, it stands for seeking truth from facts, for objective truth and for the unity of theory and practice. . . . In no case is there a possibility of a united front with any reactionary idealism. . . . New democratic culture belongs to the broad masses and is therefore democratic. It should serve the toiling masses of workers and peasants who make up more than 90 percent of the nation's population and gradually become their own.[25]

This goal of developing a new national, scientific, and mass culture for China is not a new one; it may be traced to the early revolutionary days in the 1920's when Mao first wrote the important *Hunan Report* (1927). He complained that "China has always had a landlord's culture, but never a peasant's culture."[26] Therefore he raised the question of cultural revolution in conjunction with the development of a new culture for China. Mao continued in the article *On New Democracy*:

[24]See C. P. Fitzgerald, *The Birth of Communist China* (Baltimore, Pelican Books, 1964), chapter 7.

[25]*Selected Works of Mao Tse-tung*, II, *op. cit.*, pp. 380–81

[26]*Ibid.*, pp. 371–72.

A cultural revolution is the ideological reflection of the political and economic revolution and is in their service. . . . This (new) culture can be led only by the culture and ideology of the proletariat, the ideology of communism . . . a national scientific and mass culture . . . combine the politics, the economy and the culture of the New Democracy, and you have the new-democratic republic, the Republic of China both in name and in reality, the new China we want to create.[27]

In practical politics, the new democracy offers the frustrated intellectuals as well as the oppressed peasants a way out. Not "workers of the world unite," but "workers, peasants, petty bourgeoisie and national bourgeoisie unite"—under the leadership of the Communist Party and carry out the first stage of the anti-imperialist democratic revolution. This first stage in the revolution will sweep away the power of the foreigner, the power of the bureaucratic capitalists, his lackeys, and the power of the feudal landlord, who is intimately bound up with the other two.[28] During this stage of revolution, Mao declared that China would need a "new Democratic government of a coalition nature embracing all parties and nonpartisan representatives,"[29] which could mean a coalition including the Chinese Nationalists as well as several minor parties and liberals. The coalition was to be achieved in 1949.

In summary, the birth of Maoism can be interpreted in two ways: First, on the philosophical level, Maoism becomes the variant of Marxism-Leninism and eventually develops into a new theoretical system. Secondly, Maoism serves for the Chinese people as a means to achieve a goal

[27] Ibid., pp. 373–82.

[28] C. P. Fitzgerald, op. cit., pp. 165–66.

[29] Quoted in John King Fairbank, op. cit., p. 282.

and as the day-by-day operational guide for carrying out the governmental policies. Or, as Robert J. Lifton called it, a way (*tao*), a call to a particular mode of being on behalf of a transcendent purpose. In this respect, Lifton also used the term "psychism" to denote Maoism.[30]

However, Lifton's analysis of Maoism is fundamentally critical. For example, he views ideological mobilization as an aberration which can only be counterproductive to the goals of economic and political development, without recognizing the subjective attitudes for the developmental process. Contrariwise, Joseph J. Spengler, an economist, assigned a central role to ideology when he suggested that the state of a people's politico-economic development depends largely on what is in the minds of its members, particularly the elite.[31] Or in other words, Maoism has placed primary emphasis on the reform of the mind and the spirit.[32]

Suggested Reading

CLUBB, O. EDMUND, *20th Century China*, 2nd ed. New York, Columbia University Press, 1972, chapters 5, 6, and 7.

COHEN, ARTHUR A., *The Communism of Mao Tse-tung*. Chicago, The University of Chicago Press, 1964.

COMPTON, Boyd, *Mao's China: Party Reform Documents, 1942–44*. Seattle, Washington, University of Washington Press, 1952.

FITZGERALD, C. P., *The Birth of Communist China*. Baltimore, Maryland, Pelican Books, 1964.

GITTINGS, JOHN, *The Role of the Chinese Army*. New York, Oxford University Press, 1967.

[30]Robert J. Lifton, *Revolutionary Immortality* (New York, Random House, 1968), pp. 99–126.

[31]Joseph J. Spengler, "Theory, Ideology, Non-Economic Values, and Politico-Economic Development," in Ralph Braibanti, ed., *Tradition, Values and Socio-Economic Development* (Durham, North Carolina, Duke University Press, 1961), p. 4.

[32]See Winberg Chai, *The New Politics of Communist China* (Pacific Palisades, California, Goodyear Publishing Co., 1972), Part Two.

HARRISON, JAMES PINCKNEY, *The Long March to Power*. New York, Praeger Publishers, 1972, chapters 12–17.

HSUEH, CHUN-TU, *The Chinese Communist Movement, 1937–1939*. Stanford, California, The Hoover Institution, 1962.

JOHNSON, CHALMERS A., *Peasant Nationalism and Communist Power*. Stanford, California, Stanford University Press, 1962.

LIU, F. F., *A Military History of Modern China, 1924–1949*. Princeton, New Jersey, Princeton University Press, 1956.

MCLANE, CHARLES, *Soviet Policy and the Chinese Communists, 1931–1946*. New York, Columbia University Press, 1959.

SCHRAM, STUART, *The Political Thought of Mao Tse-tung*, rev. ed. New York, Praeger Publishers, 1969.

SHELDEN, MARK, *The Yenan Way in Revolution China*. Cambridge, Massachusetts. Harvard University Press, 1971.

SNOW, EDGAR, *Random Notes on Red China, 1936–1945*. Cambridge, Massachusetts, Harvard University Press, 1957.

VAN SLYKE, LYMAN P., *The Chinese Communist Movement*. Stanford, California, Stanford University Press, 1968.

CHAPTER SIX:

THE PEOPLE'S REPUBLIC

"ON the morning of October 1, 1949," according to one eyewitness report, "hundreds of thousands of people gathered at the Tien-an-men Square in Peking. Thousands of red flags fluttered against the autumn wind, and a two-hundred-piece band played one martial song after another. The crowd was joyful and anxious. Finally, it heard the band play the familiar tune: 'The East is Red; The Sun is Rising. On the Horizon of China, appears the Great Hero Mao Tse-tung.'

"High on the Tien-an-men Tower a tall, plump man in grey uniform slowly ascended the marble stairs towards the central platform decorated with red lanterns. Flanked by other dignitaries, he at last reached the central position of the platform and, with a faint smile, turned and waved to the crowd below. Thunderous applause followed which drowned out even the loud band. By then, the band had come to the last line of the music: 'He is the Great Savior of the People.' . . ."[1] The "tall, plump man in grey uniform" was Mao Tse-tung, who was formally announcing the establishment of the Central People's Government of a new People's Republic in Peking, for which he had incessantly fought for twenty-eight years. The event is certainly a watershed of historic proportion, especially when one

[1]Quoted in Dun J. Li, *The Ageless Chinese: A History* (New York, Charles Scribner's Sons, 1965), pp. 510–11.

considers the founding of the Communist Party by a mere twelve men[2] representing only fifty-seven members. They were able to develop into a powerful organization controlling the welfare of one-quarter of the human race.

Mao Tse-tung had won the final civil war (1945–1949) against the Nationalists, in spite of the fact that at the outset, everyone outside China counseled against the revolution. Stalin wanted the Chinese Communist Party to seek a *modus vivendi* with Chiang Kai-shek, and General George Marshall argued for a coalition government between the two contending parties. And the Nationalist military strength was many times greater than that of the Communists.[3] But Mao Tse-tung had no doubt about his own strength and position in history, as he wrote his best-known poem in August, 1945, while in Chungking negotiating possible ways for a reconciliation with Chiang Kai-shek:

SNOW

to the melody of Shen Yüan Ch'un

This is the scene in that northern land;
A hundred leagues are sealed with ice,
A thousand leagues of whirling snow.
On either side of the Great Wall
One vastness is all you see.
From end to end of the great river
The rushing torrent is frozen and lost.
The mountains dance like silver snakes,
The highlands roll like waxen elephants,
As if they sought to vie with heaven in their height;
And on a sunny day
You will see a red dress thrown over the white,
Enchantingly lovely!

[2]Fourteen men attended the first Party Congress on July 1, 1921, which included two Russian delegates as guests. See Chapter One.

[3]One estimate placed Nationalist military strength as high as over eleven times that of the Communists. See Jerome Ch'en, *op. cit.*, p. 281.

Such great beauty like this in all our landscape
Has caused unnumbered heroes to bow in homage.
But alas, these heroes—Ch'in Shih Huang and Han Wu Ti
Were rather lacking in culture;
Rather lacking in literary talent
Were the emperors T'ang T'ai Tsung and Sung T'ai Tsu;
and Genghis Khan,
Beloved Son of Heaven for a day,
Only knew how to bend his bow at the golden eagle.
Now they are all past and gone;
To find men truly great and noble-hearted
We must look here in the present.[4]

I. Civil War Victories

The new People's Republic did not come into being without intensive uphill struggle. The Nationalists, especially after the Japanese attacked Pearl Harbor on December 7, 1941, were able to acquire a vast sum of U.S. money ($1.5 billion in lend-lease aid) and large quantities of military supplies.[5] Chiang Kai-shek used this newly acquired power to deploy up to half a million men to form a blockade shutting off the Communist base region in north Shensi.

At the end of World War II, there were some 2,000,000 Japanese military and civilians to be repatriated; and they occupied some 914 county-towns throughout China. When Japan surrendered on August 14, 1945, the Allied commander, General Douglas MacArthur, designated Chiang Kai-shek to accept the Japanese surrender in China (excluding Manchuria, which was to be occupied by the Russians), Formosa (Taiwan) and Indo-China north of the 16th parallel. Accepting this assignment, Chiang Kai-shek, in turn, instructed that the Chinese Communists should

[4]Mao Tse-tung, *Nineteen Poems* (Peking, Foreign Language Press, 1958), p. 22.

[5]See Barbara W. Tuchman's award-winning *Stilwell and the American Experience in China, 1911–45* (New York, Macmillan and Co., 1971).

remain in their own position and area and should not unilaterally accept the Japanese surrender. Chiang's order was promptly rejected by Chu Teh, the Commander in Chief of Communist forces.

Meanwhile, Nationalist troops were flown to many important urban centers in northern China through direct U.S. assistance. The Communists, on the other hand, began to send Lin Piao's forces into new positions in Manchuria in cooperation with Soviet forces under the command of Marshal Malinovsky under the provision of the U.S.-Soviet agreement at Yalta.[6] Other Communist forces under Chu Teh's orders began to move into former Japanese positions throughout China, in conflict with the Nationalist Army.

To avoid an immediate large-scale civil war, U.S. Ambassador Patrick J. Hurley arranged a meeting between Chiang Kai-shek and Mao Tse-tung. General Hurley flew to Yenan and escorted Mao Tse-tung to Chungking on August 28, 1945. The negotiation for a compromise lasted about two months and an interim agreement was finally reached on October 10, 1945, announcing that "civil war must be averted at all costs," and setting up a Political Consultative Conference to discuss programs for peaceful reconstruction of the country. However, there was no agreement with respect to the question of the political control of territory dominated by the Communists. At first, the Communists demanded that their eighteen "liberated areas" be recognized; then, they demanded the exclusive control of five provinces in northern China and Inner Mongolia and a share in the control of two other provinces

[6]The advance of the Soviet forces did not stop on August 14, nor did it stop at the boundaries at Manchuria. Instead, Soviet forces continued to march into the provinces of Chahar and Hopeh which linked with the Communist Chinese areas in northern China and Inner Mongolia with Manchuria. See Tang Tsou, *America's Failure in China, 1941-1950* (Chicago, The University of Chicago Press, 1963), pp. 315–16.

and three major cities. Finally, they proposed that all the "liberated areas" temporarily retain their status quo pending popular election. All these demands were rejected by the Nationalists.[7]

While these negotiations were in progress, armed clashes erupted throughout China. At this stage, on December 15, 1945, President Truman announced both the acceptance of Hurley's resignation and the appointment of General George C. Marshall as his special representative to China, with the aim "to bring about the unification (political) of China and concurrently, to effect a cessation of hostilities. . . ."[8] General Marshall arrived in China on December 19, 1945, and he immediately conveyed his instructions to the Chinese side.

Through his earnest mediation, an order for the cessation of hostilities was issued on January 10, 1946, and the Political Consultative Conference was opened on January 11, 1946. It passed a resolution, among others, on major issues on January 31, including: (1) reorganization of the national government; (2) nationalization of the armed forces; and (3) establishment of a reviewing committee to prepare a draft constitution.[9] Hopes were raised that peace might come to China through these resolutions.[10] The cold fact was, however, that no final agreement could be made on two critical issues: the legal status of the Communist military forces and the administrative status of Communist-controlled territory. Toward the end of 1946, Marshall concluded that no useful purpose could be served by his remaining in China. He left China on January 8,

[7]Tang Tsou, op. cit., p. 319.

[8]U.S. Department of State, United States Relations with China with Special Reference to the Period 1944–1949 (Washington, D.C., U.S. Printing House, 1949), p. 605.

[9]Tang Tsou, op. cit., p. 405.

[10]Carsun Chang, Third Force in China (New York, Bookman Associates, 1952), p. 147.

1947, and the country was once more in the throes of a large-scale civil war.[11]

At the outset, the Nationalists, relying on their numerical superiority and modern equipment, adopted the strategy of an all-out offensive, frantically attacking and seizing cities and territories in the hope of quickly destroying the Communists. This offensive started in June, 1946, and reached its peak when the Nationalist troops captured the Communist capital of Yenan in March, 1947. In spite of the initial military success, the Nationalist government under Chiang Kai-shek was more and more engulfed by economic and political problems. There were the usual droughts, floods, and famines throughout many parts of China. The postwar economy had been plagued by inflation, which fluctuated at an almost daily rate. There was black-marketeering and political corruption because of the new influx of American materials. And Chiang Kai-shek himself as a leader had allowed the Nationalist Party to be segmented into rival cliques that he could play off one against the other. He had always made the first criterion for his support of a subordinate the quality of personal loyalty rather than ability or devotion to any particular political or economic program. And worst of all, what was happening in the countryside, the backbone of Chinese economy, was completely ignored by the policy makers in the central government and left in the hands of local gentry or regional military commanders.[12]

The disastrous military, economic, and political developments in China had influenced the United States to adopt a new hands-off policy toward China in 1948; meanwhile, with active Soviet assistance, the Communist Party reorganized itself into a powerful military machine.[13]

[11]For a detailed analysis of Marshall's mission, see Tang Tsou, *op. cit.*, chapter X.

[12]Carsun Chang, *op. cit.*

[13]Tang Tsou, *op. cit.*, chapters XI and XII.

The 3,000,000 members of the Red Army were divided into five field armies, with Chu Teh assuming the position of Commander in Chief, with headquarters in northern China. The field armies included the following: the Northwest Field Army under P'eng Teh-huai, Ho Lung, and Hsi Chung-hsun; the Central Plains Field Army under Liu Pao-ch'eng and Teng Hsiao-p'ing; the East China Field Army under Ch'en Yi, Su Yu, and Jao Shu-shih; the Northeast China Field Army under Lin Piao, Hsiao Ching-kuang, and Lo Juan-huan; and finally, the North China Field Army under Nieh Jung-chen, Hsu Hsiang-ch'ien, and Po Yi-po. These armies were eventually reclassified as First, Second, Third, Fourth, and Fifth Field Armies, the backbone of the People's Liberation Army of China today. [14]

In the spring and summer of 1948, the Communists successively counterattacked and captured a large number of heavily fortified and strongly defended cities and towns. After September, 1948, they launched the three major campaigns of Liaohsi-Shenyang, Peking-Tientsin, and Huai-Hai, extending from Changchuan and Mukden in Manchuria to Hsuchow and Nanking in the lower Yangtze region. These three campaigns cost the Nationalists final control of China's vast countryside. In fact, the battle in Huai-Hai was the greatest engagement ever fought in Chinese history. It involved nearly a million and a quarter men, which rivals, in the number of those involved, any of the major battles of modern history. The region of Huai-Hai has always been a site of great battles between dynasties, since it is the natural passage between northern and central China. [15]

Because of military failures, Chiang Kai-shek withdrew

[14] William Whitson, "The Field Army in Chinese Communist Military Politics," *China Quarterly*, 37 (January/March, 1969).

[15] For details of civil war battles, see *Li Tsung-jen's Memoirs*, compiled by Teh-Kong Tong, to be published by the University of California Press, Berkeley.

from the Presidency in January, 1949, and subsequently took refuge in Taiwan. Vice-President Li Tsung-jen became acting President. Li sent a delegation to Peking the first four months of 1949 in search of peace.[16] But the Communists renewed their offensives against the Nationalists in April, crossing the Yangtze and occupying Nanking. Then, they advanced southward to Canton and westward to Szechwan where the last refuge of the Nationalists on the mainland was abandoned in December, 1949.

II. *Establishing the Government*

Before Mao's victorious army entered Peking, he called for the convening of a "new People's Political Consultative Conference" at the Seventh Party Central Committee meeting, from March 5 to 13, 1949. Three months later, some 134 delegates representing twenty-three organizations met in Peking to adopt "rules and provisions" for the convention of the "People's Political Consultative Conference." The conference finally opened in September with 662 delegates from forty-five representative units, including the Communist Party and several minority progressive parties, geographic regional areas, field armies, public bodies, and pro-Communist "democratic" personalities.

The conference lasted from September 21 to October 30. It adopted three important documents: the Organic Law of the People's Political Consultative Conference, the Organic Law of the Central Government, and the Common Program of the People's Political Consultative Conference, which represented a detailed statement of the theory and structure of the new government in the People's Republic.[17] The Organic Law set up the central government, defined the functions of the various state organs and their relationship

[16]*Ibid.*

[17]See *The Important Documents of the First Plenary Sessions of the Chinese People's Political Consultative Conference* (Peking, Foreign Language Press, 1949).

to one another, and the Common Program contained the guiding principles and policies of the People's Republic during the "new democratic stage," as expressed in Mao Tse-tung's early statement, *On New Democracy* (see Chapter Five). The Common Program also delineated the foreign policy of the new republic, which was to "lean to the side" of the USSR and other people's democracies. It also dealt with economic policy consisting of state-owned as well as semi-state-operated and semi-private elements.[18]

The country was to be divided into six Greater Administrative Regions: the North China Region, the Central China Region, the Northwest Region, the East China Region, the Central-South Region, and the South-west Region. In each of these a military and administrative council was established as the governing and supervisory body of the area. In addition, there were several autonomous regions, usually the former dependencies of China and areas inhabited by minority nationalities. The central government also promulgated the Electoral Law of the People's Republic on March 1, 1953, for the election of a new National Congress and local congresses to adopt a new constitution.

The Chinese election law provided voting privileges to all Chinese nationals (citizens), eighteen years or older, except when disqualified by mental illness or by reasons of being classified as "reactionaries," such as landlords or reactionary bourgeois. The electoral law provided one representative, called a deputy, to the National Congress for every 800,000 persons from a province; one for every 100,000 persons from a municipality with more than 900,000 population. There were specific numbers for the national minorities (150) and overseas Chinese community (30). A total of 1,226 deputies were elected to the First National Congress, which opened on September 15, 1954, in Peking.[19]

[18]*Ibid.*

[19]See Franklin W. Houn. "Constitution and Government," in Yuan-Li Wu, *China: A Handbook* (New York, Praeger Publishers, 1973), pp. 221–39.

The National Congress adopted the new constitution, consisting of a preamble and 106 articles in four chapters, which is, in fact, the continuation of the Organic Law and the Common Program of 1949.[20] However, the Chinese constitution contains much of the content of Western democratic constitutions. It defines functions and powers and provides for popular election of government officials; and in addition, includes a chapter on Fundamental Rights and Duties of Citizens.

In certain aspects, the Chinese constitution was copied directly from the Soviet constitution of 1936, using different terminology. For instance, the People's Republic of China is described as "a people's democratic state led by the working class and based on the alliance of workers and peasants" (Article One); whereas, according to the Soviet constitution, the "Union of Soviet Republics is a socialist state of workers and peasants" (Article One). And again, the so-called people's democratic dictatorship in the Preamble of the Chinese constitution is just another version of the Soviet Union's "proletarian dictatorship."

However, there are differences in the two governmental structures as specified in the constitution. First, the Supreme Soviet of the USSR is bicameral, providing for constituent republics, whereas the Chinese National People's Congress is unicameral. Secondly, in the USSR the Council of Ministers, including its Chairman or Premier, is appointed by the Presidium of the Supreme Soviet, whereas in the Chinese constitution, the Premier, the head of the State Council, is nominated and appointed by the Chairman of the Republic with the consent of the National People's Congress. And thirdly, the National People's Congress, like the Supreme Soviet of the USSR, is the supreme organ of state power, but it differs from the

---

[20]*The Constitution of the People's Republic of China* (Peking, Foreign Language Press, 1961).

latter in that the Chairman of its Standing Committee is not the titular head of the government, but is subordinate to the Chairman of the People's Republic of China.

Moreover, the Chairman of the People's Republic presides over the Supreme State Conference and the National Defense Council—two policy-planning organs of full constitutional status through which he can exert a dominant influence on political and military affairs of the state. Thus, the 1954 Chinese constitution creates an office for which no parallel is found in the Soviet constitution. In further examination of the state structure as provided in the new constitution, it is seen that while the National Congress is the "highest organ of the state power"(Article 21), the State Council is "the executive organ of the highest organ of state power" (Article 47). Similarly, on lower levels, the local congresses are "local organs of state power" (Article 55), and the local people's councils are "local organs of state administration" (Article 62). This parallel system of people's congresses and people's councils, which extends through the entire governmental system, is built on the distinction between "state power" as represented by the people's congresses and "state administration," as represented by the people's councils.

State administration also includes a judicial system and the "supreme people's procuratorate." The judicial system is based on a "three-level plan": the Supreme People's Court, the Provincial People's Courts, and the County People's Courts. In effect, it is a two-instance system: The County Court ordinarily functions as the court of first instance and the Provincial Court as that of the second. However, the Provincial Court can conduct the initial trial in important cases, which then are subject to appeal to the Supreme Court. In all courts the prosecution is performed by members of the Supreme People's Procuratorate, which is independent of the court system. While both the court and the procuratorate are authorized to act independently of each other, each is directly responsible to the people's congresses.[21]

Having made clear the distinction between state power and state administration, there remains the question of how this parallel system actually works in the Chinese government. The underlying spirit of the People's Republic is the principle of "democratic centralism"; that is, "centralized on the basis of democracy and democracy under centralized guidance."[22] This is in fact a system of concentration of power by the central authority, and various local people's councils only representing the downward movement of authority from the State Council at the apex of the hierarchy.[23]

In political dynamics, the real driving force behind the government is the party leadership. And the constitution is the contemporary form of the mandate by which the Chinese Communist Party had organized the public power of the Chinese state. Policies are made in the inner circle of the Central Committee. Whatever the party leaders decide on, the state machine is expected to endorse it and carry it out.

III. Setting Priorities

Because the civil war from 1945 to 1949 had exhausted China's existing resources and plunged Chinese society and economy into chaos, the primary goal for the new central government of the People's Republic was to rehabilitate the economy and restore some semblance of order. The

[21]The Chinese judicial system cannot be understood when compared with Western models; in fact it is more of a penal system for criminal justice. See Jerome Alan Cohen, *The Criminal Process in the People's Republic of China, 1949–1963: An Introduction* (Cambridge, Massachusetts, Harvard University Press, 1968).

[22]See Mao's "On Coalition Government," in *Selected Works of Mao Tse-tung*, IV, p. 272.

[23]See Carsun Chang, *op. cit.*, p. 272.

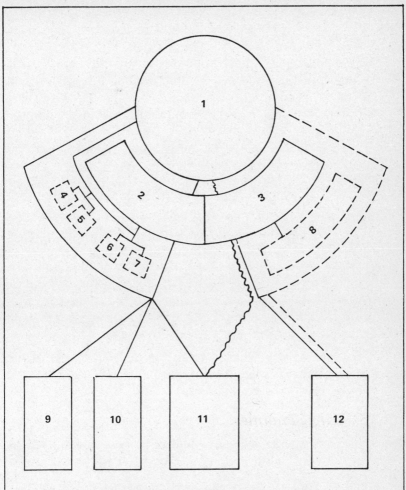

SUPREME STATE ORGANS

1. National People's Congress (NPC)
2. Standing Committee of the NPC
3. Chairman of the People's Republic of China
4. Budget Committee
5. Credentials Committee
6. Nationalities Committee
7. Bills Committee
8. Supreme State Conference
9. Supreme People's Court
10. Supreme People's Procuratorate
11. State Council
12. National Defense Council

NOTE

———————— Indicates the relationship of direction and subordination

— — — — — Indicates the relationship of election

∿∿∿∿∿∿∿∿ Indicates the relationship of nomination, appointment, and removal

SOURCE: *Chung-hwa jen min ho kwo hsien fa chiang i,* facing p. 192

government in Peking was carefully proclaiming its adherence to a coexistence policy for private sectors in the urban areas, as outlined in the Common Program, and adopting a comprehensive plan of balances specifying interindustry and intersectoral relationships with the following objectives:

1. A plan for industrial production including one for heavy industry and one for light industry.

2. A plan for agriculture including both the volume of consumption in the agricultural sector itself and the amount marketable in the nonagricultural sectors.

3. A transport plan whose objectives were to safeguard the adequate flow and distribution of industrial and farm products.

4. A plan for capital construction or investment in fixed assets.

5. A labor plan whose goal was to increase labor productivity.

6. A technological plan to ensure that all sectors of the national economy had the latest scientific and technological information at their command.

7. A cost plan to specify the standard costs for each individual segment of the economy, to fix the targets of cost reduction, and to provide guidance to the correct relationship between increase in labor productivity and increase in wages.

8. A plan for the allocation and supply of materials.

9. A plan for the flow of commodities to ensure that the industrial and farm products demanded by the urban and rural workers would be available to them in planned quantities.

10. A plan for the social and cultural welfare of the people under the guidance of Maoism.[24]

[24]Yuan-li Wu, *The Economy of Communist China* (New York, Praeger Publishers, 1965), pp. 22–25.

There were additional plans to deal with exports and imports; financial plans to deal with the national budget and the accumulation and allocation of capital funds and short-term credits; and a regional plan concerning regional specialization and the administration of enterprises under local control. To implement these national economic plans, several governmental agencies including information-gathering agencies, various planning organs, and executive departments were reorganized. In pursuit of these plans, the Chinese economy is assigned to perform five tasks:

1. Provision of essential consumer goods.
2. Generation of an economic surplus for investment or foreign aid.
3. Production of national defense goods.
4. Establishment of bases for research and development.
5. Maintenance of economic independence (self-reliance).[25]

These tasks were to be completed under several periods: (1) the period of rehabilitation, as already stated, from 1949 to 1952; (2) the First Five-Year Plan period (1953–1957), in which rapid industrialization through comprehensive planning was developed, as well as the total socialization of the industrial sector; (3) the Great Leap Forward period (1958–1960) in which heavy industry became the core of the economic development; and (4) the period of readjustment (1960–1965), which was necessitated by the failure of the Great Leap Forward and in which "agriculture became the foundation and industry was the leading factor."[26]

The highest priority was China's new agricultural policy. With 85 percent of her population living in the rural areas, China depends on agriculture to directly provide a

[25]See Nai-Ruenn Chen and Walter Galenson, *The Chinese Economy Under Communism* (Chicago, Aldine Publishing Co., 1969).

[26]Lawrence J. Lau, "Economic Development and Industrialization," in Yuan-li Wu, *China: A Handbook*, p. 533.

livelihood for at least four-fifths of her people. Agricultural products also provide the major portion of China's foreign exchange and the bulk of her raw material for light industry. The well-being of the people and the strength and stability of the government depend on the success or failure of agricultural policies.[27]

The primarily agrarian society of prerevolutionary China was confronted with three critical problems: the growing agrarian population, the scarcity of agricultural capital, and inadequate food production. The policy goal therefore involves land reform, including reclamation of land and increase in the cultivated acreage; water conservation and increase in irrigation; and intensification of existing agriculture techniques. Therefore, during the initial period of rehabilitation, a nationwide land-reform program dealing with reduction of rent and interest, and the redistribution of all was completed in 1953. Next, there was the collectivization movement, from mutual-aid teams to agricultural producers' cooperatives, under the First Five-Year Plan.

Since Chairman Mao himself was personally in favor of rapid collectivization, the party developed a system of "people's communes" during the radical period of the Great Leap Forward beginning in 1958. The commune was distinguished from a cooperative or a collective in that it was larger and it represented an organization in a "higher stage of socialism."[28] When the communes were first established throughout China, private plots and houses were placed under the collective leadership of the commune, and the utopian equalitarian system was somehow adopted. However, the peasants reacted strongly against it and modifications were made, including (1) con-

[27]See Kuo-chun Chao, *Agrarian Policy of the Chinese Communist Party* (London, Asia Publishing House, 1960). Also, K-C. Yeh, "Agricultural Policies and Performance," in Yuan-li Wu, *op. cit.*, pp. 487–529.

[28]Chih-p'u, "From Cooperative to Communes," *Red Flag*, No. 8, 1958. Quoted in K.C. Yeh, *op. cit.*, p. 507.

tinuation of some form of private ownership of property for personal use; (2) a more realistic wage system based on performance; and (3) a new form of organizational structure to permit a decentralized decision-making process.[29]

Another important priority for the new central government involved the education of several hundred million illiterates among the rural population. From 1949 to 1951, the new government in Peking held a series of national conferences on different aspects of education in order to implement the earlier recommendation of the Common Program. This included the reorganization of educational institutions and the liquidation of private schools. New policy directives provided equal opportunity of education for all, and new systems of schools under unified standards and control. An average of 7 percent of the national budget was allocated for educational programs from 1951 to 1956. The allocation increased to 10 percent by 1957.[30]

A regular school system under national control was established from the kindergarten to university level, and a part-time system with accelerated programs was also established to be maintained under local auspices. Official statistics for 1958, for instance, claimed 63 million students in elementary schools, 5 million in secondary schools, and 447,000 in universities. And an additional 81 million persons were enrolled separately in spare-time classes; 40 million in literacy classes; 26 million in spare-time grade schools; 15 million in spare-time secondary schools; and 150,000 in spare-time higher education.[31]

Spare-time education seems to have proven a major

[29]K. C. Yeh, op. cit., p. 509.

[30]See R. F. Price, Education in Communist China (New York, Praeger Publishers, 1970).

[31]Leo A. Orleans, Professional Manpower and Education (Washington, D.C., U.S. Governmental Printing House, 1960), p. 12.

success in eliminating illiteracy among the rural population. It is a useful device in adult education and it provides classes especially for workers and peasants in their time after work. Workers are asked to join the classes after work, peasants to attend winter schools in the off-seasons, and even crew members of steamers are organized for study in their extra time. In all cases, study is not to interfere with work. Since 1965, the official policy has been switching to a new work-study approach, with labor as an integral part of the total school program. Schools devoting full time to study will become less and less important, and work and study may be scheduled on alternate days or alternate weeks or at longer intervals. The goal is to integrate study with work so that it helps solve the numerous problems encountered in work.[32]

In addition to mass education, a detailed plan for the advancement of science, technology, and research was implemented. The national government allocates specific funding for science projects, some of which is distributed to the local governments in the provinces, and is to be matched by the region's contribution. For example, in 1960, the central government spent $500 million for research and development. To support research programs, China also developed a scientific and technological information base, including exchange of publications with foreign countries. In 1961, for example, China received 110,000 books and periodicals from 160 foreign countries, with 60 percent pertaining to the engineering sciences.[33]

Also, as part of China's educational policy, reforms of Chinese written characters were made: (1) adoption of a simple character to substitute for another or for several homophones; (2) reduction of a complex character to the minimum of its basic components; (3) the use of a minimal

[32]Theodore Hsi-en Chen, "Education," in Yuan-li Wu, *op. cit.*, p. 696.

[33]J. A. Berberet, "Science and Technology," in Yuan-li Wu, *op. cit.*, p. 643.

component in combination with other simple elements to create composite derivatives. The initial literacy target was set for workers at 2,000 characters and for peasants, 1,500 characters, with about 22 percent characters that have been simplified.[34] And all forms of literature, music, drama, and the other arts have been utilized to support China's educational and ideological policy of Communist revolution.[35]

China at the time of the new republic was a country with crushing health problems and with limited medical facilities. In a country with more than 450 million people in 1949, there were only 12,000 modern-trained physicians. Therefore, great priority was placed on public health, with emphasis on "learning by doing as well as learning by seeing and hearing."[36] China adopted a new medical educational policy by the amalgamation of traditional and Western medicine. She had approximately 500,000 traditional herbalist-physicians. Schools of traditional Chinese medicine were reorganized and new joint traditional and Western medical clinics were established. By 1959, there was at least one modern medical college in each province, and by 1965, there were more than 100,000 modern-trained doctors and 450,000 qualified nurses, pharmacists, and technicians.

So at long last, after two decades of constant struggle, visitors from abroad were impressed by the progress and the immense energy of the citizens of the new People's Republic. As James Reston wrote from Peking in 1971, "The extraordinary thing about this oldest civilization in the world is that it seems so young. You do not have the feeling here—so depressing and oppressive in some other

[34]S. H. Chen, "Language and Literature Under Communism," in Yun-li Wu, op. cit., p. 711.

[35]Frederick T. C. Yu, Mass Persuasion in Communist China (New York, Praeger Publishers, 1964).

[36]Robert M. Worth, "Health and Medicine," in Yun-li Wu, op. cit., p. 661.

parts of the Orient—of weariness, sickness and death, of old men and women, spent before their time, struggling against hopeless odds. . . . The people [in China] seem not only young but enthusiastic about their changing lives."[37]

Suggested Reading

ADAM, RUTH, ed., *Contemporary China.* New York, Pantheon Books, 1966.

BARNETT, A. DOAK, *Communist China: The Early Years 1945–1955.* New York, Praeger Publishers, 1964.

CHANG, CARSUN, *The Third Force in China.* New York, Bookman Associates, 1952.

CHAO, KUO-CHUN, *Agrarian Policy of the Chinese Communist Party, 1921–1959.* London, Asia Publishing House, 1960.

CHEN, NAI-RUENN and WALTER GALENSON, *The Chinese Economy Under Communism.* Chicago, Aldine Publishing House, 1969.

CHENG, CHU-YUAN, *Scientific and Engineering Manpower in Communist China.* Washington, D.C., National Science Foundation, 1965.

COHEN, JEROME ALAN, *The Criminal Process in the People's Republic of China, 1949–1963: An Introduction.* Cambridge, Massachusetts, Harvard University Press, 1968.

FAIRBANK, JOHN KING, *The United States and China,* 3rd ed. Cambridge, Massachusetts, Harvard University Press, 1971.

GOULD, SIDNEY H., ed., *Sciences in Communist China.* Washington, D.C., American Association for the Advancement of Sciences, 1961.

HU, CHANG-TU, ed., *China: Its People, Its Society, Its Culture.* New Haven, Connecticut, Human Relations Area File, 1960.

LIU, WILLIAM T., ed., *Chinese Society Under Communism: A Reader.* New York, John Wiley, 1967.

LENG, SHAO-CHUAN, *Justice in Communist China.* Dobbs Ferry, New York, Oceana Publications, 1967.

PRICE, R. F., *Education in Communist China.* New York, Praeger Publishers, 1970.

SHABAD, THEODORE, *China's Changing Map: National and Regional Development, 1949–71,* rev. ed. New York, Praeger Publishers, 1972.

TANG, PETER S. H. and JOAN M. MALONEY, *Communist China: The*

---

[37]New York *Times* (July 28, 1971).

Domestic Scene: 1949–1967. South Orange, New Jersey, Seton Hall University Press, 1967.

TANG TSOU, *America's Failure in China: 1941–1950.* Chicago, The University of Chicago Press, 1963.

TONG, TE-KONG, compiler, *Li Tsung-jen's Memoirs.* Berkeley, California, University of California Press, to be published.

TUCHMAN, BARBARA W., *Stilwell and the American Experience in China, 1911–1945.* New York, Macmillan Company, 1971.

U.S. Congress, Joint Economic Committee, *An Economic Profile of Mainland China.* 2 vols. Washington, D.C., U.S. Government Printing House, 1967.

U.S. Department of State, *United States Relations with Special Reference to the Period 1944–1949.* Washington, D.C., U.S. Government Printing House, 1949. (Also known as the White Paper on China.)

VOGEL, EZRA, *Canton Under Communism: Programs and Politics in a Provincial Capital, 1949–1968.* Cambridge, Massachusetts, Harvard University Press, 1969.

WU, YUAN-LI, ed., *China: A Handbook.* New York, Praeger Publishers, 1973.

YANG, C. K. *The Chinese Family in the Chinese Communist Revolution.* Cambridge, Massachusetts, MIT Press, 1959.

——, *A Chinese Village in Early Communist Transition.* Cambridge, Massachusetts, MIT Press, 1959.

CHAPTER SEVEN:

IDEOLOGY AND PERSONALITY

CHINESE politics is a linkage of ideological beliefs, deliberate calculations, and personal ambitions. And ideology plays the central role because it helps to integrate the various functional groups in Chinese society by laying down fundamental ethics that distinguish right from wrong. Ideology sets the general orientation of the community by defining the common purpose of political life.[1]

It has been suggested that the Chinese need a new ideology, especially after the May Fourth Movement: (1) to define a new "world view," (2) to formulate a strategy and organization for revolution, (3) to provide an alternative for traditional social values and institutions, (4) to bring about a reconstruction of society and humanity within the Chinese setting, and finally (5) to instill in the people a "faith that the reconstruction can be done and will be good for them."[2]

The Chinese Communists found that Marxism supplied the "world view" and the alternative social values and institutions, while Leninism offered the best strategy and organization for revolution. But it was Maoism that could truly rally the Chinese peasants to the support of the party to rebuild man and society in China. Accordingly, the

[1] The classic study of Chinese ideology is Franz Schurmann's *Ideology and Organization in Communist China*, new ed. (Berkeley, California, University of California Press, 1968).

[2] James Chieh Hsiung, *Ideology and Practice: The Evolution of Chinese Communism* (New York, Praeger Publishers, 1970), p. 132.

majority of Chinese Communist policies have become a reflection of these ideologies, with perhaps some necessary adjustment to reality.[3] The obvious danger of such close association of ideology with policy lies in the fact that all policies must be justified or rationalized by ideological consideration, or at least ideological arguments. And differences over policy soon become divergences in ideology, and erupt into ideological struggles and personality conflicts.

I. Ideological Campaigns

Perhaps never before in human history have systematic efforts been made, so extensive in scope and so severe in intensity, as the People's Republic's attempt to reshape the mind of man. From 1949 to the early 1970's, numerous ideological campaigns have been witnessed, such as the Thought Reform of 1950; the Three-Antis and Five-Antis campaigns of 1952; the Anti-Rightist campaigns that followed the Hundred Schools and Hundred Flowers contending campaigns of 1957; and subsequent Socialist Education campaigns in 1962; the Great Proletarian Cultural Revolution in 1966–1968; and finally the new Anti-Confucius, Anti-Lin Piao campaign of 1973–1974.[4]

The techniques used during the first Thought Reform campaign was the formation of study groups, a method continued from the Yenan days (see Chapter Five). This practice was transformed into a more coercive method of Reformative Study including new programs, such as the Three-Antis and Five-Antis campaigns, to eradicate deviant ideologies. Three-Antis included campaigns against

---

[3]Ping-ti Ho and Tang Tsou, *China in Crisis*, Vol. I, Book I (Chicago, The University of Chicago Press, 1968), p. 292.

[4]For a study of the early campaigns, see Theodore H. E. Chen, *Thought Reform of the Chinese Intellectuals* (Hong Kong, University of Hong Kong Press, 1960).

corruption, waste, and bureaucratism; and the Five-Antis were campaigns against crimes of bribery, tax evasion, fraud, theft of state assets, and leakage of state economic secrets.

These campaigns usually began with a series of articles and editorials in newspapers or on the radio. Mass accusation meetings were held, together with smaller reformative study groups in which the aim was redemption through criticism. Each group would not only discuss the facts as presented by the party, but they would also consider what kind of thought could have produced such actions. The group would then proceed to look for traces of the same in themselves. These sessions, although different in objectives, are remarkably similar to the sensitivity training used by modern American psychiatry in group therapy.[5]

Despite these rather intensified efforts to correct deviant ideology, the party became seriously disturbed by the continuing negative responses of intellectuals throughout China. In addition, there was the eruption of the Polish Communists against the Soviet Union, and the Hungarian rebellion in 1956, all of which made a considerable impact on Chairman Mao himself. He dramatically announced a new policy—Let a Hundred Flowers Blossom, Let a Hundred Schools (of thought) Contend—at the Supreme State Conference on May 2, 1956. He reaffirmed this new policy in an address entitled, "On the Correct Handling of Contradiction Among the People" on February 27, 1957.[6] His invitation of free and independent thinking generated a storm of criticism of the party by China's intellectuals. They charged the party with incompetence in leading China in science, education, and the arts; and declared that party

[5]C.F. Robert J. Lifton, *Thought Reform and the Psychology of Totalism* (New York, W.W. Norton and Co., 1963).

[6]Mao Tse-tung, *On the Correct Handling of Contradictions Among the People* (Peking, Foreign Language Press, 1960).

bureaucratism was worse than capitalism. Others even questioned the infallibility of Mao's thought as an ideology.[7]

Because of these criticisms, Mao initiated a new Anti-Rightist campaign in 1958–1960 and introduced a Three Red Flags policy: the general line for building socialism, the Great Leap Forward in economic growth, and the People's Commune in social and economic structure. But the results were disastrous and economic conditions worsened. The Soviet Union abruptly withdrew all forms of aid and technical personnel in mid-1960; China also faced the severe natural calamities of the three bad years from 1959 to 1961.

These economic disruptions led to a revision of key economic policies. The revision was known as "readjustment, consolidation, filling out and raising standards," with new emphasis on agriculture (see Chapter Six, Section III). At the same time, the party began to initiate a new Socialist Education campaign in 1962 with the goals (1) to purify ideology and rectify revisionist tendencies, and (2) to reestablish socialist, collective controls over the economy, especially in rural areas.[8]

The Socialist Education campaign passed through five discernible stages. The first stage lasted from September, 1962, through the summer of 1963, with emphasis on the general investigations of rural conditions in China. In the second stage, from 1963 to 1964, it turned the campaign into a nationwide movement, including the reorganization of the peasant associations. The third stage, which was marked by severe attacks on the deviationism of basic-level party cadres and party intellectuals, lasted from 1964 to January, 1965; and the fourth stage followed immediately with a search for new theoretical guidelines for the movement.

---

[7]Mu Fu-sheng, *The Wilting of the Hundred Flowers* (New York, Praeger Publishers, 1962).

[8]Jan. S. Prybyla, "Communist China's Strategy of Economic Development, 1961–66," *Asian Survey* (October, 1966), p. 589.

Finally, the fifth stage began in late summer and fall of 1965, with particular emphasis on the rectification of party officials at regional (county) levels. They were subjected to intensive criticism and self-criticism, in order to overcome the errors of "bureaucratism, conservatism and commandism."[9]

In the course of the Socialist Education campaign, several simultaneous mass movements were organized, such as the Four Withs, whereby party cadres were sent to rural areas to live, work, and communicate with the peasants. Another part of the campaign was called the Four Clearance movement, the purpose of which was to correct cadre corruption in respect to financial affairs, work points, accounts, and storage of produce. Still another was called the Three Fixes and One Substitution, which involved the assignment of cadres to fixed labor bases to which they had to report at fixed hours and work for a fixed length of time each day. The substitution was the requirement of learning the jobs of regular workers in order to be ready to replace the regular workers whenever necessary.[10]

In addition to these economic-related activities, the Socialist Education campaign involved the intensive study of Mao Tse-tung's thought as well as a general uplifting of the educational standards of the peasantry. There were, for example, some 19,000 sales stations established for Mao's works during the campaign and more than 12 million copies were printed for the use of peasants during the initial stage of the campaign. Moreover, many mass adult-educational schools were expanded in the rural areas, including some on a half-work, half-study basis. News, motion picture, and radio media were utilized to carry out this campaign. In 1962, for example, some 5,400 radio broadcasting stations

[9]See Richard Baum and Frederick T. Triwes, *Ssu-ch'ing: The Socialist Education Movement of 1962-66.* Center for Chinese Studies Research Monographs, No. 2 (Berkeley, California, University of California Press, 1968).

[10]Jan S. Prybyla, *op.cit.*, pp. 593-94.

were installed in villages, with 6,700,000 loudspeakers added.[11]

Whatever the success of this Socialist Education campaign in rural areas, it is clear in retrospect that in the party's intellectual community this movement encountered stiff and stubborn resistance. Mao Tse-tung himself complained in December, 1963, that in literature and art "very little had been achieved so far in socialist transformation," and termed "absurd" the fact that "many Communists showed enthusiasm in advancing feudal and capitalist art, but no zeal in promoting socialist art."[12] Again, in June, 1964, the Chairman charged that literary intellectuals within the powerful All-China Federation of Literary and Art Circles, an affiliate of the party, had "failed in the main to carry out the policies of the Party; had in recent years, even slid to the verge of revisionism; and would, if unchecked, be found at some future date to become groups like the Hungarian Petofi Club.[13]

To remedy this situation, the party launched a thoroughgoing Rectification campaign in literature and art in September, 1964, and extended it to mid-1965, which pushed the Socialist Education campaign into a new stage. Many eminent philosophers, historians, novelists, and playwrights with long years of party affiliations were deeply involved. The first important casualty was Yang Hsien-chen, President of the High Party School. Yang was an early acquaintance of Ch'ü Ch'iu-pai (see Chapter Three) when both attended the Russian Language Institute in the early 1920's. Yang later became head of the China Department of the Soviet Union's Foreign Language Press, where he was in charge of translating Soviet ideological

[11]George P. Jan, "Radio Propaganda in Chinese Villages," *Asian Survey* (May, 1967), pp. 305–15.

[12]Quoted in *The Great Socialist Cultural Revolution in China*, No. 5 (Peking, Foreign Language Press, 1966), p. 8.

[13]*Ibid.*, p. 27.

works into Chinese. Throughout his career, Yang seems to have been engaged principally in writing and lecturing on Marxism. He was elected as an alternate member of the Eighth Party Central Committee in September, 1956, in recognition of his theoretical understanding and interpretation of Marxism.[14]

During the Rectification campaign, Yang was attacked for his theory of "two combining into one" as opposed to Mao's "revolutionary dialectic of 'dividing one into two.'"[15] The essence of the controversy involves Mao's theory of contradictions, which can only be resolved by endless struggles in which the contradictory elements tend to assume the nature of each other, until at last a new unity emerges. In Maoist terms, the key to this methodology is dividing one into two, thus bringing the contradictions into the open and allowing the struggle to take place. Yang in essence agreed with this method of analysis, but rather than stressing the contradictory aspects of a problem, he argued that the differences or contradictions should be set aside and then it would be possible to reunite the common aspects into the whole. He was therefore accused by his opponents, who stated that he "harmonizes contradictions, emasculates struggle and eliminates development and change."[16]

Another important literary theorist under criticism was Shao Ch'uan-lin, formerly vice-chairman of the Chinese Writers' Union, and editor in chief of *People's Literature*. He is also the author of such popular fiction as *The Hero, The Tavern* and the *Unicorn Fortress*. As a leader of Chinese writers he advocated the theory of "deepening realism" and honored "people in the middle." Shao maintained that depicting the people in the middle, riddled

[14]Donald W. Klein and Anne B. Clark, *op.cit.*, pp. 973–75.

[15] *Red Flag*, No. 16 (1964), p. 8.

[16]Kuanming *Daily* (December 25, 1964).

with inner contradictions, summarizing "the spiritual burdens of individual peasants through centuries," and presenting the "painful stages of peasants in the transition from an individual to a collective economy" was the only realistic writing in China, or in his own words, the only way to "deepen realism."[17] But his opponents saw his writings as an attempt to criticize the Chairman's policy during the Great Leap Forward, especially with respect to the party's treatment of the peasantry; and his theory of "deepening realism" as an echo of bourgeois critical realism, containing too much of Russia's Pasternak's *Doctor Zhivago*. He was branded a revisionist and "capitalist roader."[18]

Another influential party intellectual who came under attack was the well-known professor of Marxist philosophy at Peking University, Feng Ting. He was denounced in September, 1964, for the views expounded in his works, *The Communist View of Life*, 1956, *The Commonplace Truth*, 1955, and *The Historical Mission of the Working Class*, 1953. These works had been reprinted since their first publication and had received a circulation of over 1.5 million copies. Feng graduated from Sun Yat-sen University in Moscow in 1930 and was personally involved in the Communist movement during the Sino-Japanese War. He became the deputy director of the propaganda department of the East China Bureau. In his writings, Feng held the view that social history is the history of the pursuit of happiness by all men, and at the same time he regarded the need for food and shelter as one of the main motivations of human action. Because of the views he expressed, his critics charged that he overstressed the forces of instinct and obliterated the influence of social

[17]*The Great Socialist Cultural Revolution* (1), p. 18.

[18]*Who's Who in Communist China*, Vol. 2 (Hong Kong, Union Research Institute, 1970), p. 556.

practice, thus supporting "the modern revisionist philosophy of opposing ideological orthodoxy."[19]

Prominent playwrights were also involved in the controversy, and such an important man as T'ien Han was included in the dispute. T'ien joined the party in 1932 and had been instrumental in establishing the stage as a vehicle for commentary on the political and social scene for indoctrinating children.[20] He was the founder and teacher of drama at the famous Szu Wei Children's Dramatic School in Yenan. After the founding of the People's Republic, he became director of the Bureau of Drama and Opera Improvement at the Ministry of Culture in Peking. He translated *Romeo and Juliet, Hamlet,* and Wilde's *Salome* into Chinese, and was the author of dozens of new plays including *The Song of Spring Return, The Will to Live, Tumultuous Toll, Night Talks in Soochow, The Dance of the Fire,* and the *Legend of the White Snake.* However, when he published his play *Hsieh Yao-huan* in 1961, he was severely criticized. The play centered around a female court attendant of the T'ang empress. By lauding the empress' liberal rules against the exploitation of the peasantry by corrupt local bureaucrats, T'ien Han was charged with using the historical analogy to criticize the party treatment of the peasantry during the Great Leap Forward. T'ien Han and many other similar writers were purged or banished to the countryside to participate in "productive labor."[21] And there was the sudden halt of virtually all literary publications by late 1966, in the midst of a new and more powerful phase of ideological campaign, the Great Proletarian Cultural Revolution.

[19]Kuanming *Daily* (December 25, 1964).

[20]*Who's Who in Communist China,* Vol. 2, pp. 621–22.

[21]Merle Goldman, *Literary Dissent in Communist China* (Cambridge, Massachusetts, Harvard University Press, 1967).

II. The Cultural Revolution

Although the Great Proletarian Cultural Revolution can be viewed as a logical extension of the rectification campaign against the party intellectuals in 1964, it differs from all the previous ideological movements in that it did not enjoy the support of the majority of the ruling Central Committee of the party.[22] As the events unfolded, the Cultural Revolution turned against the party itself and became a titantic power struggle.

The use of the world "cultural" in the new volcanic movement is significant: It recalls the traditional Chinese belief in the didactic function of all forms of culture, and in cultural regeneration as the key to social or national regeneration.[23] After all, Mao Tse-tung raised the question of cultural revolution as early as 1940 (see Chapter Five). Therefore, in truth, the Cultural Revolution was a spirited attempt to rectify the thinking of the entire nation through an all-out assault on revisionism and capitalism for the final achievement of Mao's goal: a national, scientific, and mass culture and a new stage of social development for China. Thus, in the largest sense the Cultural Revolution denoted a philosophy of selfless struggle as well as reforms in arts and letters.[24]

Moreover, the Cultural Revolution also served as a great mass mobilization, with its intensive indoctrination and involvement in the study and application of Mao's thought. It was led by millions of young students, known as the Red Guards, and each of them was carrying the Little Red Book

[22]See *Peking Review* (December 9, 1966), p. 9. For a comprehensive study of the Cultural Revolution, see Thomas Robinson, *et al., The Cultural Revolution in China* (Berkeley, California, University of California Press, 1971).

[23]James Chieh Hsiung, *op. cit.*, chapters 12–13.

[24]William Hinton, *Turning Point in China* (New York, Monthly Review Press, 1972).

of the quotations of Chairman Mao.[25] The intensity and religious fervor in the study of Mao's works can be seen from the fact that in 1967, 350 million copies of the Little Red Book were distributed throughout China. Mao's writings, in this sense, had become the Bible of Chinese Communism; and there is no question that the Maoists in China intended to indoctrinate the youth as successors, and thus perpetuate the revolutionary cause.

As the Cultural Revolution developed into four major phases, it failed miserably because of the chaos and violence it created throughout China. The first phase, which lasted until the autumn of 1966, might be regarded as the warming-up period in which forces were mobilized and gradually steered in the desired direction. The second phase saw the beginning of a clarification of the issues and the widening of the struggle from Peking to the countryside. The third phase began about the end of January, 1967, and lasted until September, 1968. It was a period of intense chaos and violence from time to time in one area to another. Finally, Mao Tse-tung ordered the army to take control of all the future activities of the Red Guards and restored the country to some semblance of order. The following table probably best details the monthly chronology of events during the Cultural Revolution in China.

DEVELOPMENT OF THE CULTURAL REVOLUTION
1966–1968

Date	Events
1966	
August	Party officially adopted the resolution on the Cultural Revolution on August 8; Red Guards organized in Peking to support the revolution.

[25]The Little Red Book was first issued under orders of Lin Piao and published by the People's Liberation Army. A facsimile of a special statement: "Study Chairman Mao's writings, follow his teachings and act according to his instructions," written by Lin Piao in his own handwriting, appeared on the front page after Chairman Mao's picture.

September	Expansion of Red Guards' activities through major Chinese cities; various party factions competed for power.
October	Red Guards headquarters organized and its activities further expanded; Liu Shao-ch'i allegedly made a "self-criticism."
November	Central Cultural Revolution Committee organized; Red Guards continued to expand activities into provinces; fighting erupted.
December	Red Guards adopted terrorism; P'eng Chen, mayor of Peking, purged; Chiang Ching, Mao's wife, emerged as a new leader in the movement.
1967 January	Lin Piao gained more power; revolution gained momentum in Shanghai; Red Guards exhorted to seize power throughout China; Heilungkiang organized China's first revolutionary committee to replace party organization.
February	"February Adverse Current" because of counterrevolutionary moves by party regulars; Chou En-Lai issued orders to protect State Council; Shanghai, Kweichow, and Shantung organized revolutionary committees.
March	Army instructed to support agriculture; Peking opened conference of revolutionary workers; Shansi established revolutionary committee.
April	Liu Shao-ch'i officially denounced as "China's Khrushchev"; Party Secretary-General Teng Hsiao-ping condemned for "revisionism"; Chairman Mao ordered army to support the "Left"; Peking formed revolutionary committee.

May   "White terror" (anti-Maoists) reported
                            throughout China; Hong Kong workers rioted.

June   China explodes first hydrogen bomb; Lin Piao
                            seen frequently with Chairman Mao.

July   Liu Shao-ch'i made new "self-criticism";
                            Wu-han region military rebelled against Red
                            Guards; Chou En-lai mediated disputes.

August   Lin Piao issued new directives on Cultural
                            Revolution; Red Guards temporarily seized
                            China's Foreign Ministry; Tsinghai organized
                            revolutionary committee.

September   Mao Tse-tung toured China issuing latest
                            instructions urging rebel factions to reconcile
                            differences.

October   Indonesia suspended diplomatic relations with
                            China; thousands of Chinese there slaugh-
                            tered.

November   Mao Tse-tung, Lin Piao, Chou En-lai, and
                            other top leaders demonstrated unity in
                            Peking; Inner Mongolia revolutionary
                            committee organized.

December   *People's Daily* editorials stressed the impor-
                            tance of unity; Tientsin revolutionary commit-
                            tee organized.

1968
January   New themes advanced to consolidate "three-
                            in-one alliance" (army-revolutionary cadres-
                            masses), to support the army and to promote
                            revolutionary committees; Kiangsi, Kansu,
                            and Honan formed revolutionary committees.

February   Army again instructed to support the "Left";
                            and three more revolutionary committees
                            organized in Hopeh, Hupeh and Kwangtung.

March	Mao Tse-tung issued new directives demanding new strategic plans; purges within the army ranks with Chief of Staff Yang Cheng-wu resigning. Kirin, Kiangsu, and Chekiang formed revolutionary committees.
April	Public security forces took over Supreme People's Court; Hunan, Ninghsia, and Anhwei revolutionary committees established.
May	Leftists, Red Guards stepped up new demonstrations; Shensi, Liaoning, Szechuan provincial revolutionary committees established.
June	Violence again on upswing throughout China; sixty-three active members and seventy-two alternate members of the ruling Central Committee of the party purged.
July	Lin Piao strengthened army's control; Mao began to criticize Red Guards for lack of discipline.
August	Mao ordered army to restore order; three new revolutionary committees formed in Yunnan, Fukien and Kwangsi.
September	Some Red Guard leaders arrested; China completed all new revolutionary committee organizations including Tibet and Sinkiang.
October	*People's Daily* editorials urged "rebuilding of the party"; Cultural Revolution came to an end.

The full impact of the Great Proletarian Cultural Revolution on Chinese society is yet to be measured, but the immediate results in 1969 can be summarized as follows: (1) The destruction of party organizations throughout China's provinces and rural areas and their replacement by the hastily organized interim "revolutionary committees"; (2) The ascendancy of the military, especially with new allocation of power and authority into the hands of regional military commanders; (3) The complete breakdown of the educational process with most of China's educational institutions suspended during the Cultural Revolution and students marching throughout the urban centers and countryside; (4) Decreases in industrial and agricultural production in all areas; and finally; (5) The isolation of China in international affairs including the danger of war with both the United States and the Soviet Union. In fact, more than 400 military border skirmishes occurred between the Chinese and Soviet forces in 1969. The largest was in March, in conflict over Chenpao Island (Russia's Damansky Island) in the Ussuri River.[26]

While the Cultural Revolution restored the position of Chairman Mao Tse-tung as the charismatic leader, and his thought as a guiding ideology for China, it weakened the party as an institution and delayed the process of routinization. The subtle but important change in the interrelationship of the leader, the ideology, and the organization will make institutionalization in the political sphere more difficult than before, and it will render precarious the political stability achieved at any particular time.

III. Personality and Factional Conflicts

Nothing has been more damaging to party unity in China than personality and factional conflicts resulting from policy or ideological differences. We have already discussed some of the early factionalism within the party (see Chapter Three), which resulted in great splits such as

[26]New York *Times* (March 21, 1969).

the charges against party founder Ch'en Tu-hsiu's "opportunism" in 1928 and Chang Kuo-t'ao's "rebellion against the party" in 1938.[27] The more vivid examples of personality conflicts may be seen from the purges of Kao Kang and Jao Shu-shih in 1953–1954.[28]

Kao Kang was born in 1891 in Hengshan, Shensi, an area of great importance to Mao after the Long March. In 1927 he and Liu Chih-tan established a soviet base area in the northwest, persisted in guerrilla operations in the Shensi-Kansu-Ninghsia border area, and formed several revolutionary bases, which became the fountainhead for Mao Tse-tung in 1935. Kao held many influential posts under Mao and after the founding of the new Republic, he became chairman of the Northeast (Manchuria) People's Government (regional government).

Apparently, Kao was dissatisfied with his new post as well as with the rapid ascendancy of Liu Shao-ch'i, Teng Hsiao-p'ing, and Chou En-lai over him within the Central People's Government in Peking. He insisted that he be given a more responsible position, because he spent more time in the "Red area" during the war, while others, including Chou En-lai, were in the "White areas" and should therefore have taken secondary positions. (White areas were those parts of China under the rule of the Kuomintang after the Communists moved into the soviet bases in rural China, the "Red area," in the late 1920's.) Liu Shao-ch'i did serve as the party's Labor organizer in various Nationalist-held areas, but he was finally returned to Yenan in 1943 to conduct the Party's Rectification campaigns.

Kao's insistence on elevating his own leadership position

[27]Peter S. H. Tang, *Communist China Today* (Washington, D.C., Research Institute of the Sino-Soviet Bloc, 1961), p. 88

[28]*Documents of the National Conference of the Communist Party of China, March, 1955* (Peking, Foreign Language Press, 1955).

confronted Chairman Mao with a serious problem, since Liu and Chou En-lai, among others, were Mao's personal choices at the founding of the People's Republic. Kao enlisted Jao Shu-shih, a powerful party secretary of the East China Bureau, in a showdown at the 1954 Central Committee meeting; but their fate was already decided at the Politburo meeting in December, 1953. Both Kao Kang and Jao Shu-shih were expelled from the party; Kao committed suicide and Jao was put in prison.[29] Thereafter, Mao supervised the drafting of a state constitution to stabilize the leadership positions of Liu Shao-ch'i, Chou En-lai, and other party members of his choice.

No serious personality conflicts occurred after Kao's purge until 1958, during the controversial Great Leap Forward. The man who questioned Mao's policies then was Marshal P'eng Teh-huai, the Vice-Premier of the State Council and Minister of Defense. P'eng had a brilliant career within the Communist movement. He was born in a village in Hunan, the same district where Mao Tse-tung was born. Although he came from a rich peasant family, he left home and joined a provincial army because of a quarrel with his family. During the northern expedition, he joined the Communisty Party. He led an uprising against the Nationalist Army in 1928 and soon after joined forces with Red Army units led by Chu Teh and Mao Tse-tung. He was a leader in the Long March and became the deputy commander in chief of the People's Liberation Army in 1945. He also commanded the Chinese People's Volunteers in the Korean War and was awarded the title of "Hero," the highest honor awarded by North Korea.[30]

As a soldier, P'eng had championed the cause of professional armed forces in China. He allegedly argued for

[29]Chu-yuan Cheng, "Power Struggle in Red China," *Asian Survey* (September, 1966).

[30]Donald W. Klein and Anne B. Clark, *op.cit.*, pp. 727–37.

the following principles: (1) putting the "army before the party"; (2) counterposing "regularization and modernization" against "proletarian revolutionization" of the army; (3) substituting the "system of one-man leadership" for the "collective leadership of the party committee" in the army; and finally, (4) placing "military technique" in the first place in building the army.[31]

During the initial phase of the Great Leap Forward in 1958, P'eng also attacked Mao's new approach to economic development. He questioned the wisdom of putting "politics in command" over economic construction and the establishment of rural communes throughout China. When, apparently, P'eng felt that Mao was not about to modify his radical policy, he went to the Soviet Union in late April, 1959, and solicited support from Premier Khrushchev.[32] On returning to China, he initiated an attack on Mao's leadership and questioned the validity of Mao's policy on a number of issues among top party leaders. Finally, P'eng wrote a letter to Chairman Mao on July 14, 1959, demanding reexamination at the expanded Politburo session of "objective lessons gained by the Great Leap Forward" with the goal of "distinguishing right from wrong" and thus "uniting the whole Party."[33]

Mao called the Central Committee to convene at Lushan August 2 to 16, 1959. Instead of discussing the issues raised by P'eng, Mao concentrated on denigrating P'eng's character and impugning his motives, characterizing him as "essentially a representative of the bourgeoisie."[34]

[31]Philip Bridgham, "Factionalism in the Central Committee," in John Wilson Lewis, ed., *Party Leadership and Revolutionary Power* (New York, Oxford University Press, 1971), p. 216.

[32]See David A. Charles, "The Dismissal of Marshal P'eng Teh-huai," *China Quarterly*, 8 (October–December, 1961).

[33]Philip Bridgham, *op. cit.*, p. 214.

[34]*Ibid.*, p. 215.

Confronted in effect with the necessity of choosing between the two personalities, Mao or P'eng, the Central Committee members chose Mao. P'eng and his supporters, including Chief of Staff Huang Ko-cheng, were replaced by Lin Piao and Lo Jui-ching, a former Minister of Public Security. But Mao's own position was considerably weakened since he had already given up his Chairmanship of the republic to Liu Shao-ch'i, at the Sixth Plenum, November 28–December 10, 1958.

The crucial Lushan meeting saw the rise of a relatively "young" Army officer, Lin Piao, who was then only fifty-two. (See the next chapter with respect to Lin's personality.) He immediately set out to reorganize the Chinese Liberation Army, utilizing the strategy of "propagating" Mao Tse-tung's thought. He abolished the system of rank in the military so as to gain the support and confidence of the lower cadres and soldiers. He introduced a new system of political departments, not only in the army, but also in industry, communications, trade, financial units, and educational and scientific research organizations. He also appointed regional army commanders as new party secretaries in charge of the party's six regional bureaus. In addition, he enlisted Mao's wife, Chiang Ch'ing, a former actress, to help him advance the cause of promoting the "study of Chairman Mao's thought" and to "combat revisionism."

Liu Shao-ch'i, on the other hand, is also an old revolutionary who emerged as a new power center at the Lushan meeting. He was already named to succeed Mao as Chairman of the Republic. He began to consolidate his forces among regular party cadres to compete for power positions in the government. Liu earned a reputation as a specialist in organization and he helped Mao in Yenan in Mao's famous *"cheng-feng"* campaigns. Later, his own position in the party became second only to that of Mao. Liu wrote an important work, *How to be a Good*

Communist, which for more than twenty years served as a basic statement of the model of ideal Communist behavior. In this work, Liu encouraged party members to discipline themselves according to the Chinese tradition of self-cultivation, as expressed in passages from Confucian classics.[35]

Liu organized a very important Central Work Expansion Conference in Peking in 1962, which included 7,000 leading party cadres from all parts of China. During this conference, the possibility of making Mao an honorary Chairman was discussed. After the conference Liu began to exercise firmer and greater control of administrative affairs of the government and took personal command of China's foreign policy, limiting the role formerly played by Premier Chou En-lai, and the foreign minister, Ch'en Yi. Liu traveled to many foreign states, including the Soviet Union and Eastern European countries in 1960. He visited Burma, Cambodia, North Korea, and North Vietnam in 1963. And from May 21 to June 5, 1965, Chairman Liu was in Indonesia conferring with President Sukarno for the proposed "Peking-Djakarta axis," a role that should have been taken by Premier Chou En-lai.[36]

In addition, Liu Shao-ch'i began to develop a different political strategy and policy lines from those advanced by Chairman Mao and his supporters. Mao insisted on Rectification campaigns supported by mass movements to eradicate ideological deviations, whereas Liu preferred a milder form of persuasion by party "work teams" consisting of veteran cadres. In foreign policy considerations, Mao argued for a protracted "people's war" (in Vietnam at that time) while Liu allegedly preferred a united

[35]Liu Shao-chi, *How to be a Good Communist* (Peking, Foreign Language Press, 1964).

[36]Liu was the first Chinese Chief of State to visit a non-Communist country (Mao never has). See Harold C. Hinton, *China's Turbulent Quest* (Bloomington, Indiana University Press, 1972), p. 182.

front solution in cooperation with the Soviet Union.[37] These differences in policy matters soon developed into personality conflicts as Mao Tse-tung becoming increasingly annoyed over Liu Shao-ch'i's inability to galvanize the party machinery and to generate revolutionary momentum.

The Maoists, under the leadership of Lin Piao, Chiang Ch'ing, Chang Chun-ch'iao, and Yao Wen-yuan, used the Cultural Revolution to their advantage and planned a complicated strategy against Liu Shao-ch'i and his colleagues, P'eng Chen, Teng Hsiao-ping and Lo Jui-ching, among others. The Maoists found a convenient tool to accomplish their goal in the form of a popular play written by Wu Han, a scholar specializing in Ming history and a close friend of P'eng Chen. Wu in 1961 wrote a play, *The Dismissal of Hai Jui,* which dealt with a benevolent Chinese official in the sixteenth century who "always fought with all his might against corrupt officials and therefore lost favor with the Emperor."[38] Wu Han portrayed Hai Jui as a just and honest official with moral integrity and the courage to resist unjust pressures from his superiors. What made the incident noteworthy was the accusation that Wu Han was actually writing an allegory based on the dismissal of P'eng Teh-huai.

From November, 1965, to April, 1966, many articles appeared in the newspapers bitterly denouncing Wu Han. Mao himself had left Peking for Shanghai sometime in November, to direct the complicated plot against Wu Han. P'eng Chen, apparently without realizing the seriousness of the plot, came to Wu's rescue, as the Maoists expected. He had also asked two prominent party ideologists, Teng T'o, then editor in chief of the *People's Daily,* and Liao Mo-sha, head of the United Front Department of the party, to

[37]Uri Ra'anan, "Peking's Foreign Policy Debates, 1965–1966," in Ho Ping-ti and Tang Tsou, *China in Crisis,* Vol. 2, pp. 23-71.

[38]Quoted in Chu-yuan Cheng, "Power Struggle in Red China," *op. cit.*

defend Wu Han and his work. For awhile Liu Shao-chi felt that his position was quite secure and he left Peking with his wife on March 26, 1966, for another state visit to Pakistan and Afghanistan. His absence afforded his opponents the opportunity to complete their power play. With the positions of Liu Shao-ch'i's group publicly exposed, the Maoists opened fire. First, the *Liberation Army Daily* published fierce attacks on these men, as did the official party paper, the *People's Daily*, which had been taken over by the Maoists. The Maoists asserted that "this anti-Party small clique is not an incidental and isolated phenomenon" and urged a nationwide movement so that the group could be dealt with "thoroughly and merciless-ly."[39] With Mao's encouragement, a nationwide campaign was launched attacking Liu Shao-ch'i's colleagues. Although Liu returned to China immediately thereafter, there was no publicized reception for him in Peking, and his political career was coming to an end. Liu died of cancer in Peking in 1974.

Suggested Reading

BARNETT, A. DOAK, *Cadres, Bureaucracy and Political Power in Communist China.* New York, Columbia University Press, 1967.

BAUM, RICHARD, and FREDERICK C. TEIWES, *Ssu-Ch'ing: The Socialist Movement of 1962–1966.* Berkeley, California, University of California Press, 1968.

CHAI, WINBERG, "The Reorganization of the Chinese Communist Party, 1966–1968." *Asian Survey,* November, 1968.

——, *Essential Works of Chinese Communism,* rev. ed. New York, Bantam Books, 1972.

CHEN, THEODORE H. E., *Thought Reform of the Chinese Intellectuals.* Hong Kong, University of Hong Kong Press, 1960.

GOLDMAN, MERLE, *Literary Dissent in Communist China.* Cambridge, Massachusetts, Harvard University Press, 1967.

HO PING-TI and TANG TSOU, eds., *China in Crisis.* 2 vols. Chicago, The University of Chicago Press, 1968.

[39]Quoted in Chu-yuan Cheng, *op.cit.*

HSIUNG, JAMES CHIEH, *Ideology and Practice.* New York, Praeger Publishers, 1970.

HSUEH, CHUN-TU, ed., *Revolutionary Leaders of Modern China.* New York, Oxford University Press, 1971.

JOHNSON, CHALMER, ed., *Ideology and Politics in Contemporary China.* Seattle, Washington, University of Washington Press, 1973.

KLEIN, DONALD, and ANNE B. CLARK, *Biographical Dictionary of Chinese Communism, 1921–1965.* Cambridge, Massachusetts, Harvard University Press, 1971.

LEWIS, JOHN WILSON, ed., *Party Leadership and Revolutionary Power in China.* New York, Cambridge University Press, 1970.

LING, KEN (pseudonym), *The Revenge of Heaven—Journal of a Young Chinese.* New York, G. P. Putnam's Sons, 1972.

ROBINSON , THOMAS, *et al., The Cultural Revolution in China.* Berkeley, California, University of California Press, 1971.

SCALAPINO, ROBERT A., ed., *Elites in the People's Republic of China.* Seattle, Washington, University of Washington Press, 1972.

SCHURMANN, FRANZ, *Ideology and Organization in Communist China,* new enlarged ed. Berkeley, California, University of California Press, 1968.

SCHWARTZ, BENJAMIN I., *Communism and China: Ideology in Flux.* Cambridge, Massachusetts, Harvard University Press, 1968.

TOWNSEND, JAMES R., *Political Participation in Communist China.* Berkeley, California, University of California Press, 1967.

VAN NESS, PETER, *Revolution and Chinese Foreign Policy.* Berkeley, California, University of California Press, 1970.

Who's Who in Communist China. 2 vols. Hong Kong, Union Research Institute, 1970.

CHAPTER EIGHT:
POST-CULTURAL REVOLUTION POLITICS

THE search for a reintegrated political community in China has suffered a serious setback because of the opposition Mao Tse-tung created within the Communist Party organization during the Cultural Revolution. It has been estimated that the Chairman could not count on support from more than 30 percent of the 1967 membership in the ruling Central Committee (52 out of 172 members).[1] In fact, this was the first time in the history of the Chinese Communist Party that the Chairman of the party completely violated the norms and prescribed procedures of the party in order to carry out the activities of the Cultural Revolution.[2]

The extent of opposition to the Maoists can also be seen in the purges of party officials. The publication of a list of 127 prominent leaders as "monsters and demons" or "black gangsters" in November, 1966, reveals the vindictiveness of the purge.[3] During 1967 an additional 316 high party officials were removed from office. They included 91 persons from party apparatuses, 87 from governmental organizations, 43 from the People's

---

[1]*Studies on Chinese Communism* (May, 1967), pp. 1–18 and (October, 1967), pp. 1–3.

[2]Winberg Chai, "The Reorganization of the Chinese Communist Party, 1966–1968," *Asian Survey* (November, 1968), pp. 901–10.

[3]Asia Research Center, *The Great Cultural Revolution in China* (Hong Kong, Asia Research Center, 1967), pp. 116–93.

Liberation Army, 51 from educational and scientific institutions, and 44 from cultural establishments.[4]

At the end of the Cultural Revolution, 34 members had been purged and 9 out of the remaining 63 active members of the Central Committee had been sharply criticized. In addition, 27 out of 72 active alternate members were purged and 29 were under criticism from the leftist Maoists. And across China, there are only 9 out of 45 party secretaries of the first and second regional party secretaries still known to be active in party affairs.[5]

By the time the Ninth Party Congress convened in Peking on April 1, 1969, newcomers accounted for 72 percent of the 177 full members of the Central Committee (123 members); and they were elected for the first time to this policy-making body. Lin Piao was named as Mao's successor, but the tenuity of his position and the weakness of the party were exposed when Lin was the target of a new purge in 1971. Thereafter, the Ninth Party Central Committee was replaced by yet another new Tenth Central Committee in August, 1973.

The Tenth Congress was the first that Chairman Mao attended but did not address. There was no clear hierarchy of leadership established. No successor to Chairman Mao was named and no Secretary-General of the party was appointed. With yet another political campaign to criticize Lin Piao and Confucius in 1973–1974, the struggles continue for ideology, power, and priorities in the new China into the middle of the 1970's.[6]

I. The Rise and Fall of Lin Piao

One of the most controversial events in post-Cultural Revolution politics in China involves the rise and fall of Lin

[4]For a complete list, see *Studies of Chinese Communism*, Vol. II, No. 1 (January, 1968) and No. 2 (February, 1968).

[5]New York *Times* (June 24, 1968).

[6]*Peking Review* (September 7, 1973).

Piao; and Lin's life pattern from the time of his entrance into the party reads like the broader history of the party and its army.[7] Lin shared a common socioeconomic background with many other great Communist leaders who were of nonpeasant, petty bourgeois origin and were subjected to modernizing foreign influences from an early age, and who witnessed some of the major nationalistic movements in China.

Lin was born in a village near Wuhan in 1907.[8] While attending middle school in Wuchang, he joined the Nationalist Party. Later he went to Shanghai where he joined the Communist Youth League, which helped him to gain admission to the Whampoa Military Academy. There he became a Communist through the influence of Chou En-lai. He was present at the Nanchang uprisings in 1927 and accompanied Chu Teh back to Chingkang Mountain to join the historic linkup with Mao Tse-tung. He became a leader of the Long March and led his column of soldiers through the grasslands to reach Shensi. (See Chapter Four.) There he commanded the Communist forces fighting against the Japanese and was severely wounded in battle.

Lin was sent to the Soviet Union to recover and returned to Yenan just in time to participate in the important *cheng-feng* movement. Later he joined with Chou En-lai and participated in negotiations with Chiang Kai-shek in Chungking. He was instrumental in formulating strategies to defeat the Nationalists during the civil war, and became one of Mao Tse-tung's trusted lieutenants. He was elected a member of the party's Seventh Central Committee in June, 1945, and within a few years was elected to the membership of the Central People's Government Council, the People's Revolutionary Military Council, and the Standing Committee of the Political Consultative Council;

[7]Thomas W. Robinson, "Lin Piao, as an Elite Type," in Robert A. Scalapino, ed., *Elites in the People's Republic of China* (Seattle, University of Washington Press, 1972).

[8]Donald W. Klein and Anne B. Clark, *op. cit.*, pp. 553–67.

all three organizations chaired by Mao Tse-tung. Meanwhile, he retained the top post in the central-south military region of China until he was requested to command the Chinese Volunteer Army during the Korean War. He was again seriously wounded and forced to retire from active political life until 1956 when he was elected to the Politburo.

In a recent study of Lin Piao, he was described as "quiet, reserved, nontalkative, calm, unemotional and modest; [and] at the same time, clever, calculating, deliberate, and astute."[9] It is suggested that he liked to bury himself in the details of his work and to pursue a matter, once begun, to its conclusion. With respect to his ideological background, he believed in Marxism-Leninism to the extent that he was familiar with it, but it did not appear to have "penetrated to the center of his being."[10] In fact, what does become clear is that from the very beginning, Lin Piao was "a nearly xenophobic nationalist."[11]

However, Lin gained international prominence in the autumn of 1965 when he published his essay, *Long Live the Victory of the People's War,* in commemoration of the twentieth anniversary of victory against Japan. This essay had been widely publicized as "a comprehensive, systematic and profound analysis of Comrade Mao Tse-tung's theory and strategic concept of people's war and provides the revolutionary people of the whole world with a powerful ideological weapon in the fight against imperialism and modern revisionism."[12] It was in this article that Lin became an internationalist in that he outlined Mao's "village-encircle-city" strategy for carrying out the worldwide Communist revolution.

[9]Thomas W. Robinson, *op. cit.*, p. 165.

[10] *Ibid.*, p. 169.

[11] *Ibid.*, p. 170.

[12]*Long Live the Victory of the People's War* (Peking, Foreign Language Press, 1965).

After 1965, Lin appeared to be a blind follower of Mao. He had pledged "eternal allegiance to Mao" personally and the construction of a new state machine "forever loyal to the thought of Mao Tse-tung.[13] For his loyalty and dedication, Lin was elevated officially as Mao Tse-tung's "close comrade-in-arms and successor" in the official constitution of the party in 1969.[14]

In spite of all the glorification of personality in the cult of Mao, the Chairman became dismayed at both the military ascendancy and the personal power of his designated successor, Lin Piao. He was now convinced that he would have "to remove his designated successor as the leader of a 'disloyal opposition' in order to regain 'effective control' over the political apparatus in China."[15] The ensuing power struggle began at the Second Plenum of the Ninth Central Committee in August, 1970, through the summer of 1971. The issues were the drafting of a new state constitution to replace the 1954 constitution, and the naming of a new Chairman of the Republic.[16] Lin Piao's supporters at the plenum, with his wife, Yeh Chun, as the leading activist, proposed that Lin be appointed Chairman of the Republic, implying that this was the wish of Chairman Mao. However, Lin's strategy failed when Mao himself rejected the proposal and delivered instead a very strong criticism of Lin for his extreme impatience in bidding for the leadership.

By this time, Lin realized that his hope for supreme power was unattainable as long as Chairman Mao was an

[13]Thomas W. Robinson, op. cit., pp. 175–76.

[14]Winberg Chai, ed., Essential Works of Chinese Communism (New York, Bantam Books, 1972), p. 431.

[15]Philip Bridgham, "The Fall of Lin Piao," China Quarterly, 55, (July/September, 1973), p. 427.

[16]The draft constitution was never published. For a translation of the secret draft, see Winberg Chai, Essential Works of Chinese Communism, op. cit., pp. 514–20.

obstacle. He planned a number of secret plots and urged a coup d'etat against the Chairman.[17] Meanwhile Mao sought assurances of support from various regional military leaders in August and September, 1971. According to the Chinese account:

On September 12, 1971, Mao was returning to Peking from Shanghai by train. Lin had arranged to blow up the train somewhere north of Nanking. If anything went wrong a second attempt would be made further along the line. . . .

The officer in charge of the first attempt had misgivings at being ordered to perform such an extraordinary task. He was torn between the iron discipline of a PLA [People's Liberation Army] man to obey orders, and revulsion at being asked to blow up a passenger coach. He confided to his wife, a doctor and Party member. She was horrified . . . and gave him an injection [before he could touch off the explosion]. And his wife informed her Party branch committee. . . . So Mao travelled over the first charge safely, unaware of any danger. Messages were flashed to Peking after the doctor's warning. A few stations before the second charge was to be exploded, the train was halted; Mao was urged to descend rapidly and moved into a car, ordered by Chou En-lai, to bring him to Peking with an appropriate escort. Thus the first two assassination attempts failed. . . . Lin Piao, learning of the failure of the plot, took his family and fled by airplane to the Soviet Union via Mongolia. The plane later ran out of fuel and crashed in Mongolia, killing everyone aboard. . . .[18]

Because of Lin Piao's alleged plot against the Chairman, many of his former associates and colleagues were purged,

[17]A number of secret documents were later released by the party. See the Appendix 3 of this book.

[18]See Wilfred Burchett, "Lin Piao's Plot—The Full Story," *Far Eastern Economic Review* (August 20, 1973), pp. 22–24.

including members of the powerful Politburo and top military leadership in Peking.[19] Named as co-conspirators were Chief of the General Staff Huang Yung-sheng, Air Force Commander in Chief Wu Fa-hsien, and Naval Commander in Chief Li Tso-p'eng, as well as Commander in Chief of Logistics Ch'iu Hui-tso. Since power in a Communist society is so highly concentrated and wielded so extensively and intensively, the death of a ruling leader poses a particularly difficult problem for the system to handle. The purge of Lin Piao illustrated the gravity of the problem China faces in search of an eventual successor to Chairman Mao, who was eighty years of age on December 26, 1973.

II. The Uncertain Role of the Military

One of the significant developments during the post-Cultural Revolution period involves the rise of the military as a competitor for political power and authority within Chinese Communist politics.

During the early years, Chinese military units were not involved in party politics and they were standardized on the Soviet model. Territorial commands were divided into administrative regions through which the Central Committee exercised its political authority under unified area commands responsible to the Military Affairs Committee. And with the adoption of the new constitution in 1954, the military changed from a party organ to an agency of the government.[20]

The military was placed under the firm control of the Ministry of National Defense, which was divided into various general staff departments serving as military

[19]For detailed listings, see Chang Ching-wen, "Mao's Purge of Lin Piao's Faction," *Issues and Studies* (April, 1973), pp. 19–27.

[20]*The Constitution of the People's Republic of China*, chapter 9.

headquarters. Thirteen military districts for ground operation were established, plus nine air regions for air defense and three naval districts to control fleet operations in the Yellow, East China, and South China seas.[21] Military manpower is drawn selectively from every segment of society under a national annual conscription program. All males eighteen years of age, plus a small number of females, are subject to the draft, provided they pass a rigorous political, educational, and physical examination. Preference is given to poor, lower-middle peasant, and fishermen families from rural areas, and to worker-laborer families in the cities.

There are no commissioned officers in the People's Liberation Army, as the system of ranks and grades was abolished in 1965. The function of leadership remains, however, and is discharged by men who are simply referred to by job titles. Since leadership positions are maintained, there are prescribed procedures and channels through which the status of leader may be achieved. In addition, the men are judged by their active participation in various rectification campaigns.

For example, there was the so-called "Three-Eight" Working-Style campaign in 1960. This is derived from Mao Tse-tung's three famous phrases (firm, correct, political orientation; a plain, hardworking style; and flexibility in strategy and tactics), and eight additional Chinese characters, which in English mean "unity," "alertness," "earnestness," and "liveliness." In the spring of 1961, it burgeoned into a nationwide campaign to build what was known as the "Four Good Company." All units on the company level were urged to become good in four aspects of their work and rated accordingly: good in "Three-Eight"

---

[21]See John Gittings, *The Role of the Chinese Army* (New York, Oxford University Press, 1967).

Working Style; good in military training; and good in management of army livelihood. The last one is most interesting, because in the past fifteen years, soldiers of the People's Liberation Army have had to devote considerable time to raising some portion of their own food.[22]

The army has a total strength of something under 2.5 million. Military practice seems to follow task force, rather than rigid, formal principles of organization. In addition, the militia, a vast organization of armed civilians between eighteen and fifty years of age, forms the basic reserve for the regular armed forces.

We do not know the precise role the military played in struggles within the party during the early years; however, in recent major purges, there have always been accompanying shifts of combat troops, transfers of military and public-security commanders, and changes in the Peking garrison command. These changes usually begin before the purge is announced or even takes place, apparently as preparation for anticipated resistance. The army was called to play a central role during the Cultural Revolution, including purging of high officials, restoring order, and imposing administrative control. The following table may illustrate the role of the military in carrying out the purges of Liu Shao-ch'i and Lin Piao:[23]

In the immediate post-Cultural Revolution period, especially during the Ninth Party Congress in April, 1959, there was a dramatic shift of power from the party to the military. There were 123 military men elected to the 279-member Central Committee. In the Politburo, at least 10 of the 21 full members and 2 of the 4 alternates were

[22]*Peking Review* (March 15, 1968).

[23] Michael Pillsbury, "Patterns of Chinese Power Struggles: Three Models," paper presented at university seminar on modern China, Columbia University, New York City, March 27, 1974.

MAIN FORCE TRANSFERS BETWEEN
MILITARY REGIONS FROM 1967 TO 1970

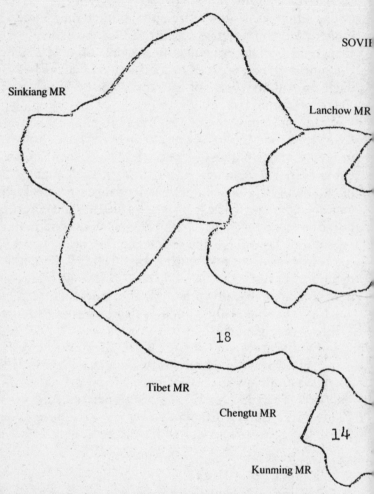

SOVIE

Sinkiang MR

Lanchow MR

18

Tibet MR

Chengtu MR

14

Kunming MR

Sources: 21st: *Issues and Studies,* April, 1968, p. 21. 38th: SCMP No. 4227, p.8.
50th: SCMP No. 4181, pp. 1–6. 13th and 54th: *Issues and Studies,* August, 1970, p.
12. Prepared by Michael Pillsbury.

References to locations of PRC main force units from *PLA Unit History*
(Washington, D.C., Office of the Chief of Military History, Department of the
Army, no date) which is a translation of a Taiwan government publication
released in 1966. MR denotes Military Region of People's Republic of China.

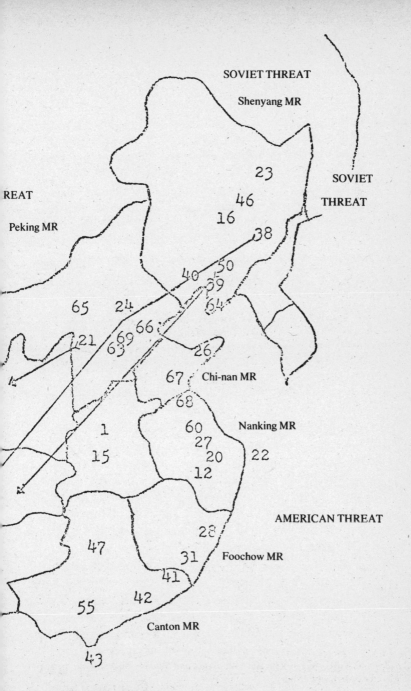

	The Purges of	
	Liu Shao-ch'i	Lin Piao
Shift of Peking garrison commander	Tseng Mei replaced by Li Chia-yi	Wen Yu-ch'eng replaced by Yang Chun-sheng
Shift of Peking military regional commander	Yang Yung replaced by Cheng Wei-shan	Cheng Wei-shan replaced by T'eng Hai-ch'ing
Transfer of public security officer	Yu Sang named new vice-minister	Li Chen named new vice-minister
Shift of troops to capital area	38th Corps transferred	27th and 28th Corps transferred
Escort of purge victim while abroad	Liu visited Pakistan with Wang Tung-hsing	Lin visited North Korea with Huang Yung-sheng

from the military. Of the 29 revolutionary committees established in the provinces, 20 were chaired by military men. And 94, or 60 percent of a total of 158 new regional party leaders were military men. In fact, among the 189 special administrative districts below the provincial level, 160 were headed by military cadres; and out of 2,359 counties, 2,000 were captured by the military during this period. Consultations with the military leadership became a regular feature of the policy decision-making process in post-Cultural revolution politics.

The ascendancy of military power and the steady erosion of the authority of regular party organizations again brought intraparty conflicts into a new dimension. By the time of the Tenth Party Congress, in 1973, the military representation in the Central Committee was reduced from 123 to 100 members; and changes were also made in the commands of eight of eleven military regions throughout China, which diminished their hold on the provincial party apparatus.

The shifts were announced in January, 1974, and involved the uprooting of two powerful Politburo members, Hsu Shih-yu at Nanking in the east, and Ch'en Hsi-lien at Shenyang, in the northeast, who had held sway in their large strategic bailiwicks for twenty and fifteen years, respectively. Hsu was transferred to command the Canton military region and Ch'en was put in charge of the Peking military region. In the case of Hsu's transfer, it may have destroyed the alliance between the Nanking regional military leaders and Shanghai cadres high in the party.

Other changes included moving Ting Shen from Canton to Nanking; Tseng Ssu-yu of the Wuhan region exchanging places with Yang Teh-chih of the Tsinan military region; Han Hsien-chu of the Foochow region exchanging positions with Pi Ting-chun of the Lanchow military region. Yang Yung, Chin Chi-wei, and Wang Pi-cheng continued their posts in Sinkiang, Chengtu, and Kunming respectively. Chairman Mao once told his party members, "Every Communist must grasp the truth, political power grows out of the barrel of a gun"; but he added, "the Party controls the gun and the gun shall never be allowed to control the Party."[24] The future role of the military is yet to be determined.

III. Politics of Political Succession

During the visits by members of the American Society of Newspaper Editors in Peking in late October, 1972, Premier Chou En-lai spoke freely and frankly about the problem of who will succeed Chairman Mao Tse-tung and Premier Chou. One of the of the American editors quoted Mr. Chou as saying, "With such a big country and the problems facing us, how can you have only one successor?"[25]

Both the Chairman and Premier Chou are of advanced

[24]*Selected Works of Mao Tse-tung*, II, p. 224.

[25]Reuters dispatch from Peking (October 16, 1972).

age, eighty-one and seventy-six respectively in 1974, and obviously time is not on their side. Twice before, Chairman Mao has made arrangements for a peaceful succession, and twice has failed, with his efforts resulting in violence. Both would-be successors, Liu Shao-ch'i in 1958 and Lin Piao in 1969, played havoc with party politics. The last heir, as we have mentioned in previous sections, was an alleged conspirator in numerous secret plots and coups including an assassination attempt against the Chairman.

After the disqualification and death of Lin Piao, the Chairman apparently considered promoting Premier Chou En-lai as his third and interim successor. Chou has continuously held the position of Premier of the Chinese government since its inception in Peking in 1949. Chou far surpasses Mao in knowledge of world affairs because of his personal participation in many international negotiations and conferences. He attended the successful 1954 Geneva Conference on Indochina; and in an interlude, Chou visited New Delhi and Rangoon and issued the famous policy of "Five Principles of Peaceful Coexistence," which then became a dominant theme in China's diplomacy with countries in the Third World. Chou had also participated in the important Bandung Conference in April, 1955, in Indonesia, where he used his diplomatic skills to create a new image of China in the eyes of the developing nations.

In domestic affairs, Chou En-lai demonstrated his administrative ability when he was able to achieve a near-total recovery for China from the dislocations of the Cultural Revolution. Mass organizations were set back into place, government ministries seemed to be fully manned, the educational system was functioning at all levels, and a new Five-Year Plan was promoted. Agriculture was given top priority. There was also large-scale investment in infrastructure such as transport, utilities, and resource development.[26]

[26]Thomas W. Robinson, "China in 1973," *Asian Survey* (January, 1974), p. 1.

In party politics, Chou En-lai had faced strong and recurrent opposition from various groups and was well aware that Chinese politics is factional in character. Rumor, character assassination, bargaining, power play, and deception are always brewing. Although Chou En-lai chaired a new Tenth Party Congress from August 24 to 28, 1973, and presented an official report on behalf of the party, the Tenth Congress clearly created a fragile structure that papered over many divisive issues.

Moreover, the Tenth Party Congress did not give Premier Chou a working majority. Instead, there is a balance between several factions. Among the 195 members and 124 alternate members elected to the Central Committee, the military occupies 32 percent, party and government cadres 28 percent, and representatives of the Leftist "revolutionary masses" control 40 percent of total membership. The Central Committee memberships include nearly all the important central and regional military leaders, all provincial party committee heads, and most provincial trade union leaders.

Twenty-one members are elected to the Politburo, which is a balanced factional system representing three or four major interest groups:

1. *Central bureaucrats:* Chou En-lai, Yeh Chien-ying, Chu Teh, Liu Pao-ch'eng (military bureaucrats); Tung Pi-wu, Teng Hsiao-ping, Li Hsien-nien, and Wu Teh (political bureaucrats).

2. *Leftist radicals:* Chiang Ch'ing (Chairman Mao's wife); K'ang Sheng, Wang Tung-hsiang (internal security apparatus); Chang Ch'un-ch'iao, Yao Wen-yuan and Wang Hung-wen (Shanghai propaganda group).

3. *Military representatives:* Li Teh-sheng (head of the General Political Department of the army and Anhwei provincial chief); Ch'en Hsi-lien (formerly head of the Shenyang military region, now commands Peking region); Hsu Shih-yu (formerly Nanking military region chief, now in charge of Canton).

4. *Regional representatives:* Wei Kuo-ch'ing from Kwangsi; Hua Kuo-feng from Hunan; Wu Teh from Peking; and Ch'en Yung-kuei from the rural model commune, Tachai.

The most powerful factional group appears to be under the personal direction of Chairman Mao's wife, Chiang Ching. They launched an Anti-Lin Piao and Anti-Confucius campaign which gained considerable momentum at the end of 1973. The campaign suggested that such time-honored concepts as filial piety was Confucius' way of keeping the "slaves in line."[27] With this new campaign as a rallying point, the "Leftists" began to reorganize students and peasants alike to bring about another "Cultural Revolution."[28]

Premier Chou has always been the lone balancer in Chinese politics; and is a veteran survivor of many purges chiefly because of his ability to anticipate and swim with the political current. He has wielded no power threats, and has displayed great loyalty and appreciation of the Chairman. His expertise in foreign affairs is unique among Chinese leaders. But Chou's unexpected illness in spring, 1974, has shattered Chairman Mao's plan for an orderly transition of the Chinese government. The vacuum now created by his illness threatens a new political crisis and a disturbance to the process of routinization of post-Cultural Revolution politics in China.

Chairman Mao's ambitious wife, Chiang Ch'ing, apparently is the likely candidate to succeed Premier Chou. Outspoken and dominant, she has enjoyed her role within the inner circle of leaders since the downfall of Liu Shao-ch'i. She heads the powerful "Leftist Radical faction" within the party, including the control of internal public security forces as well as regional propaganda

[27]*Peking Review* (October 12, 1973), pp. 5–10.

[28]New York *Times* (June 14, 1974).

groups. A rather rigid personality, nearly devoid of humor, she has no experience of foreign affairs.

In second place as a possible candidate for succeeding Chou chould be the young (late thirties) Wang Hung-wen, who rose from the ranks of Red Guards in Shanghai.[29] He is alleged to be one of the first party members in a Shanghai cotton mill where he worked to put up a poster attacking the "capitalist powerholders" of their factory. He is also attributed with the recruitment of thirty workers who journeyed to Peking in the early stage of the Culture Revolution to present their petitions to Chairman Mao and his wife. After the new Shanghai Municipal Revolutionary Committee was established, he was appointed a "leading member" and subsequently named a deputy chairman under Chang Ch'un-ch'iao.

Wang became a member of the Presidium and was elected to the Central Committee at the Ninth Party Congress. At the Tenth Party Congress, he was named a Second Vice-Chairman of the party. A protégé of Chiang Ch'ing, he enjoys a nearly father-son relationship with Chairman Mao. He is often seen in photographs at the side of the Chairman receiving foreign guests, and is gaining rapidly in the play for administrative power.

Premier Chou's personal choices for successors are his Deputy Premiers Teng Hsiao-ping and Li Hsien-nien, already acting on his behalf. Both men belong to the "central bureaucrat faction" headed by Chou. Teng's exceptional administrative experience includes having served as Secretary-General of the party. Li was for a number of years China's chief economic planner. Unfortunately, neither of these men enjoys the unreserved confidence of the Chairman and his powerful wife. There are a number of important military leaders in the Politburo

[29]See Parris H. Chang, "Political Profiles: Wang Hung-wen and Li Teh-sheng," *The China Quarterly*, No. 57 (January/March, 1974).

who could very well succeed Premier Chou. However, after the coup of Lin Piao in 1971, it is unlikely that Chairman Mao will entrust another general with such political power.

One Western analyst suggested that eight traits seem useful in the selection process for a successor in China: (1) ideological purity; (2) charisma and existence of a personal following; (3) career stability and authority; (4) power base—institutional or geographic; (5) ability to effectively conduct political infighting; (6) ability to conciliate different factions; (7) demonstrated literary and forensic ability; and finally, (8) relative youth, *i.e.*, not more than sixty years of age.[30] One perhaps could add (9) strong administrative experience and (10) ability to negotiate with foreign countries. For the moment Chairman Mao has not found such a person.

No one can tell what will happen in China in a post-Mao Tse-tung era, except that the successors to Mao, at least for a short time, will be evaluated in terms of his (or her) comparative fidelity to Mao's life and work. However, in time Mao's thought will (and must) come to be regarded as "pure" ideology rather than "practical" ideology as it was in 1974. In terms of Franz Schurmann's distinction, "pure" ideology states "values: moral and ethical conceptions about right and wrong"; and "practical" ideology denotes "norms: rules which prescribe behavior and thus are expected to have direct action consequences."[31]

A new "practical" ideology will then arise in post-Mao China to deal with new political and economic issues. The weight of the whole history of the party and Chinese culture will surely be a lasting influence on the Chinese people.

---

[30] Thomas W. Robinson, paper presented at Columbia University seminar on modern China, May 1, 1974.

[31] Franz Schurmann, *Ideology and Organization in Communist China* (Berkeley, University of California Press, 1968), pp. 38–39.

SUGGESTED READING

BARNETT, A. DOAK, *Uncertain Passage—China's Transition to the Post-Mao Era*. Washington, D.C., The Brookings Institution, 1974.

Bulletin of the Atomic Scientists, *China After the Cultural Revolution*. New York, Random House, 1969.

CHAI, WINBERG, *New Politics of Communist China: Modernization Process of a Developing Nation*. Pacific Palisades, California, Goodyear Publishing Co., 1972.

——, ed., *The Foreign Relations of the People's Republic of China*. New York, G. P. Putnam's Sons, 1972.

CLUBB, O. EDMUND, *China and Russia, the Great Game*. New York, Columbia University Press, 1970.

Committee of Concerned Asian Scholars, *China! Inside the People's Republic*. New York, Bantam Books, 1972.

Far Eastern Economic Review Yearbook, Hong Kong, published annually.

GALBRAITH, JOHN KENNETH, *A China Passage*. Boston, Houghton Mifflin, 1973.

GURTOV, MELVIN, *China and Southeast Asia—the Politics of Survival*. Lexington, Massachusetts, Heath Lexington Books, 1971.

HART, THOMAS G., *The Dynamics of Revolution*. Stockholm, Stockholm University, 1971.

HINTON, HAROLD C., *China's Turbulent Quest: An Analysis of China's Foreign Relations Since 1949*, rev. ed. Bloomington, Indiana University Press, 1972.

HSIAO, GENE T., ed., *Sino-American Détente and Its Policy Implication*. New York, Praeger Publishers, 1974.

HSIUNG, JAMES CHIEH, *Law and Policy in China's Foreign Relations*. New York, Columbia University Press, 1972.

LINDBECK, JOHN M. H., ed., *China: Management of a Revolutionary Society*. Seattle, University of Washington Press, 1971.

MACCIOCCHI, MARIA ANTONIETTA, *Daily Life in Revolutionary China*. New York, Monthly Review Press, 1972.

MYRDAL, JAN, and GUN KESSLE, *China: The Revolution Continued*. New York, Pantheon Books, 1970.

OKSENBERG, MICHEL, ed., *China's Developmental Experience*. New York, Praeger Publishers, 1973.

SCALAPINO, ROBERT A., *Elites in the People's Republic of China*. Seattle, University of Washington Press, 1972.

SIMMONDS, J. D., *China's World: The Foreign Policy of a Developing State*. New York, Columbia University Press, 1971.

SNOW, EDGAR, *The Long Revolution.* New York, Random House, 1972.

WHITSON, WILLIAM, *The Chinese High Command: A History of Communist Military Politics: 1927–1971.* New York, Praeger Publishers, 1973.

Serial Publications (in English only):

American Consulate-General of Hong Kong publications:
  Survey of China Mainland Press (daily translations since 1950).
  Current Background (weekly extracts from mainland press since 1950).
  Selections from China Mainland Magazines (since 1955).
  Extracts from China Mainland Publications (since 1962).
  Current Scene (authoritative analysis since 1961—bi-weekly).
  Problem of Communism (USIA authoritative analysis).
Asian Survey (monthly publication of the University of California Press).
The China Quarterly (scholarly analysis of the Contemporary China Institute, London).
China Trade Report (monthly publication of the *Far Eastern Economic Review* of Hong Kong).
Far Eastern Economic Review (weekly news analysis from Hong Kong).
Union Research Institute (Hong Kong) publications:
  Biographical Service (since 1956).
  Communist China Annual (since 1955).
  Communist China Problem Research Series (since 1953).
  Union Research Service (bi-weekly since 1966).
Chinese Communist Publications:
  China Reconstruct (monthly).
  China Pictorial (monthly).
  Chinese Literature (monthly).
  Hsinhua New Bulletin (daily).
  Peking Review (weekly).
  Ta-kung Pao Weekly Supplement (Hong Kong).
Chinese Nationalist Publications:
  Issue and Studies (monthly),
  What's Happening on the Chinese Mainland (bi-weekly).

APPENDICES

DOCUMENTS ON
POST-CULTURAL REVOLUTION CHINA

APPENDIX 1: THE CONSTITUTION OF THE COMMUNIST PARTY OF CHINA
(April, 1969)*

[This is the first revised constitution of the party since the 1956 constitution adopted by the Eighth Party Congress on September 26, 1956. The purpose of a party constitution deals mainly with the party structure and system; it formalizes internal relationships, methods of operation, and hierarchy of authority. However, this constitution, approved by the post-Cultural Revolution Ninth Party Congress on April 14, 1969, is much shorter and more generalized than the 1956 constitution, which consisted of a General Program and sixty articles arranged in nine chapters. In the General Program of the 1956 constitution the party is defined as "the vanguard of the Chinese working class," guided by the "principles of Marxism-Leninism." In the 1969 constitution "the thought of Mao Tse-tung" is restored as the official party ideology and Lin Piao is named as the successor to Mao Tse-tung. And party organization now permits more flexibility of the central leadership than the 1956 constitution.]

CHAPTER I

GENERAL PROGRAMME

The Communist Party of China is the political party of the proletariat.

The basic programme of the Communist Party of China is the complete overthrow of the bourgeoisie and all other exploiting classes, the establishment of the dictatorship of the proletariat in

*From *Peking Review*, 18 (April 30, 1969), pp. 36–39.

place of the dictatorship of the bourgeoisie and the triumph of socialism over capitalism. The ultimate aim of the Party is the realization of communism.

The Communist Party of China is composed of the advanced elements of the proletariat; it is a vigorous vanguard organization leading the proletariat and the revolutionary masses in the fight against the class enemy.

The Communist Party of China takes Marxism-Leninism-Mao Tse-tung Thought as the theoretical basis guiding its thinking. Mao Tse-tung Thought is Marxism-Leninism of the era in which imperialism is heading for total collapse and socialism is advancing to world-wide victory.

For half a century now, in leading China's great struggle for accomplishing the new-democratic revolution, in leading her great struggle for socialist revolution and socialist construction and in the great struggle of the contemporary international communist movement against imperialism, modern revisionism and the reactionaries of various countries, Comrade Mao Tse-tung has integrated the universal truth of Marxism-Leninism with the concrete practice of revolution, inherited, defended and developed Marxism-Leninism and has brought it to a higher and completely new stage.

Comrade Lin Piao has consistently held high the great red banner of Mao Tse-tung Thought and has most loyally and resolutely carried out and defended Comrade Mao Tse-tung's proletarian revolutionary line. Comrade Lin Piao is Comrade Mao Tse-tung's close comrade-in-arms and successor.

The Communist Party of China with Comrade Mao Tse-tung as its leader is a great, glorious and correct Party and is the core of leadership of the Chinese people. The Party has been tempered through long years of class struggle for the seizure and consolidation of state power by armed force, it has strengthened itself and grown in the course of the struggle against both Right and "Left" opportunist lines, and it is valiantly advancing with supreme confidence along the road of socialist revolution and socialist construction.

Socialist society covers a fairly long historical period. Throughout this historical period, there are classes, class contradictions and class struggle, there is the struggle between the socialist road and the capitalist road, there is the danger of capitalist restoration and there is the threat of subversion and aggression by imperialism and modern revisionism. These contradictions can be resolved only by depending on the Marxist theory of continued revolution and on practice under its guidance. Such is China's Great Proletarian Cultural Revolution, a great political revolution carried out under the conditions of socialism by the proletariat against the bourgeoisie and all other exploiting classes.

The whole Party must hold high the great red banner of Marxism-Leninism-Mao Tse-tung Thought and lead the hundreds of millions of the people of all the nationalities of our country in carrying on the three great revolutionary movements of class struggle, the struggle for production and scientific experiment, in strengthing and consolidating the dictatorship of the proletariat and in building socialism independently and with the initiative in our own hands, through self-reliance and hard struggle and by going all out, aiming high and achieving greater, faster, better and more economical results.

The Communist Party of China upholds proletarian internationalism; it firmly unites with the genuine Marxist-Leninist Parties and groups the world over, unites with the proletariat, the oppressed people and nations of the whole world and fights together with them to overthrow imperialism headed by the United States, modern revisionism with the Soviet revisionist renegade clique as its centre and the reactionaries of all countries, and to abolish the system of exploitation of man by man on the globe, so that all mankind will be emancipated.

Members of the Communist Party of China, who dedicate their lives to the struggle for communism, must be resolute, fear no sacrifice and surmount every difficulty to win victory!

Chapter II

MEMBERSHIP

Article 1: Any Chinese worker, poor peasant, lower-middle peasant, revolutionary armyman or any other revolutionary element who has reached the age of 18 and who accepts the Constitution of the Party, joins a Party organization and works actively in it, carries out the Party's decisions, observes Party discipline and pays membership dues may become a member of the Communist Party of China.

Article 2:   Applicants for Party membership must go through the procedure for admission individually. An applicant must be recommended by two Party members, fill out an application form for Party membership and be examined by a Party branch, which must seek the opinions of the broad masses inside and outside the Party. Application is subject to acceptance by the general membership meeting of the Party branch and approval by the next higher Party committee.

Article 3:   Members of the Communist Party of China must:

(1) Study and apply Marxism-Leninism-Mao Tse-tung Thought in a living way;

(2) Work for the interests of the vast majority of the people of China and the world;

(3) Be able at uniting with the great majority, including those who have wrongly opposed them but are sincerely correcting their mistakes; however, special vigilance must be maintained against careerists, conspirators and double-dealers so as to prevent such bad elements from usurping the leadership of the Party and the state at any level and guarantee that the leadership of the Party and the state always remains in the hands of Marxist revolutionaries;

(4) Consult with the masses when matters arise;

(5) Be bold in making criticism and self-criticism.

Article 4:   When Party members violate Party discipline, the Party organizations at the levels concerned shall, within their functions and powers and on the merits of each case, take appropriate disciplinary measures—warning, serious warning, removal from posts in the Party, placing on probation within the Party, or expulsion from the Party.

The period for which a Party member is placed on probation shall not exceed two years. During this period, he has no right to vote or elect or be elected.

A Party member who becomes politically apathetic and makes no change despite education should be persuaded to withdraw from the Party.

When a Party member asks to withdraw from the Party, the Party branch concerned shall, with the approval of its general membership meeting, remove his name from the Party rolls and report the matter to the next higher Party committee for the record. When necessary, this should be made public to the masses outside the Party.

Proven renegades, enemy agents, absolutely unrepentant persons in power taking the capitalist road, degenerates and alien class elements must be cleared out of the Party and not be re-admitted.

CHAPTER III

ORGANIZATIONAL PRINCIPLE OF THE PARTY

Article 5: The organizational principle of the Party is democratic centralism.

The leading bodies of the Party at all levels are elected through democratic consultation.

The whole Party must observe unified discipline: The individual is subordinate to the organization, the minority is subordinate to the majority, the lower level is subordinate to the higher level, and the entire Party is subordinate to the Central Committee.

Leading bodies of the Party at all levels shall regularly report on their work to congresses or general membership meetings, constantly listen to the opinions of the masses both inside and outside the Party and accept their supervision. Party members have the right to criticize Party organizations and leading members at all levels and make proposals to them. If a Party member holds different views with regard to the decisions or directives of the Party organizations, he is allowed to reserve his views and has the right to bypass the immediate leadership and report directly to higher levels, up to and including the Central Committee and the Chairman of the Central Committee. It is essential to create a political situation in which there are both centralism and democracy, both discipline and freedom, both unity of will and personal ease of mind and liveliness.

The organs of state power of the dictatorship of the proletariat, the People's Liberation Army, and the Communist Youth League and other revolutionary mass organizations, such as those of the workers, the poor and lower-middle peasants and the Red Guards, must all accept the leadership of the Party.

Article 6: The highest leading body of the Party is the National Party Congress and, when it is not in session, the Central Committee elected by it. The leading bodies of Party organizations in the localities, in army units and in various departments are the Party congresses or general membership meetings at their respective levels and the Party committees elected by them. Party congresses at all levels are convened by Party committees at their respective levels.

The convening of Party congresses in the localities and army units and their elected Party committee members are subject to approval by the higher Party organizations.

Article 7: Party committees at all levels shall set up their working bodies or dispatch their representative organs in accordance with the principles of unified leadership, close ties with the masses and simple and efficient structure.

CHAPTER IV

CENTRAL ORGANIZATIONS
OF THE PARTY

Article 8: The National Party Congress shall be convened every five years. Under special circumstances, it may be convened before its due date or postponed.

Article 9: The plenary session of the Central Committee of the Party elects the Political Bureau of the Central Committee, the Standing Committee of the Political Bureau of the Central Committee and the Chairman and Vice-Chairman of the Central Committee.

The plenary session of the Central Committee of the Party is convened by the Political Bureau of the Central Committee.

When the Central Committee is not in plenary session, the

Political Bureau of the Central Committee and its Standing Committee exercise the functions and powers of the Central Committee.

Under the leadership of the Chairman, the Vice-Chairman and the Standing Committee of the Political Bureau of the Central Committee, a number of necessary organs, which are compact and efficient, shall be set up to attend to the day-to-day work of the Party, the government and the army in a centralized way.

CHAPTER V

PARTY ORGANIZATIONS IN THE LOCALITIES AND THE ARMY UNITS

Article 10: Local Party congresses at the county level and upwards and Party congresses in the People's Liberation Army at the regimental level and upwards shall be convened every three years. Under special circumstances, they may be convened before their due date or postponed.

Party committees at all levels in the localities and the army units elect their standing committees, secretaries and deputy secretaries.

CHAPTER VI

PRIMARY ORGANIZATIONS OF THE PARTY

Article 11: In general, Party branches are formed in factories, mines and other enterprises, people's communes, offices, schools, shops, neighbourhoods, companies of the People's Liberation Army and other primary units; general Party branches or primary Party committees may also be set up where there is a relatively large membership or where the revolutionary struggle requires.

Primary Party organizations shall hold elections once a year. Under special circumstances, the election may take place before its due date or be postponed.

Article 12: Primary Party organizations must hold high the great red banner of Marxism-Leninism-Mao Tse-tung Thought, give prominence to proletarian politics and develop the style of integrating theory with practice, maintaining close ties with the masses of the people and practising criticism and self-criticism. Their main tasks are:

(1) To lead the Party members and the broad revolutionary masses in studying and applying Marxism-Leninism-Mao Tse-tung Thought in a living way;

(2) To give constant education to the Party members and the broad revolutionary masses concerning class struggle and the struggle between the two lines and lead them in fighting resolutely against the class enemy;

(3) To propagate and carry out the policies of the Party, implement its decisions and fulfil every task assigned by the Party and the state;

(4) To maintain close ties with the masses, constantly listen to their opinions and demands and wage an active ideological struggle within the Party so as to keep Party life vigorous;

(5) To take in new Party members, enforce Party discipline, constantly consolidate the Party organizations and get rid of the stale and take in the fresh so as to maintain the purity of the Party ranks.

APPENDIX 2: LIN PIAO: REPORT TO THE NINTH NATIONAL CONGRESS OF THE COMMUNIST PARTY OF CHINA (April, 1969)*

[This report was delivered on April 1, 1969, at the Ninth Party Congress to legitimize all the changes in China during the Cultural Revolution from 1966 to 1968. Lin Piao summed up the experiences of the Cultural Revolution, analyzed the domestic and international situation, and put forward new tasks for the party as he sees it. This report was in fact delivered at the height of Lin's power in China and was adopted, together with the constitution, on April 14 by the 1,512 delegates attending the congress.]

Comrades!

The Ninth National Congress of the Communist Party of China will be a congress with a far-reaching influence in the history of our Party.

Our present congress is convened at a time when great victory has been won in the Great Proletarian Cultural Revolution personally initiated and led by Chairman Mao. This great revolutionary storm has shattered the bourgeois headquarters headed by the renegade, hidden traitor and scab Liu Shao-chi, exposed the handful of renegades, enemy agents and absolutely unrepentant persons in power taking the capitalist road within the Party, with Liu Shao-chi as their arch-representative, and smashed their plot to restore capitalism; it has tremendously strengthened the dictatorship of the proletariat of our country, tremendously strengthened our Party and thus prepared ample conditions for this congress politically, ideologically and organizationally.

*From *Peking Review*, 18 (April 30, 1969), pp. 16–35.

I. ON THE PREPARATION FOR THE GREAT PROLETARIAN CULTURAL REVOLUTION

The Great Proletarian Cultural Revolution of our country is a genuine proletarian revolution on an immense scale.

Chairman Mao has explained the necessity of the current great revolution in concise terms: "The current Great Proletarian Cultural Revolution is absolutely necessary and most timely for consolidating the dictatorship of the proletariat, preventing capitalist restoration and building socialism."

In order to comprehend this scientific thesis of Chairman Mao's fully, we should have a deep understanding of his theory of continuing the revolution under the dictatorship of the proletariat.

In 1957, shortly after the conclusion of the Party's Eighth National Congress, Chairman Mao published his great work *On the Correct Handling of Contradictions Among the People*, in which, following his *Report to the Second Plenary Session of the Seventh Central Committee of the Communist Party of China*, he comprehensively set forth the existence of contradictions, classes and class struggle under the conditions of the dictatorship of the proletariat, set forth the thesis of the existence of two different types of contradictions in socialist society, those between ourselves and the enemy and those among the people, and set forth the great theory of continuing the revolution under the dictatorship of the proletariat. Like a radiant beacon, this great work illuminates the course of China's socialist revolution and socialist construction and has laid the theoretical foundation for the current Great Proletarian Cultural Revolution.

In order to have a deeper understanding of Chairman Mao's great historic contribution, it is necessary briefly to review the historical experience of the international communist movement.

In 1852, Marx said:

Long before me bourgeois historians had described the historical development of this class struggle and bourgeois economists the economic anatomy of the classes. What I did that was new was to prove: 1) that the *existence of classes* is only bound up with *particular historical phases in the development of production*, 2) that the class struggle necessarily leads to the *dictatorship of the proletariat*, 3) that this dictatorship itself only constitutes the transition to the *abolition of all classes* and to a *classless society*. (Marx and Engels, *Selected Correspondence*, Chinese ed., p. 63.)

Marx's theory of the dictatorship of the proletariat clearly distinguished scientific socialism from utopian socialism and sham socialism of every kind. Marx and Engels fought all their lives for this theory and for its realization.

After the death of Marx and Engels, almost all the parties of the Second International betrayed Marxism, with the exception of the Bolshevik Party led by Lenin. Lenin inherited, defended and developed Marxism in the struggle against the revisionism of the Second International. The struggle focused on the question of the dictatorship of the proletariat. In denouncing the old revisionists, Lenin time and again stated: "Those who recognize *only* the class struggle are not yet Marxists. . . . Only he is a Marxist who *extends* the recognition of the class struggle to the recognition of the *dictatorship of the proletariat*." (Lenin, *Collected Works*, Chinese ed., Vol. 25, p. 399.)

Lenin led the proletariat of Russia in winning the victory of the Great October Socialist Revolution and founding the first socialist state. Through his great revolutionary practice in leading the dictatorship of the proletariat, Lenin perceived the danger of the restoration of capitalism and the protracted nature of class struggle: "The transition from capitalism to Communism represents an entire historical epoch. Until this epoch has terminated, the exploiters inevitably cherish the hope of restoration, and this *hope* is converted into *attempts* at restoration." (Lenin, *Collected Works*, Chinese ed., Vol. 28, p. 235.)

Lenin stated:

. . . the bourgeoisie, whose resistance is increased *tenfold* by its overthrow (even if only in one country), and whose power lies not only in the strength of international capital, in the strength and durability of the international connections of the bourgeoisie, but also in the *force of habit*, in the strength of *small production*. For, unfortunately, small production is still very, very widespread in the world, and small production *engenders* capitalism and the bourgeoisie continuously, daily, hourly, spontaneously, and on a mass scale. (Lenin, *Collected Works*, Chinese ed., Vol. 31, p. 6.)

His conclusion was: "For all these reasons the dictatorship of the proletariat is essential." (*Ibid.*)

Lenin also stated that "the new bourgeoisie" was "arising from among our Soviet government employees." (Lenin, *Collected Works*, Chinese ed., Vol. 29, p. 162.)

He pointed out that the danger of restoration also came from capitalist encirclement: The imperialist countries "will never miss an opportunity for military intervention, as they put it, i.e., to strangle Soviet power." (Lenin, *Collected Works*, Chinese ed., Vol. 31, p. 423.)

The Soviet revisionist renegade clique has completely betrayed these brilliant teachings of Lenin's. From Khrushchov to Brezhnev and company, they are all persons in power taking the capitalist road, who have long concealed themselves in the Communist Party of the Soviet Union. As soon as they came to power, they turned the bourgeoisie's "hope of restoration" into "*attempts* at restoration," usurped the leadership of the Party of Lenin and Stalin and, through "peaceful evolution," turned the world's first state of the dictatorship of the proletariat into a dark fascist state of the dictatorship of the bourgeoisie.

Chairman Mao has waged a tit-for-tat struggle against modern revisionism with the Soviet revisionist renegade clique as its centre and has inherited, defended and developed the Marxist-Leninist theory of proletarian revolution and the dictatorship of the proletariat. Chairman Mao has comprehensively summed up the historical experience of the dictatorship of the proletariat both in the positive and negative aspects and, in order to prevent the restoration of capitalism, has put forward the theory of continuing the revolution under the dictatorship of the proletariat.

As early as March 1949, on the eve of the transition of the Chinese revolution from the new-democratic revolution to the socialist revolution, Chairman Mao explicitly pointed out in his report to the Second Plenary Session of the Seventh Central Committee of the Party: After the country-wide seizure of power by the proletariat, the principal internal contradiction is "the contradiction between the working class and the bourgeoisie." The heart of the struggle is still the question of state power. Chairman Mao especially reminded us: "After the enemies with guns have been wiped out, there will still be enemies without guns; they are bound to struggle desperately against us, and we must never regard these enemies lightly. If we do not now raise and understand the problem in this way, we shall commit the gravest mistakes."

Having foreseen the protracted and complex nature of the class struggle between the proletariat and the bourgeoisie after the establishment of the dictatorship of the proletariat, Chairman Mao set the whole Party the militant task of fighting imperialism, the Kuomintang and the bourgeoisie in the political, ideological, economic, cultural and diplomatic spheres.

Our Party waged intense battles in accordance with the resolution of the Second Plenary Session of the Seventh Central Committee and the Party's general line for the transition period formulated by Chairman Mao. In 1956, the socialist transformation of the ownership of the means of production in agriculture, handicrafts and capitalist industry and commerce was in the main completed. That was the crucial moment for the question of whether the socialist revolution could continue to advance. In view of the rampancy of revisionism in the international communist movement and the new trends of class struggle in our country, Chairman Mao, in his great work *On the Correct Handling of Contradictions Among the People*, called the attention of the whole Party to the following fact: "In China, although in the main socialist transformation has been completed with respect to the system of ownership . . . there are still remnants of the overthrown landlord and comprador classes, there is still a bourgeoisie, and the remoulding of the petty bourgeoisie has only just started."

Countering the fallacy put forward by Liu Shao-chi in 1956 that "in China, the question of which wins out, socialism or capitalism, is already solved," Chairman Mao specifically pointed out: "The question of which will win out, socialism or capitalism, is still not really settled. The class struggle between the proletariat and the bourgeoisie, the class struggle between the different political forces, and the class struggle in the ideological field between the proletariat and the bourgeoisie will continue to be long and tortuous and at times will even become very acute."

Thus, for the first time in the theory and practice of the international communist movement, it was pointed out explicitly that classes and class struggle still exist after the socialist transformation of the ownership of the means of production has been in the main completed, and that the proletariat must continue the revolution.

The proletarian headquarters headed by Chairman Mao led the broad masses in carrying on the great struggle in the direction he indicated. From the struggle against the bourgeois rightists in 1957 to the struggle to uncover Peng Teh-huai's anti-Party clique at the Lushan Meeting in 1959, from the great debate on the general line of the Party in building socialism to the struggle between the two lines in the socialist education movement—the focus of the struggle was the question of whether to take the socialist road or to take the capitalist road, whether to uphold the dictatorship of the proletariat or to restore the dictatorship of the bourgeoisie.

Every single victory of Chairman Mao's proletarian revolutionary line, every victory in every major campaign launched by the Party against the bourgeoisie, was gained only after smashing the revisionist line represented by Liu Shao-chi, which either was Right or was "Left" in form but Right in essence.

Now it has been proved through investigation that as far back as the First Revolutionary Civil War period Liu Shao-chi betrayed the Party, capitulated to the enemy and became a hidden traitor and scab, that he was a crime-steeped lackey of the imperialists, modern revisionists and Kuomintang reactionaries and that he was the arch-representative of the persons in power taking the capitalist road. He had a political line by which he vainly attempted to restore capitalism in China and turn her into an imperialist and revisionist colony. In addition, he had an organizational line to serve his counter-revolutionary political line. For many years, recruiting deserters and turncoats, Liu Shao-chi gathered together a gang of renegades, enemy agents, and capitalist-roaders in power. They covered up their counter-revolutionary political records, shielded each other, colluded in doing evil, usurped important Party and government posts and controlled the leadership in many central and local units, thus forming an underground bourgeois headquarters in opposition to the proletarian headquarters headed by Chairman Mao. They collaborated with the imperialists, modern revisionists and Kuomintang reactionaries and played the kind of disruptive role that the U.S. imperialists, the Soviet revisionists and the reactionaries of various countries were not in a position to do.

In 1939, when the War of Resistance Against Japan and for National Liberation led by Chairman Mao was vigorously surging forward, Liu Shao-chi dished up his sinister book *Self-Cultivation*. The core of that book was the betrayal of the dictatorship of the proletariat. It did not touch at all upon the questions of defeating Japanese imperialism and of waging the struggle against the Kuomintang reactionaries, nor did it touch upon the fundamental Marxist-Leninist principle of seizing state power by armed force; on the contrary, it urged Communist Party members to depart from the great practice of revolution and indulge in idealistic "self-cultivation," which actually meant that Communists should "cultivate" themselves into willing slaves going down on their knees before the counter-revolutionary dictatorship of the imperialists and the Kuomintang reactionaries.

After the victory of the War of Resistance Against Japan, when the U.S. imperialists were arming Chiang Kai-shek's counter-revolutionary troops in preparation for launching an all-out offensive against the liberated areas, Liu Shao-chi, catering to the needs of the U.S.-Chiang reactionaries, dished up the capitulationist line, alleging that "China has entered the new stage of peace and democracy." It was designed to oppose Chairman Mao's general line of "go all out to mobilize the masses, expand the people's forces and, under the leadership of our Party, defeat the aggressor and build a new China," and to oppose Chairman Mao's policy of "give tit for tat and fight for every inch of land," which was adopted to counter the offensive of the U.S.-Chiang reactionaries. Liu Shao-chi preached that "at present the main form of the struggle of the Chinese revolution has changed from armed struggle to non-armed and mass parliamentary struggle." He tried to abolish the Party's leadership over the people's armed forces and to "unify" the Eighth Route Army and the New Fourth Army, predecessors of the People's Liberation Army, into Chiang Kai-shek's "national army" and to demobilize large numbers of worker and peasant soldiers led by the Party in a vain attempt to eradicate the people's armed forces, strangle the Chinese revolution and hand over to the Kuomintang the fruits of victory which the Chinese people had won in blood.

In April 1949, on the eve of the country-wide victory of China's new-democratic revolution when the Chinese People's Liberation Army was preparing to cross the Yangtse River, Liu Shao-chi hurried to Tientsin and threw himself into the arms of the capitalists. He wildly opposed the policy of utilizing, restricting and transforming private capitalist industry, a policy decided upon by the Second Plenary Session of the Seventh Central Committee of the Party which had just concluded. He clamoured that "capitalism in China today is still in its youth," that it needed an unlimited "big expansion" and that "capitalist exploitation today is no crime, it is a merit." He shamelessly praised the capitalist class, saying that "the more they exploit, the greater their merit," and feverishly advertised the revisionist theory of productive forces. He did all this in his futile attempt to lead China onto the capitalist road.

In short, at the many important historical junctures of the new-democratic revolution and the socialist revolution, Liu Shao-chi and his gang always wantonly opposed Chairman Mao's proletarian revolutionary line and engaged in counter-revolutionary conspiratorial and disruptive activities. However, since they were counter-revolutionaries, their plots were bound to come to light. When Khrushchov came to power, and especially when the Soviet revisionists ganged up with the U.S. imperialists and the reactionaries of India and other countries in whipping up a large-scale anti-China campaign, Liu Shao-chi and his gang became all the more rabid.

Chairman Mao was the first to perceive the danger of the counter-revolutionary plots of Liu Shao-chi and his gang. At the working conference of the Central Committee in January 1962, Chairman Mao pointed out the necessity of guarding against the emergence of revisionism. At the working conference of the Central Committee at Peitaiho in August 1962 and at the Tenth Plenary Session of the Eighth Central Committee of the Party in September of the same year, Chairman Mao put forward more comprehensively the basic line of our Party for the whole historical period of socialism. Chairman Mao pointed out:

Socialist society covers a fairly long historical period. In the historical period of socialism, there are still classes, class contradictions and class struggle, there is the struggle between the socialist road and the capitalist road, and there is the danger of capitalist restoration. We must recognize the protracted and complex nature of this struggle. We must heighten our vigilance. We must conduct socialist education. We must correctly understand and handle class contradictions and class struggle, distinguish the contradictions between ourselves and the enemy from those among the people and handle them correctly. Otherwise a socialist country like ours will turn into its opposite and degenerate, and a capitalist restoration will take place. From now on we must remind ourselves of this every year, every month and every day so that we can retain a rather sober understanding of this problem and have a Marxist-Leninist line.

This Marxist-Leninist line advanced by Chairman Mao is the lifeline of our Party.

Following this, in May 1963, under the direction of Chairman Mao, the *Draft Decision of the Central Committee of the Chinese Communist Party on Certain Problems in Our Present Rural Work (i.e., the 10-Point Decision)* was worked out, which laid down the line, principles and policies of the Party for the socialist education movement. Chairman Mao again warned the whole Party: If classes and class struggle were forgotten and if the dictatorship of the proletariat were forgotten, then it would not be long, perhaps only several years or a decade, or several decades at most, before a counter-revolutionary restoration on a national scale would inevitably occur, the Marxist-Leninist party would undoubtedly become a revisionist party or a fascist party, and the whole of China would change its colour. Comrades, please think it over. What a dangerous situation this would be!

Thus, Chairman Mao still more sharply showed the whole Party and the whole nation the danger of the restoration of capitalism.

All these warnings and struggles did not and could not in the least change the reactionary class nature of Liu Shao-chi and his gang. In 1964, in the great socialist education movement, Liu Shao-chi came out to repress the masses, shield the capitalist-roaders in power and openly attack the Marxist scientific method of investigating and studying social conditions initiated by Chairman Mao, branding it as "outdated." He raved that whoever refused to carry out his line was "not qualified to hold a leading post." He and his gang were working against time to restore capitalism. At the end of 1964, Chairman Mao convened a working conference of the Central Committee and, under his direction, the document *Some Current Problems Raised in the Socialist Education Movement in the Rural Areas (i.e.,* the *23-Point Document)* was drawn up. He denounced Liu Shao-chi's bourgeois reactionary line which was "Left" in form but Right in essence and repudiated Liu Shao-chi's absurdities, such as "the intertwining of the contradictions inside and outside the Party" and "the contradiction between the 'four cleans' and the 'four uncleans'." And for the first time Chairman Mao specifically indicated: "The main target of the present movement is those Party persons in power taking the capitalist road." This new conclusion drawn by Chairman Mao after summing up the historical experience of the dictatorship of the proletariat, domestic and international, set right the course of the socialist education movement and clearly showed the orientation for the approaching Great Proletarian Cultural Revolution.

Reviewing the history of this period, we can see that the

current Great Proletarian Cultural Revolution with the participation of hundreds of millions of revolutionary people has by no means occurred accidentally. It is the inevitable result of the protracted and sharp struggle between the two classes, the two roads and the two lines in socialist society. The Great Proletarian Cultural Revolution is

> a great political revolution carried out by the proletariat against the bourgeoisie and all other exploiting classes; it is a continuation of the prolonged struggle waged by the Chinese Communist Party and the masses of revolutionary people under its leadership against the Kuomintang reactionaries, a continuation of the class struggle between the proletariat and the bourgeoisie.

The heroic Chinese proletariat, poor and lower-middle peasants, People's Liberation Army, revolutionary cadres and revolutionary intellectuals, who were all determined to follow the great leader Chairman Mao closely in taking the socialist road, could no longer tolerate the restoration activities of Liu Shao-chi and his gang, and so a great class battle was unavoidable.

As Chairman Mao pointed out in his talk in February 1967: "In the past we waged struggles in rural areas, in factories, in the cultural field, and we carried out the socialist education movement. But all this failed to solve the problem because we did not find a form, a method, to arouse the broad masses to expose our dark aspect openly, in an all-round way and from below."

Now we have found this form—it is the Great Proletarian Cultural Revolution. It is only by arousing the masses in their hundreds of millions to air their views freely, write big-character posters and hold great debates that the renegades, enemy agents, and capitalist-roaders in power who have wormed their way into the Party can be exposed and their plots to restore capitalism smashed. It is precisely with the participation of the broad masses in the examination of Liu Shao-chi's case that his true features as an old-line counter-revolutionary, renegade, hidden traitor and scab were brought to light. The Enlarged Twelfth Plenary Session of the Eighth Central Committee of the Party decided to dismiss Liu Shao-chi from all posts both inside and outside the Party and to expel him from the Party once and for all. This was a great victory for the hundreds of millions of the people. On the basis of the theory of continuing the revolution under the dictatorship of the proletariat, our great teacher Chairman Mao has personally initiated and led the Great Proletarian Cultural Revolution. This is indeed "absolutely necessary and most timely" and it is a new and great contribution to the theory and practice of Marxism-Leninism.

II.   ON THE COURSE OF THE GREAT PROLETARIAN CULTURAL REVOLUTION

The Great Proletarian Cultural Revolution is a great political revolution personally initiated and led by our great leader Chairman Mao under the conditions of the dictatorship of the proletariat, a great revolution in the realm of the superstructure. Our aim is to smash revisionism, seize back that portion of power usurped by the bourgeoisie, exercise all-round dictatorship of the proletariat in the superstructure, including all spheres of culture, and strengthen and consolidate the economic base of socialism so as to ensure that our country continues to advance in giant strides along the road of socialism.

Back in 1962, at the Tenth Plenary Session of the Eighth Central Committee of the Party, Chairman Mao pointed out: "To overthrow a political power, it is always necessary first of all to create public opinion, to do work in the ideological sphere. This is true for the revolutionary class as well as for the counter-revolutionary class."

This statement of Chairman Mao's hit the Liu Shao-chi counter-revolutionary revisionist clique right on the head. It was solely for the purpose of creating public opinion to prepare for the overthrow of the dictatorship of the proletariat that they spared no effort in seizing upon the field of ideology and the superstructure, violently exercising counter-revolutionary dictatorship over the proletariat in the various departments they controlled and wildly spreading poisonous weeds. To overthrow them politically, we must likewise first vanquish their counter-revolutionary public opinion by revolutionary public opinion.

Chairman Mao has always attached major importance to the struggle in ideology. After the liberation of our country, he initiated on different occasions the criticism of the film *The Life of Wu Hsun*, the Hu Feng counter-revolutionary clique, *Studies of "The Dream of the Red Chamber,"* etc. And this time it was Chairman Mao again who led the whole Party in launching the offensive on the bourgeois positions occupied by Liu Shao-chi and his gang. Chairman Mao wrote the celebrated essay *Where Do Correct Ideas Come From?* and other documents, in which he criticized Liu Shao-chi's bourgeois idealism and metaphysics, criticized the departments of literature and art under Liu Shao-chi's control as being "still dominated by 'the dead'," criticized the Ministry of Culture by saying that "if it refuses to change, it should be renamed the Ministry of Emperors, Kings, Generals and Prime Ministers, the Ministry of Scholars and Beauties or the Ministry of Foreign Mummies" and said that the Ministry of Health should likewise be renamed the "Ministry of Health for Urban Overlords." At the call of Chairman Mao, the proletariat first launched a revolution in the spheres of Peking Opera, the ballet and symphonic music, spheres that had been regarded as sacred and inviolable by the landlord and capitalist classes. It was a fight at close quarters. Despite every possible kind of resistance and sabotage by Liu Shao-chi and his gang, the proletariat finally scored important successes after arduous struggles. A number of splendid model revolutionary theatrical works came into being and the heroic images of the workers, peasants and soldiers finally rose aloft on the stage. After that, Chairman Mao initiated the criticism of *Hai Jui Dismissed From Office* and other poisonous weeds, focusing the attack right on the den of the revisionist clique—that impenetrable and watertight "independent kingdom" under Liu Shao-chi's control, the old Peking Municipal Party Committee.

The *Circular* of May 16, 1966, worked out under Chairman Mao's personal guidance laid down the theory, line, principles and policies for the Great Proletarian Cultural Revolution and constituted the great programme for the whole movement. The *Circular* thoroughly criticized the "February Outline" turned out by Liu Shao-chi's bourgeois headquarters for the purpose of suppressing this great revolution. It called upon the whole Party and the whole nation to direct the spearhead of struggle against the representatives of the bourgeoisie who had sneaked into the Party and to pay special attention to unmasking "persons like Khrushchov . . . who are still nestling beside us." This was a great call mobilizing the people of the whole country to unfold a great political revolution. The Cultural Revolution Group Under the Central Committee, which was set up by decision of the *Circular,* has firmly carried out Chairman Mao's proletarian revolutionary line.

Under the guidance of Chairman Mao's proletarian revolutionary line, the broad revolutionary masses plunged into the fight. In Peking University a big-character poster was written in response to the call of the Central Committee. And soon big-character posters criticizing reactionary bourgeois ideas mushroomed all over the country. Then Red Guards rose and came forward in large numbers and revolutionary young people became courageous and daring pathbreakers. Thrown into a panic, the Liu Shao-chi clique hastily hurled forth the bourgeois reactionary line, cruelly suppressing the revolutionary movement of the student youth. However, this did not win them much time in their death-bed struggle. Chairman Mao called and presided over the Eleventh Plenary Session of the Eighth Central Committee of the Party. The Plenary Session adopted the programmatic document, *Decision of the Central Committee of the Chinese Communist Party Concerning the Great Proletarian Cultural Revolution (i.e.,* the *16-Point Decision).* Chairman Mao put up his big-character poster *Bombard the Headquarters,* thus taking the lid off Liu Shao-chi's bourgeois headquarters. In his letter to the Red Guards, Chairman Mao said that the revolutionary actions of the Red Guards

> express your wrath against and your denunciation of the landlord class, the bourgeoisie, the imperialists, the revisionists and their running dogs, all of whom exploit and oppress the workers, peasants, revolutionary intellectuals and revolutionary parties and groups. They show that it is right to rebel against reactionaries. I warmly support you.

Afterwards, Chairman Mao received 13 million Red Guards and other revolutionary masses from all parts of the country on

eight occasions at Tien An Men in the capital, which heightened
the revolutionary fighting will of the people of the whole country.
The revolutionary movements of the workers, peasants and
revolutionary functionaries developed rapidly. Increasing
numbers of big-character posters spread like raging prairie fire
and roared like guns; the slogan "It is right to rebel against
reactionaries" resounded throughout the land. And the battle of
the hundreds of millions of the people to bombard Liu Shao-chi's
bourgeois headquarters developed vigorously.

No reactionary class will ever step down from the stage of
history of its own accord. When the revolution touched that
portion of power usurped by the bourgeoisie, the class struggle
became all the more acute. After Liu Shao-chi's downfall, his
revisionist clique and his agents in various places changed their
tactics time and again, putting forward slogans which were
"Left" in form but Right in essence such as "suspecting all" and
"overthrowing all," in a futile attempt to go on hitting hard at the
many and protecting their own handful. Moreover, they created
splits among the revolutionary masses and manipulated and
hoodwinked a section of the masses so as to protect themselves.
When these schemes were shattered by the proletarian revolutionaries, they launched another frenzied counter-attack, and
that is the adverse current lasting from the winter of 1966 to the
spring of 1967.

This adverse current was directed against the proletarian
headquarters headed by Chairman Mao. Its general programme
boiled down to this: to overthrow the decisions adopted by the
Eleventh Plenary Session of the Eighth Central Committee of the
Party, reversing the verdict on the overthrown bourgeois
headquarters headed by Liu Shao-chi, reversing the verdict on
the bourgeois reactionary line, which had already been
thoroughly repudiated and discredited by the broad masses, and
repressing and retaliating on the revolutionary mass movement.
However, this adverse current was seriously criticized by
Chairman Mao and resisted by the broad revolutionary masses; it
could not prevent the main current of the revolutionary mass
movement from surging forward.

The twists and reversals in the revolutionary movement
further brought home to the broad masses the importance of
political power: the main reason why Liu Shao-chi and his gang

could do evil was that they had usurped the power of the proletariat in many units and localities and the main reason why the revolutionary masses were repressed was that power was not in the hands of the proletariat in those places. In some units, the socialist system of ownership existed only in form, but in reality the leadership had been usurped by a handful of renegades, enemy agents, and capitalist-roaders in power, or it remained in the hands of former capitalists. Especially when the capitalist-roaders in power whipped up the evil counter-revolutionary wind of economism after failing in their scheme to suppress the revolution on the pretext of "grasping production," the broad masses came to understand still better that only by recapturing the lost power was it possible for them to defeat the capitalist-roaders in power completely. Under the leadership and with the support of Chairman Mao and the proletarian headquarters headed by him, the working class in Shanghai with its revolutionary tradition came forward courageously and, uniting with the broad revolutionary masses and revolutionary cadres, seized power from below in January 1967 from the capitalist-roaders in power in the former Municipal Party Committee and Municipal People's Council.

Chairman Mao summed up in good time the experience of the January storm of revolution in Shanghai and issued his call to the whole nation: "Proletarian revolutionaries, unite and seize power from the handful of Party persons in power taking the capitalist road!" Following that, Chairman Mao gave the instruction: "The People's Liberation Army should support the broad masses of the Left." He went on to sum up the experience of Heilungkiang Province and other provinces and municipalities and laid down the principles and policies for the establishment of the revolutionary committee which embraces representatives of the revolutionary cadres, representatives of the People's Liberation Army and representatives of the revolutionary masses, constituting a revolutionary three-in-one combination, thus pushing forward the nation-wide struggle for the seizure of power.

The struggle between the proletariat and the bourgeoisie for the seizure and counter-seizure of power was a life-and-death struggle. During the one year and nine months from Shanghai's

January storm of revolution in 1967 to the establishment of the revolutionary committees of Tibet and Sinkiang in September 1968, repeated trials of political strength took place between the two classes and the two lines, fierce struggles went on between proletarian and non-proletarian ideas and an extremely complicated situation emerged. As Chairman Mao has said:

> In the past, we fought north and south; it was easy to fight such wars. For the enemy was obvious. The present Great Proletarian Cultural Revolution is much more difficult than that kind of war.
> The problem is that those who commit ideological errors are mixed up with those whose contradiction with us is one between ourselves and the enemy, and for a time it is hard to sort them out.

Nevertheless, relying on the wise leadership of Chairman Mao, we finally overcame this difficulty. In the summer of 1967, Chairman Mao made an inspection tour north and south of the Yangtse River and issued extremely important instructions, guiding the broad revolutionary masses to distinguish gradually the contradictions between ourselves and the enemy from those among the people and to further bring about the revolutionary great alliance and the revolutionary three-in-one combination and guiding people with petty-bourgeois ideas onto the path of the proletarian revolution. Consequently, it was only the enemy who was thrown into disorder while the broad masses were steeled in the course of the struggle.

The handful of renegades, enemy agents, unreformed landlords, rich peasants, counter-revolutionaries, bad elements and rightists, active counter-revolutionaries, bourgeois careerists and double-dealers who had hidden themselves among the masses would not reveal their colours until the climate suited them. In the summer of 1967 and the spring of 1968, they again fanned up a reactionary evil wind to reverse correct verdicts both from the Right and the extreme "Left." They directed their spearhead against the proletarian headquarters headed by Chairman Mao, against the People's Liberation Army and against the new-born revolutionary committees. In the meantime, they incited the masses to struggle against each other and organized counter-revolutionary conspiratorial cliques in a vain attempt to stage a counter-seizure of power from the proletariat. However, like their chieftain Liu Shao-chi, this handful of bad people was finally exposed. This was an important victory for the Great Proletarian Cultural Revolution.

III. ON CARRYING OUT THE TASKS OF STRUGGLE-CRITICISM-TRANSFORMATION CONSCIENTIOUSLY

As in all other revolutions, the fundamental question in the current great revolution in the realm of the superstructure is the question of political power, a question of which class holds leadership. The establishment of revolutionary committees in all provinces, municipalities and autonomous regions throughout the country (with the exception of Taiwan Province) marks the great, decisive victory achieved by this revolution. However, the revolution is not yet over. The proletariat must continue to advance, "carry out the tasks of struggle-criticism-transformation conscientiously" and carry the socialist revolution in the realm of the superstructure through to the end.

Chairman Mao says:

> Struggle-criticism-transformation in a factory, on the whole, goes through the following stages: Establishing a three-in-one revolutionary committee; carrying out mass criticism and repudiation; purifying the class ranks; consolidating the Party organization; and simplifying the administrative structure, changing irrational rules and regulations and sending office workers to the workshops.

We must act on Chairman Mao's instruction and fulfil these tasks in every single factory, every single school, every single commune and every single unit in a deep-going, meticulous, down-to-earth and appropriate way.

Confronted with a thousand and one tasks, a revolutionary committee must grasp the fundamental: it must put the living study and application of Mao Tsetung Thought above all work and place Mao Tsetung Thought in command of everything. For decades, Mao Tsetung Thought has been showing the orientation of the revolution to the whole party and the whole nation. However, as Liu Shao-chi and his gang of counter-revolutionary revisionists blocked Chairman Mao's instructions, the broad revolutionary masses could hardly hear Chairman Mao's voice directly. The storm of the present great revolution has destroyed the "palaces of hell-rulers," big and small, and has made it possible for Mao Tsetung Thought to reach the broad revolutionary masses directly. This is a great victory. This wide dissemination of Mao Tsetung Thought in a big country with a population of 700 million is the most significant achievement of the Great Proletarian Cultural Revolution. In this revolution, hundreds of millions of people always carry with them *Quotations From Chairman Mao Tsetung*, which they study and apply conscientiously. As soon as a new instruction of Chairman Mao's is issued, they propagate it and go into action. This most valuable practice must be maintained and persevered in. We should carry on in a deep-going way the mass movement for the living study and application of Mao Tsetung Thought, continue to run well the Mao Tsetung Thought study classes of all types and, in the light of Chairman Mao's *May 7 Directive* of 1966, truly turn the whole country into a great school of Mao Tsetung Thought.

All revolutionary comrades must be clearly aware that class struggle will by no means cease in the ideological and political spheres. The struggle between the proletariat and the bourgeoisie by no means dies out with our seizure of power. We must continue to hold high the banner of revolutionary mass criticism and use Mao Tsetung Thought to criticize the bourgeoisie, to criticize revisionism and all kinds of Right or extreme "Left" erroneous ideas which run counter to Chairman Mao's proletarian revolutionary line and to criticize bourgeois individualism and the theory of "many centres," that is, the theory of "no centre." We must continue to criticize thoroughly and discredit completely the stuff of the renegade, hidden traitor and scab Liu Shao-chi such as the slavish comprador philosophy and the doctrine of trailing behind at a snail's pace, and must firmly establish among the cadres and the masses of the people Chairman Mao's concept of "maintaining independence and keeping the initiative in our own hands and relying on our own efforts," so as to ensure that our cause will continue to advance in the direction indicated by Chairman Mao.

Chairman Mao points out: "The revolutionary committee should exercise unified leadership, eliminate duplication in the administrative structure, follow the policy of 'better troops and simpler administration' and organize itself into a revolutionized leading group which maintains close ties with the masses."

This is a basic principle which enables the superstructure to serve its socialist economic base still better. A duplicate administrative structure divorced from the masses, scholasticism which suppresses and binds their revolutionary initiative, and a landlord and bourgeois style of formality and ostentation—all these are destructive to the socialist economic base, advantageous to capitalism and disadvantageous to socialism. In accordance with Chairman Mao's instructions, organs of state power at all levels and other organizations must keep close ties with the masses, first of all with the basic masses—the working class and the poor and lower-middle peasants. Cadres, old and new, must constantly sweep away the dust of bureaucracy and must not catch the bad habit of "acting as bureaucrats and overlords." They must keep on practising frugality in carrying out revolution, run all socialist undertakings industriously and thriftily, oppose extravagance and waste and guard against the bourgeois attacks with sugar-coated bullets. They must maintain the system of cadre participation in collective productive labour. They must be concerned with the well-being of the masses. They must themselves make investigation and study in accordance with Chairman Mao's teachings, dissect one or several "sparrows" and constantly sum up experiences. They must make criticism and self-criticism regularly and, in line with the five requirements for the successors to the revolution as set forth by Chairman Mao, "fight self, criticize revisionism" and conscientiously remould their world outlook.

The People's Liberation Army is the mighty pillar of the dictatorship of the proletariat. Chairman Mao has pointed out many times: From the Marxist point of view the main component of the state is the army. The Chinese People's Liberation Army personally founded and led by Chairman Mao is an army of the workers and peasants, an army of the proletariat. It has performed great historic feats in the struggle for overthrowing the three big mountains of imperialism, feudalism and bureaucrat-capitalism, and in the struggles for defending the motherland, for resisting U.S. aggression and aiding Korea and for smashing aggression by imperialism, revisionism and the reactionaries. In the Great Proletarian Cultural Revolution, large numbers of commanders and fighters have taken part in the work of "three supports and two militaries" (*i.e.,* support industry, support agriculture, support the broad masses of the Left, military control, political and military training) and representatives of the army have taken part in the three-in-one combination; they have tempered themselves in the class struggle, strengthened their ties with the masses, promoted the ideological revolutionization of the army, and made new contributions to the people. And this is also the best preparation against war. We must carry forward the glorious tradition of "supporting the government and cherishing the people," "supporting the army and cherishing the people," strengthen the unity between the army and the people, strengthen the building of the militia and of national defence and do a still better job in all our work. For the past three years, it is precisely because the people have supported the army and the army has protected the people that renegades, enemy agents, absolutely unrepentant persons in power taking the capitalist road and counter-revolutionaries have failed in their attempts to undermine this great people's army of ours.

Departments of culture, art, education, the press, health, etc., occupy an extremely important position in the realm of the superstructure. The line "We must whole-heartedly rely on the working class" was decided upon at the Second Plenary Session of the Seventh Central Committee. And now, at Chairman Mao's call that "The working class must exercise leadership in everything," the working class, which is the main force in the proletarian revolution, and its staunch ally the poor and lower-middle peasants have mounted the political stage of struggle-criticism-transformation in the superstructure. From July 27, 1968, mighty contingents of the working class marched to places long dominated by the persons in power taking the capitalist road and to all places where intellectuals were predominant in number. It was a great revolutionary action. Whether the proletariat is able to take firm root in the positions of culture and education and transform them with Mao Tsetung Thought is the key question in carrying the Great Proletarian Cultural Revolution through to the end. Chairman Mao has attached profound importance to our work in this connection and personally grasped typicals, thus setting us a brilliant example. We must overcome the wrong tendency among some comrades who make light of the ideological, cultural and educational front; we must closely follow Chairman Mao and consistently do arduous and meticulous work. "On its part, the working class should always raise its political consciousness in the course of struggle," sum up the experience in leading the struggle-criticism-transformation in the superstructure and win the battle on this front.

IV. ON THE POLICIES OF THE GREAT PROLETARIAN CULTURAL REVOLUTION

In order to continue the revolution in the realm of the superstructure, it is imperative to carry out conscientiously all Chairman Mao's proletarian policies.

Policies for the Great Proletarian Cultural Revolution were early explicitly stipulated in the *Circular* of May 16, 1966, and the *16-Point Decision* of August 1966. The series of Chairman Mao's latest instructions including "serious attention must be paid to policy in the stage of struggle-criticism-transformation in the Great Proletarian Cultural Revolution" have further specified the various policies.

The main question at present is to carry them out to the letter.

The Party's policies, including those towards the intellectuals, the cadres, "the sons and daughters that can be educated" [The sons and daughters of those who have committed crimes or mistakes.—*Translator*], the mass organizations, the struggle against the enemy and the economic policy—all these policies come under the general subject of the correct handling of the two different types of contradictions, those between ourselves and the enemy and those among the people.

The majority or the vast majority of the intellectuals trained in the old type of schools and colleges are able or willing to integrate themselves with the workers, peasants and soldiers. They should be "re-educated" by the workers, peasants and soldiers under the guidance of Chairman Mao's correct line, and encouragement should be given to those who have done well in the integration and to the Red Guards and educated young people who are active in going to the countryside or mountainous areas.

Chairman Mao has taught us many times: "Help more people by educating them and narrow the target of attack" and "carry out Marx's teaching that only by emancipating all mankind can the proletariat achieve its own final emancipation." With regard to people who have made mistakes, stress must be laid on giving them education and re-education, doing patient and careful ideological and political work and truly acting "on the principle of 'learning from past mistakes to avoid future ones' and 'curing the sickness to save the patient,' in order to achieve the twofold objective of clarity in ideology and unity among comrades." With regard to good people who committed the errors characteristic of the capitalist-roader in power but have now raised their political consciousness and gained the understanding of the masses, they should be promptly "liberated," assigned to suitable work and encouraged to go among the masses of the workers and peasants to remould their world outlook. As for those who have made a little progress and become to some extent awakened, we should continue to help them, proceeding from the viewpoint of unity. Chairman Mao has recently pointed out:

> The proletariat is the greatest class in the history of mankind. It is the most powerful revolutionary class ideologically, politically and in strength. It can and must unite the overwhelming majority of people around itself so as to isolate the handful of enemies to the maximum and attack them.

In the struggle against the enemy, we must carry out the policy "make use of contradictions, win over the many, oppose the few and crush our enemies one by one" which Chairman Mao has always advocated. "Stress should be laid on the weight of evidence and on investigation and study, and it is strictly forbidden to obtain confessions by compulsion and to give them credence." We must implement Chairman Mao's policies of "leniency towards those who confess their crimes and severe punishment of those who refuse to do so" and of "giving a way out." We rely mainly on the broad masses of the people in exercising dictatorship over the enemy. As for bad people or suspects ferreted out through investigation in the movement for purifying the class ranks, the policy of "killing none and not arresting most" should be applied to all except the active counter-revolutionaries against whom there is conclusive evidence of crimes such as murder, arson or poisoning, and who should be dealt with in accordance with the law.

As for the bourgeois reactionary academic authorities, we should either criticize them and see, or criticize them and give them work to do, or criticize them and provide them with a proper livelihood. In short, we should criticize their ideology and at the same time give them a way out. To handle this part of the contradictions between ourselves and the enemy in the manner of handling contradictions among the people is beneficial to the consolidation of the dictatorship of the proletariat and to the disintegration of the enemy ranks.

In carrying out the policies of the Party, it is necessary to study the specific conditions of the unit concerned. In places where the revolutionary great alliance has not yet been sufficiently consolidated, it is necessary to help the revolutionary masses bring about, in accordance with revolutionary principles, the revolutionary great alliance on the basis of different fields of work, trades and school classes so that they will become united against the enemy. In units where the work of purifying the class ranks has not yet started or has only just started, it is imperative to grasp the work firmly and do it well in accordance with the Party's policies. In units where the purification of the class ranks is by and large completed, it is necessary to take firm hold of other tasks in keeping with Chairman Mao's instructions concerning the various stages of struggle-criticism-transformation. At the same time, it is necessary to pay close attention to new trends in the class struggle. What if the bad people go wild again? Chairman Mao has a well-known saying: "Thoroughgoing materialists are fearless." If the class enemies stir up trouble again, just arouse the masses and strike them down again.

As the *16-Point Decision* indicates, "The Great Proletarian Cultural Revolution is a powerful motive force for the development of the social productive forces in our country." Our country has seen good harvests in agricultural production for years running and there is also a thriving situation in industrial production and science and technology. The enthusiasm of the broad masses of the working people both in revolution and production has soared to unprecedented heights. Many factories, mines and other enterprises have time and again topped their production records, creating all-time highs in production. The technical revolution is making constant progress. The market is flourishing and prices are stable. By the end of 1968 we had redeemed all the national bonds. Our country is now a socialist country with neither internal nor external debts.

"Grasp revolution, promote production"—this principle is absolutely correct. It correctly explains the relationship between revolution and production, between consciousness and matter, between the superstructure and the economic base and between the relations of production and the productive forces. Chairman Mao always teaches us: "Political work is the life-blood of all economic work." Lenin denounced the opportunists who were opposed to approaching problems politically: "Politics cannot but have precedence over economics. To argue differently means forgetting the ABC of Marxism." (Lenin, *Collected Works*, Chinese ed., Vol. 32, p. 72.) Lenin again stated: To put politics on a par with economics also means "forgetting the ABC of Marxism." (*Ibid.*) Politics is the concentrated expression of economics. If we fail to make revolution in the superstructure, fail to arouse the broad masses of the workers and peasants, fail to criticize the revisionist line, fail to expose the handful of renegades, enemy agents, capitalist-roaders in power and counter-revolutionaries and fail to consolidate the leadership of the proletariat, how can we further consolidate the socialist economic base and further develop the socialist productive forces? This is not to replace production by revolution but to use revolution to command production, promote it and lead it forward. We must make investigation and study, and actively and properly solve the many problems of policy in struggle-criticism-transformation on the economic front in accordance with Chairman Mao's general line of "Going all out, aiming high and achieving greater, faster, better and more economical results in building socialism" and in accordance with his great strategic concept "Be prepared against war, be prepared against natural disasters, and do everything for the people" and with the series of principles such as "take agriculture as the foundation and industry as the leading factor." We must bring the revolutionary initiative and creativeness of the people of all nationalities into full play, firmly grasp revolution and energetically promote production and fulfil and overfulfil our plans for developing the national economy. It is certain that the great victory of the Great Proletarian Cultural Revolution will continue to bring about new leaps forward on the economic front and in our cause of socialist construction as a whole.

V. ON THE FINAL VICTORY OF THE REVOLUTION IN OUR COUNTRY

The victory of the Great Proletarian Cultural Revolution of our country is very great indeed. But we must in no way think that we may sit back and relax. Chairman Mao pointed out in his talk in October 1968:

> We have won great victory. But the defeated class will still struggle. These people are still around and this class still exists. Therefore, we cannot speak of final victory. Not even for decades. We must not lose our vigilance. According to the Leninist viewpoint, the final victory of a socialist country not only requires the efforts of the proletariat and the broad masses of the people at home, but also involves the victory of the world revolution and the abolition of the system of exploitation of man by man on the whole globe, upon which all mankind will be emancipated. Therefore, it is wrong to speak lightly of the final victory of the revolution in our country; it runs counter to Leninism and does not conform to facts.

There will be reversals in the class struggle. We must never forget class struggle and never forget the dictatorship of the proletariat. In the course of carrying out our policies at present, there still exists the struggle between the two lines and there is interference from the "Left" or the Right. It still calls for much effort to accomplish the tasks for all the stages of struggle-criticism-transformation. We must closely follow Chairman Mao and steadfastly rely on the broad revolutionary masses to surmount the difficulties and twists and turns on our way forward and seize still greater victories in the cause of socialism.

VI. ON THE CONSOLIDATION AND BUILDING OF THE PARTY

The victory of the Great Proletarian Cultural Revolution has provided us with valuable experience on how we should build the Party under the conditions of the dictatorship of the proletariat. As Chairman Mao has indicated to the whole Party,

> The Party organization should be composed of the advanced elements of the proletariat; it should be a vigorous vanguard organization capable of leading the proletariat and the revolutionary masses in the fight against the class enemy.

Chairman Mao's instruction has determined our political orientation for consolidating and building the Party.

The Communist Party of China has been nurtured and built up by our great leader Chairman Mao. Since its birth in 1921, our Party has gone through long years of struggle for the seizure of state power and the consolidation of the dictatorship of the proletariat by armed force. Led by Chairman Mao, our Party has always stood in the forefront of revolutionary wars and struggles. Under the guidance of Chairman Mao's correct line, our Party has, in the face of extremely strong domestic and foreign enemies and in the most complex circumstances, led the proletariat and the broad masses of the people of China in adhering to the principle of maintaining independence and keeping the initiative in our own hands and relying on our own efforts, in upholding proletarian internationalism and in waging heroic struggles with one stepping into the breach as another fell, and it is only thus that our Party has grown from Communist groups with only a few dozen members at the outset into the great, glorious and correct Party leading the powerful People's Republic of China today. We deeply understand that without the armed struggle of the people, there would not be the Communist Party of China today and there would not be the People's Republic of China today. We must forever bear in mind Chairman Mao's teaching: "Comrades throughout the Party must never forget this experience for which we have paid in blood."

The Communist Party of China owes all its achievements to the wise leadership of Chairman Mao and these achievements constitute victories for Mao Tsetung Thought. For half a century now, in leading the great struggle of the people of all the nationalities of China for accomplishing the new-democratic revolution, in leading China's great struggle for socialist revolution and socialist construction and in the great struggle of the contemporary international communist movement against imperialism, modern revisionism and reactionaries of various countries, Chairman Mao has integrated the universal truth of Marxism-Leninism with the concrete practice of revolution, has inherited, defended and developed Marxism-Leninism in the political, military, economic, cultural and philosophical spheres, and has brought Marxism-Leninism to a higher and completely new stage. Mao Tsetung Thought is Marxism-Leninism of the era in which imperialism is heading for total collapse and socialism is advancing to world-wide victory. The entire history of our Party has borne out this truth: Departing from the leadership of Chairman Mao and Mao Tsetung Thought, our Party will suffer setbacks and defeats; following Chairman Mao closely and acting on Mao Tsetung Thought, our Party will advance and triumph. We must forever remember this lesson. Whoever opposes Chairman Mao, whoever opposes Mao Tsetung Thought, at any time or under any circumstances, will be condemned and punished by the whole Party and the whole nation.

Discussing the consolidation and building of the Party, Chairman Mao has said:

A human being has arteries and veins through which the heart makes the blood circulate, and he breathes with his lungs, exhaling carbon dioxide and inhaling fresh oxygen, that is, getting rid of the stale and taking in the fresh. A proletarian party must also get rid of the stale and take in the fresh, for only thus can it be full of vitality. Without eliminating waste matter and absorbing fresh blood the Party has no vigour.

With this vivid analogy, Chairman Mao has expounded the dialectics of inter-Party contradiction. "The law of contradiction in things, that is, the law of the unity of opposites, is the basic law of materialist dialectics." Opposition and struggle between the two lines within the Party are a reflection inside the Party of contradictions between classes and between the new and the old in society. If there were no contradictions in the Party and no struggles to resolve them, and if the Party did not get rid of the stale and take in the fresh, the Party's life would come to an end. Chairman Mao's theory on inner-Party contradiction is and will be the fundamental guiding thinking for the consolidation and building of the Party.

The history of the Communist Party of China is one in which Chairman Mao's Marxist-Leninist line combats the Right and "Left" opportunist lines in the Party. Under the leadership of Chairman Mao, our Party defeated Chen Tu-hsiu's Right opportunist line, defeated the "Left" opportunist lines of Chu Chiu-pai and Li Li-san, defeated Wang Ming's first "Left" and then Right opportunist lines, defeated Chang Kuo-tao's line of splitting the Red Army, defeated the Right opportunist anti-Party bloc of Peng Teh-huai, Kao Kang, Jao Shu-shih and others and after long years of struggle, has shattered Liu Shao-chi's counter-revolutionary revisionist line. Our Party has consolidated itself, developed and grown in strength precisely in the struggle between the two lines, especially in the struggles to defeat the three renegade cliques of Chen Tu-hsiu, Wang Ming and Liu Shao-chi which did the gravest harm to the Party.

In the new historical period of the dictatorship of the proletariat, the proletariat enforces its dictatorship and exercises its leadership in every field of work through its vanguard the Communist Party. Departing from the dictatorship of the proletariat and from continuing the revolution under the dictatorship of the proletariat, it is impossible to solve correctly the question of Party building, the question of building what kind of Party and how to build it.

Liu Shao-chi's revisionist line on Party building betrayed the very essence of the Marxist-Leninist teaching on the dictatorship of the proletariat and of the Marxist-Leninist theory on Party building. At the crucial moment when China's socialist revolution was deepening and the class struggle was extraordinary acute, Liu Shao-chi had his sinister book *Self-Cultivation* re-published and it was precisely his aim to overthrow the dictatorship of the proletariat in our country and restore the dictatorship of the bourgeoisie. When he copied the passage from Lenin on the necessity of the dictatorship of the proletariat, which we quoted earlier in this report, Liu Shao-chi once again deliberately omitted the most important conclusion that "the dictatorship of the proletariat is essential," thereby clearly revealing his own counter-revolutionary features as a renegade to the dictatorship of the proletariat. Moreover, Liu Shao-chi went on spreading such reactionary fallacies as the theory of "the dying out of class struggle," the theory of "docile tools," the theory that "the masses are backward," the theory of "joining the Party in order to climb up," the theory of "inner-Party peace" and the theory of "merging private and public interests" (*i.e.*, "losing a little to gain much"), in a vain attempt to corrupt and disintegrate our Party, so that the more the Party members "cultivated" themselves, the more revisionist they would become and so that the Marxist-Leninist Party would "evolve peacefully" into a revisionist party and the dictatorship of the proletariat into the dictatorship of the bourgeoisie. We should carry on revolutionary mass criticism and repudiation and thoroughly eliminate the pernicious influence of Liu Shao-chi's reactionary fallacies.

The Great Proletarian Cultural Revolution is the most broad and deep-going movement for Party consolidation in the history of our Party. The Party organizations at various levels and the broad masses of Communists have experienced the acute struggle between the two lines, gone through the test in the large-scale class struggle and undergone examination by the revolutionary masses both inside and outside the Party. In this way, the Party members and cadres have faced the world and braved the storm and have raised their class consciousness and their consciousness of the struggle between the two lines. This great revolution tells us: Under the dictatorship of the proletariat, we must educate the masses of Party members on classes, on class struggle, on the struggle between the two lines and on continuing the revolution. We must fight revisionism both inside and outside the Party, clear the Party of renegades, enemy agents and other elements representing the interests of the exploiting classes, and admit into the Party the genuine advanced elements of the proletariat who have been tested in the great storm. We must strive to ensure that the leadership of the Party organizations at all levels is truly in the hands of Marxists. We must see to it that the Party members really integrate theory with practice, maintain close ties with the masses and are bold in making criticism and self-criticism. We must see to it that the Party members will always keep to the style of being modest, prudent and free from arrogance and rashness and to the style of arduous struggle and plain living. Only thus will the Party be able to lead the proletariat and the revolutionary masses in carrying the socialist revolution through to the end.

Chairman Mao teaches us: "Historical experience merits attention. A line or a point must be explained constantly and repeatedly. It won't do to explain them only to a few people; they must be made known to the broad revolutionary masses."

The study and spread of the basic experience of the Great Proletarian Cultural Revolution, the study and spread of the history of the struggle between the two lines and the study and spread of Chairman Mao's theory of continuing the revolution under the dictatorship of the proletariat must be conducted not just once but should be repeated every year, every month, every day. Only thus will it be possible for the masses of Party members and the people to criticize and resist erroneous lines and tendencies the moment they emerge, and will it be possible to guarantee that our Party will always forge ahead victoriously along the correct course charted by Chairman Mao.

The revision of the Party Constitution is an important item on the agenda of the Ninth National Congress of the Party. The Central Committee has submitted the draft Party Constitution to the congress for discussion. This draft was worked out jointly by the whole Party and the revolutionary masses throughout the country. Since November 1967 when Chairman Mao proposed that basic Party organizations take part in the revision of the Party Constitution, the Central Committee has received several thousand drafts. On this basis the Enlarged Twelfth Plenary Session of the Eighth Central Committee of the Party drew up the draft Party Constitution, upon which the whole Party, the whole army and the revolutionary masses throughout the country once again held enthusiastic and earnest discussions. It may be said that the draft of the new Party Constitution is the product of the integration of the great leader Chairman Mao's wise leadership with the broad masses; it reflects the will of the whole Party, the whole army and the revolutionary masses throughout the country and gives a vivid demonstration of the democratic centralism and the mass line to which the Party has always adhered. Especially important is the fact that the draft Party Constitution has clearly reaffirmed that Marxism-Leninism-Mao Tsetung Thought is the theoretical basis guiding the Party's thinking. This is a great victory for the Great Proletarian Cultural Revolution in smashing Liu Shao-chi's revisionist line on Party building, a great victory for Marxism-Leninism-Mao Tsetung Thought. The Central Committee is convinced that, after the discussion and adoption of the new Party Constitution by the congress, our Party will, in accordance with its provisions, surely be built into a still greater, still more glorious and still more correct Party.

VII. ON CHINA'S RELATIONS WITH FOREIGN COUNTRIES

Now we shall go on specifically to discuss China's relations with foreign countries.

The revolutionary struggles of the proletariat and the oppressed people and nations of the world always support each other. The Albanian Party of Labour and all other genuine fraternal Marxist-Leninist Parties and organizations, the broad masses of the proletariat and revolutionary people throughout the world as well as many friendly countries, organizations and personages have all warmly acclaimed and supported the Great Proletarian Cultural Revolution of our country. On behalf of the great leader Chairman Mao and the Ninth National Congress of the Party, I hereby express our heartfelt thanks to them. We firmly pledge that we the Communist Party of China and the Chinese people are determined to fulfil our proletarian internationalist duty and, together with them, carry through to the end the great struggle against imperalism, modern revisionism and all reaction.

The general trend of the world today is still as Chairman Mao described it: "The enemy rots with every passing day, while for us things are getting better daily." On the one hand, the revolutionary movement of the proletariat of the world and of the people of various countries is vigorously surging forward. The armed struggles of the people of southern Vietnam, Laos, Thailand, Burma, Malaya, Indonesia, India, Palestine and other countries and regions in Asia, Africa and Latin America are steadly growing in strength. The truth that "Political power grows out of the barrel of a gun" is being grasped by ever broader masses of the oppressed people and nations. An unprecedentedly gigantic revolutionary mass movement has broken out in Japan, Western Europe and North America, the "heartlands" of capitalism. More and more people are awakening. The genuine fraternal Marxist-Leninist Parties and organizations are growing steadily in the course of integrating Marxism-Leninism with the concrete practice of revolution in their own countries. On the other hand, U.S. imperialism and Soviet revisionist social-imperialism are bogged down in political and economic crises, beset with difficulties both at home and abroad and find themselves in an impasse. They collude and at the same time contend with each other in a vain attempt to re-divide the world. They act in co-ordination and work hand in glove in opposing China, opposing communism and opposing the people, in suppressing the national liberation movement and in launching wars of aggression. They scheme against each other and get locked in strife for raw materials, markets, dependencies, important strategic points and spheres of influence. They are both stepping up arms expansion and war preparations, each trying to realize its own ambitions.

Lenin pointed out: Imperialism means war. " . . . imperialist wars are absolutely inevitable under *such* an economic system, *as long as* private property in the means of production exists."

(Lenin, *Collected Works*, Chinese ed., Vol. 22, p. 182.) Lenin further pointed out: "Imperialist war is the eve of socialist revolution." (Lenin, *Collected Works*, Chinese ed., Vol. 25, p. 349.) These scientific theses of Lenin's are by no means out of date.

Chairman Mao has recently pointed out, "With regard to the question of world war, there are but two possibilities: One is that the war will give rise to revolution and the other is that revolution will prevent the war." This is because there are four major contradictions in the world today: The contradiction between the oppressed nations on the one hand and imperialism and social-imperialism on the other; the contradiction between the proletariat and the bourgeoisie in the capitalist and revisionist countries; the contradiction between imperialist and social-imperialist countries and among the imperialist countries; and the contradiction between socialist countries on the one hand and imperialism and social-imperialism on the other. The existence and development of these contradictions are bound to give rise to revolution. According to the historical experience of World War I and World War II, it can be said with certainty that if the imperialists, revisionists and reactionaries should impose a third world war on the people of the world, it would only greatly accelerate the development of the contradictions and help arouse the people of the world to rise in revolution and send the whole pack of imperialists, revisionists and reactionaries to their graves.

Chairman Mao teaches us: "All reactionaries are paper tigers." "Strategically we should despise all our enemies, but tactically we should take them all seriously." This great truth enunciated by Chairman Mao heightens the revolutionary militancy of the people of the whole world and guides us from victory to victory in the struggle against imperialism, revisionism and all reaction.

The nature of U.S. imperialism as a paper tiger has long since been laid bare by the people throughout the world. U.S. imperialism, the most ferocious enemy of the people of the whole world, is going downhill more and more. Since he took office, Nixon has been confronted with a hopeless mess and an insoluble economic crisis, with the strong resistance of the masses of the people at home and throughout the world and with the predicament in which the imperialist countries are disintegrating and the baton of U.S. imperialism is getting less and less effective. Unable to produce any solution to these problems, Nixon, like his predecessors, cannot but continue to play the counter-revolutionary dual tactics, ostensibly assuming a "peace-loving" appearance while in fact engaging in arms expansion and war preparations on a still larger scale. The military expenditures of the United States have been increasing year by year. To date the U.S. imperialists still occupy our territory Taiwan. They have dispatched aggressor troops to many countries and have also set up hundreds upon hundreds of military bases and military installations in different parts of the world. They have made so many airplanes and guns, so many nuclear bombs and guided missiles. What is all this for? To frighten, suppress and slaughter the people and dominate the world. By doing so they make themselves the enemy of the people everywhere and find themselves besieged and battered by the broad masses of the proletariat and the people all over the world, and this will definitely lead to revolutions throughout the world on a still larger scale.

The Soviet revisionist renegade clique is a paper tiger, too. It has revealed its social-imperialist features more and more clearly. When Khrushchov revisionism was just beginning to emerge, our great leader Chairman Mao foresaw what serious harm modern revisionism would do to the cause of world revolution. Chairman Mao led the whole Party in waging resolute struggles in the ideological, theoretical and political spheres, together with the Albanian Party of Labour headed by the great Marxist-Leninist Comrade Enver Hoxha and with the genuine Marxist-Leninists of the world, against modern revisionism with Soviet revisionism as its centre. This has enabled the people all over the world to learn gradually in struggle how to distinguish genuine Marxism-Leninism from sham Marxism-Leninism and genuine socialism from sham socialism and brought about the bankruptcy of Khrushchov revisionism. At the same time, Chairman Mao led our Party in resolutely criticizing Liu Shao-chi's revisionist line of capitulation to imperialism, revisionism and reaction and of suppression of revolutionary movements in various countries and in destroying Liu Shao-chi's counter-revolutionary revisionist clique. All this has been done in the fulfilment of our Party's proletarian internationalist duty.

Since Brezhnev came to power, with its baton becoming less and less effective and its difficulties at home and abroad growing more and more serious, the Soviet revisionist renegade clique has been practising social-imperialism and social-fascism more frantically than ever. Internally, it has intensified its suppression of the Soviet people and speeded up the all-round restoration of capitalism. Externally, it has stepped up its collusion with U.S. imperialism and its suppression of the revolutionary struggles of the people of various countries, intensified its control over and its exploitation of various East European countries and the People's Republic of Mongolia, intensified its contention with U.S. imperialism over the Middle East and other regions and intensified its threat of aggression against China. Its dispatch of hundreds of thousands of troops to occupy Czechoslovakia and its armed provocations against China on our territory Chenpao Island are two foul performances staged recently by Soviet revisionism. In order to justify its aggression and plunder, the Soviet revisionist renegade clique trumpets the so-called theory of "limited sovereignty," the theory of "international dictatorship" and the theory of "socialist community." What does all this stuff mean? It means that your sovereignty is "limited," while his is unlimited. You won't obey him? He will exercise "international dictatorship" over you—dictatorship over the people of other countries, in order to form the "socialist community" ruled by the new tsars, that is, colonies of social-imperialism, just like the "New Order of Europe" of Hitler, the "Greater East Asia Co-prosperity Sphere" of Japanese militarism and the "Free World Community" of the United States. Lenin denounced the renegades of the Second International: "Socialism in words, imperialism in deeds, *the growth of opportunism into imperialism.*" (Lenin, *Collected Works*, Chinese ed., Vol. 29, p. 458.) This applies perfectly to the Soviet revisionist renegade clique of today which is composed of a handful of capitalist-roaders in power. We firmly believe that the proletariat and the broad masses of the people in the Soviet Union with their glorious revolutionary tradition will surely rise and overthrow this clique consisting of a handful of renegades. As Chairman Mao points out:

> The Soviet Union was the first socialist state and the Communist Party of the Soviet Union was created by Lenin. Although the leadership of the Soviet Party and state has now been usurped by revisionists, I would advise comrades to remain firm in the conviction that the masses of the Soviet people and of Party members and cadres are good, that they desire revolution and that revisionist rule will not last long.

Now that the Soviet government has created the incident of armed encroachment on the Chinese territory Chenpao Island, the Sino-Soviet boundary question has caught the attention of the whole world. Like boundary questions between China and some of her other neighbouring countries, the Sino-Soviet boundary question is also one left over by history. As regards these questions, our Party and Government have consistently stood for negotiations through diplomatic channels to reach a fair and reasonable settlement. Pending a settlement, the status quo of the boundary should be maintained and conflicts avoided. Proceeding from this stand, China has satisfactorily and successively settled boundary questions with neighbouring countries such as Burma, Nepal, Pakistan, the People's Republic of Mongolia and Afghanistan. Only the boundary questions between the Soviet Union and China and between India and China remain unsettled to this day.

The Chinese Government held repeated negotiations with the Indian government on the Sino-Indian boundary question. As the reactionary Indian government had taken over the British imperialist policy of aggression, it insisted that we recognize the illegal "McMahon line" which even the reactionary governments of different periods in old China had not recognized, and moreover, it went a step further and vainly attempted to occupy the Aksai Chin area, which has always been under Chinese jurisdiction, thereby disrupting the Sino-Indian boundary negotiations. This is known to all.

The Sino-Soviet boundary question is the product of tsarist

Russian imperialist aggression against China. In the latter half of the 19th century when power was not in the hands of the Chinese and Russian people, the tsarist government took imperialist acts of aggression to carve up China, imposed a series of unequal treaties on her, annexed vast expanses of her territory and, moreover, crossed the boundary line stipulated by the unequal treaties, in many places, and occupied still more Chinese territory. This gangster behavior was indignantly condemned by Marx, Engels and Lenin. On September 27, 1920, the Government of Soviets led by the great Lenin solemnly proclaimed: It "declares null and void all the treaties concluded with China by the former Governments of Russia, renounces all seizure of Chinese territory and all Russian concessions in China and restores to China, without any compensation and forever, all that had been predatorily seized from her by the Tsar's Government and the Russian bourgeoisie." (See *Declaration of the Government of the Russian Socialist Federated Soviet Republic to the Chinese Government.*) Owing to the historical conditions of the time, this proletarian policy of Lenin's was not realized.

As early as August 22 and September 21, 1960, the Chinese Government, proceeding from its consistent stand on boundary questions, twice took the initiative in proposing to the Soviet government that negotiations be held to settle the Sino-Soviet boundary question. In 1964, negotiations between the two sides started in Peking. The treaties relating to the present Sino-Soviet boundary are unequal treaties imposed on the Chinese people by the tsars, but out of the desire to safeguard the revolutionary friendship between the Chinese and Soviet people, we still maintained that these treaties be taken as the basis for the settlement of the boundary question. However, betraying Lenin's proletarian policy and clinging to its new-tsarist social-imperialist stand, the Soviet revisionist renegade clique refused to recognize these treaties as unequal and, moreover, it insisted that China recognize as belonging to the Soviet Union all the Chinese territory which they had occupied or attempted to occupy in violation of the treaties. This great-power chauvinist and social-imperialist stand of the Soviet government led to the disruption of the negotiations.

Since Brezhnev came to power, the Soviet revisionist renegade clique has frenziedly stepped up its disruption of the status quo of the boundary and repeatedly provoked border incidents, shooting and killing our unarmed fishermen and peasants and encroaching upon China's sovereignty. Recently it has gone further and made successive armed intrusions into our territory Chenpao Island. Driven beyond the limits of their forbearance, our frontier guards have fought back in self-defence, dealing the aggressors well-deserved blows and triumphantly safeguarding our sacred territory. In an effort to extricate them from their predicament, Kosygin asked on March 21 to communicate with our leaders by telephone. Immediately on March 22, our Government replied with a memorandum, in which it was made clear that, "In view of the present relations between China and the Soviet Union, it is unsuitable to communicate by telephone. If the Soviet government has anything to say, it is asked to put it forward officially to the Chinese Government through diplomatic channels." On March 29, the Soviet government issued a statement still clinging to its obstinate aggressor stand, while expressing willingness to resume "consultations." Our Government is considering its reply to this.

The foreign policy of our Party and Government is consistent. It is: To develop relations of friendship, mutual assistance and co-operation with socialist countries on the principle of proletarian internationalism; to support and assist the revolutionary struggles of all the oppressed people and nations: to strive for peaceful coexistence with countries having different social systems on the basis of the Five Principles of mutual respect for territorial integrity and sovereignty, mutual non-aggression, non-interference in each other's internal affairs, equality and mutual benefit, and peaceful coexistence, and to oppose the imperialist policies of aggression and war. Our proletarian foreign policy is not based on expediency; it is a policy in which we have long persisted. This is what we did in the past and we will persist in doing the same in the future.

We have always held that the internal affairs of each country should be settled by its own people. The relations between all countries and between all parties, big or small, must be built on the principles of equality and non-interference in each other's international affairs. To safeguard these Marxist-Leninist principles, the Communist Party of China has waged a long struggle against the sinister great-power chauvinism of the Soviet revisionist renegade clique. This is a fact known to all. The Soviet revisionist renegade clique glibly talks of "fraternal parties" and "fraternal countries," but in fact it regards itself as the patriarchal party, and as the new tsar, who is free to invade and occupy the territory of other countries. They conduct sabotage and subversion against the Chinese Communist Party, the Albanian Party of Labour and other genuine Marxist-Leninist Parties. Moreover, when any party or any country in their so-called "socialist community" holds a slightly different view, they act ferociously and stop at nothing in suppressing, sabotaging and subverting and even sending troops to invade and occupy their so-called "fraternal countries" and kidnapping members of their so-called "fraternal parties." These fascist piratical acts have sealed their doom.

U.S. imperialism and Soviet revisionism are always trying to "isolate" China; this is China's honour. Their rabid opposition to China cannot do us the slightest harm. On the contrary, it serves to further arouse our people's determination to maintain independence and keep the initiative in our own hands, rely on our own efforts and work hard to make our country prosperous and powerful; it serves to prove to the whole world that China has drawn a clear line between herself on the one hand and U.S. imperialism and Soviet revisionism on the other. Today, it is not imperialism, revisionism and reaction but the proletariat and the revolutionary people of all countries that determine the destiny of the world. The genuine Marxist-Leninist Parties and organizations of various countries, which are composed of the advanced elements of the proletariat, are a new rising force that has infinitely broad prospects. The Communist Party of China is determined to unite and fight together with them. We firmly support the Albanian people in their struggle against imperialism and revisionism; we firmly support the Vietnamese people in carrying their war of resistance against U.S. aggression and for national salvation through to the end; we firmly support the revolutionary struggles of the people of Laos, Thailand, Burma, Malaya, Indonesia, India, Palestine and other countries and regions in Asia, Africa and Latin America; we firmly support the proletariat, the students and youth and the masses of the Black people of the United States in their just struggle against the U.S. ruling clique; we firmly support the proletariat and the labouring people of the Soviet Union in their just struggle to overthrow the Soviet revisionist renegade clique; we firmly support the people of Czechoslovakia and other countries in their just struggle against Soviet revisionist social-imperialism; we firmly support the revolutionary struggles of the people of Japan and the West European and Oceanian countries; we firmly support the revolutionary struggles of the people of all countries; and we firmly support all the just struggles of resistance against aggression and oppression by U.S. imperialism and Soviet revisionism. All countries and people subjected to aggression, control, intervention or bullying by U.S. imperialism and Soviet revisionism, unite and form the broadest possible united front and overthrow our common enemies!

On no account must we relax our revolutionary vigilance because of victory or ignore the danger of U.S. imperialism and Soviet revisionism launching a large-scale war of aggression. We must make full preparations, preparations against their launching a big war and against their launching a war at an early date, preparations against their launching a conventional war and against their launching a large-scale nuclear war. In short, we must be prepared. Chairman Mao said long ago: We will not attack unless we are attacked; if we are attacked, we will certainly counter-attack. If they insist on fighting, we will keep them company and fight to the finish. The Chinese revolution won out on the battlefield. Armed with Mao Tsetung Thought, tempered in the Great Proletarian Cultural Revolution, and with full confidence in victory, the Chinese people in their hundreds of millions, and the Chinese People's Liberation Army are determined to liberate their sacred territory Taiwan and resolutely, thoroughly, wholly and completely wipe out all aggressors who dare to come!

Our great leader Chairman Mao points out:

Working hand in glove, Soviet revisionism and U.S. imperialism have done so many foul and evil things that the revolutionary people the world over will not let them go unpunished. The people of all countries are rising. A new historical period of opposing U.S. imperialism and Soviet revisionism has begun.

Whether the war gives rise to revolution or revolution prevents the war, U.S. imperialism and Soviet revisionism will not last long! Workers of all countries, unite! Proletarians and oppressed people and nations of the world, unite! Bury U.S. imperialism, Soviet revisionism and their lackeys!

VIII. THE WHOLE PARTY, THE WHOLE NATION UNITE TO WIN STILL GREATER VICTORIES

The Ninth National Congress of the Party is being held at an important moment in the historical development of our Party, at an important moment in the consolidation and development of the dictatorship of the proletariat in our country and at an important moment in the development of the international communist movement and world revolution. Among the delegates to the congress are proletarian revolutionaries of the older generation and also a large number of fresh blood. In the previous congresses of our Party there have never been such great numbers of delegates of Party members from among the industrial workers, poor and lower-middle peasants, and of women delegates. Among the delegates from the Party members in the People's Liberation Army, there are veteran Red Army fighters as well as new fighters. The delegates of Party members from among Red Guards are attending a national congress of the Party for the first time. The fact that so many delegates have come to Peking from all corners of the country and gathered around the great leader Chairman Mao to discuss and decide on the affairs of the Party and state signifies that our congress is a congress full of vitality, a congress of unity and a congress of victory.

Chairman Mao teaches us: "The unification of our country, the unity of our people and the unity of our various nationalities

—these are the basic guarantees of the sure triumph of our cause."

Through the Great Proletarian Cultural Revolution our motherland has become unprecedentedly unified and our people have achieved a great revolutionary unity on an extremely broad scale under the great red banner of Mao Tsetung Thought. This great unity is under the leadership of the proletariat and is based on the worker-peasant alliance; it embraces all the fraternal nationalities, the patriotic democrats who for a long time have done useful work for the cause of the revolution and construction of our motherland, the vast numbers of patriotic overseas Chinese and our patriotic compatriots in Hongkong and Macao, our patriotic compatriots in Taiwan who are oppressed and exploited by the U.S.-Chiang reactionaries, and all those who support socialism and love our socialist motherland. We are convinced that after the present national congress of our Party, the people of all the nationalities of our country will certainly unite still more closely under the leadership of the great leader Chairman Mao and win still greater victories in the struggle against our common enemy and in the cause of building our powerful socialist motherland.

Chairman Mao said in 1962:

The next 50 to 100 years, beginning from now, will be a great era of radical change in the social system throughout the world, an earthshaking era without equal in any previous historical period. Living in such an era, we must be prepared to engage in great struggles which will have many features different in form from those of the past.

This magnificent prospect far-sightedly envisioned by Chairman Mao illuminates our path of advance in the days to come and inspires all genuine Marxist-Leninists to fight valiantly for the realization of the grand ideal of communism.

Let the whole Party unite, let the whole nation unite, hold high the great red banner of Mao Tsetung Thought, be resolute, fear no sacrifice and surmount every difficulty to win victory!

Long live the great victory of the Great Proletarian Cultural Revolution!

Long live the dictatorship of the proletariat!

Long live the Ninth National Congress of the Party!

Long live the great, glorious and correct Communist Party of China!

Long live great Marxism-Leninism-Mao Tsetung Thought!

Long live our great leader Chairman Mao! A long, long life to Chairman Mao!

APPENDIX 3: SECRET DOCUMENTS ON THE "LIN PIAO AFFAIR"*

[The purge of Lin Piao in 1971 illustrated the complexities of Chinese politics and the danger of close association of ideology with policy that can erupt into ideological struggles and personality conflicts. Since the "Lin Piao Affair" involved the purges of power holders in the post-Cultural Revolution party hierarchy, it posed a particularly difficult problem for the system to handle. To soften the obvious adverse impact on the party membership, a number of top secret documents were distributed within the party to initiate discussion and consideration by its leadership at several levels.

The first example given here involves one of the private letters written by Chairman Mao to Chiang Ching, dated July 8, 1966, to disclose Mao's mistrust of Lin Piao in the initial stage of the Cultural Revolution. The second document, supposedly a captured document written by Lin Piao, outlined his coup plan against the Chairman. Lin used the code name "Five-Seven-One Project" because in Chinese these words sounded the same as "armed uprising." The third document gives a summary of Chairman Mao's talks with military leaders during his inspection tour in August–September, 1971. The final document presents the Communist Party's collected evidences of Lin Piao's "anti-party" plans.]

---

*These documents were released for limited distribution within the Communist Party and were not published inside China. However, some of them were obtained by the Nationalist Chinese intelligence community in Taiwan and published by the Institute of International Relations, Taipei.

221

A. Mao Tse-tung's Private Letter to Chiang Ching (July, 1966).*

CHIANG CH'ING:

Your letter of June 29 has been received. It is better for you to stay there longer as suggested by Comrade Wei[1] and Comrade Ch'en.[2] This month I shall have to give audience to two foreign guests. I will tell you my schedule after the audience. Since I left Wulin on June 15, I stayed in a cave in the west for some ten days. There the communication was not very good. I arrived at Paiyun Huang Ho on June 28. Since then, ten days have elapsed. Here I read materials every day; it is an interesting work. The situation changes from a great upheaval to a great peace once every seven or eight years. Ghosts and monsters jumped out by themselves. Their destiny being decided by their own class, they had to jump out. The Central urged me to publish the address of my friend,[3] and I have prepared to agree with it.

His address was devoted entirely to a political coup. There has never been any address like his before. I was quite uneasy at some of his thinking. I have never believed that the several

*From *Issues and Studies* (January, 1973), pp. 94–96.

[1] Comrade Wei refers to Wei Wen-po, secretary of CCP Shanghai Municipal Committee and concurrently secretary of Eastern China Bureau of CCP Central Committee during the Cultural Revolution.

[2] Comrade Ch'en refers to Ch'en P'i-hsien, first secretary of CCP Shanghai Municipal Committee, and concurrently secretary of Eastern China Bureau of CCP Central Committee and first political commissar of Shanghai Garrison District Command. Both Wei Wen-po and Ch'en P'i-hsien were criticized, struggled against and paraded by the Red Guards and rebels during the power-seizure struggle in January 1967.

[3] The "friend" refers to Lin Piao, and the "address of my friend" to Lin Piao's address at the enlarged meeting of the CCP Central Politburo held on May 18, 1966. In the address, Lin dealt with the crisis of a possible political coup at the highest level of the Communist regime and Mao's efforts to put the clamp on it. Lin also flattered Mao as being a "genius" of modern Marxism-Leninism and called for a mass movement for living study and application of Mao's works. This address, listed by the CCP Central as an important document of the Cultural Revolution, was published on September 22, 1966, for study, discussion and application by the whole Party and the Army. (For the text of the address, see *Issues & Studies*, Vol. VI, No. 5, February 1970, pp. 81–91.)

booklets I wrote would have so much supernatural power. Now after he exaggerated them, the whole nation has exaggerated them just as Wang P'o bragged about the melons she sold. I was driven by them to join the Liangshan Mountain rebels.[4] It seems that I have to concur with them. It is the first time in my life that I unwillingly concur with others on major questions. I have to do things against my own will! Yüan Chi[5] of the Chin Dynasty was opposed to Liu Pang.[6] Yüan traveled from Loyang to Chengkao. A humble man as he was became renowned because there were no heroes in the world at that time. Lu Hsün had corrected his own articles. He and I are of one mind; I like his straightforwardness. He said that he "anatomized himself more strictly than others." After having fallen down several times, I often do as he did. But our comrades often do not believe it. I have self-confidence but also some doubt. I once said when I was in my teens: I believed I could live two hundred years and sweep three thousand *lis*.[7] I was haughty in appearance and attitude. But somewhat I doubt myself and always feel that when tigers are absent from the mountain, the monkey there professes himself a king. I have become such a king. But it does not mean eclecticism. In my mind there is some air of tiger which is primary, and also some air of monkey which is secondary. I once quoted Li Ku's letter[8] to Huang Ch'iung[9] of the Han Dynasty as saying "A tall thing is easy to break; a white thing is easy to stain. The white snow in spring can hardly find its match; a high reputation is difficult to live up to." The last two sentences refer exactly to me. I have also read these passages at one of the standing committee meetings of the Central Politburo.

[4]"Driven to join the Liangshan Mountain rebels"—an old Chinese saying derived from the Chinese classic novel *All Men Are Brothers*. Most of the characters in this novel were good men originally, but later joined the bandits on Liangshan because of persecution by corrupt government officials.

[5]Yüan Chi—One of the noted scholars in the Chin Dynasty (265–419 A.D.).

[6]Liu Pang—The first emperor of the Han Dynasty (206 B.C.–220 A.D.).

[7]*Li*—A unit of Chinese measure equal to about 600 meters.

[8]Li Ku—Alias Tzu Chien, defense minister during the reign of Emperor Chung (145–146 A.D.).

[9]Huang Ch'iung—Alias Shih Ying, a noted statesman during the reign of Emperor Shun (126–144 A.D.).

It is valuable to know oneself. At the Hangchow Conference[10] held in April this year, I expressed my opinion which was different from that of my friend's. I could do nothing else. In the conference held in May in Peking, he spoke in the same manner. The press spoke even more so, describing me as a god. In that situation, I could only go up to Liangshan.

I guessed that their very intention was to strike the ghosts by the help of Chung K'uei.[11] I became Chung K'uei of the Communist Party as early as in the 1960's. Things always go toward the opposite side. The higher a thing is blown up, the more serious it is hurt at the fall. I am now prepared to be broken to pieces. This does not bother me. For the matter can never be destroyed; I may become pieces, that's all. There are more than one hundred parties[12] in the world. Most of the parties no longer believe in Marxism. Even Marx and Lenin have been smashed by them, much less we. I suggest that you should also pay attention to this problem and should not become dizzy with success.[13] You should remind yourself often of your weak points, shortcomings and mistakes. On this I have talked with you numerous times, and I did so last April in Shanghai. The above seem to be black words.

[10]"Hangchow Conference" refers to the Enlarged Meeting of the Standing Committee, CCP Central Politburo, held in April–May, 1966. The meeting was first presided over by Mao in Hangchow, and later removed to Peiping and was chaired by Lin Piao. It was in these two conferences that the criticism in the press was transformed into actions. Resolutions adopted in the meeting included (1) rescinding the "February Outline" drafted by P'eng Chen and others, deactivating the five-man "Cultural Revolution Group" and establishing the "Central Cultural Revolution Group" under the Standing Committee, Central Politburo; (2) reorganizing CCP Peking Municipal Committee and dismissing P'eng Chen and others from the Party offices; (3) reorganizing the Propaganda Department of the CCP Central Committee, dismissing Lu Ting-i and others from offices, and reorganizing the People's Daily; and (4) determining the crimes of "counterrevolutionary revisionists" P'eng Chen, Lu Ting-i, Lo Jui-ch'ing, and Yang Shang-k'un.

[11]Chung K'uei—A character in Chinese legend, said to be a Chin Shih (equivalent to Ph.D.) that Emperor Hsuan Tsung (713–741 A.D.) met in his dream. According to the emperor, Chung K'uei had power to repel ghosts and evil spirits. After he awoke, the emperor ordered a painter to draw Chung K'uei's picture based on his impression in the dream. The picture later was reproduced and adopted by civilians who posted it on their doors on the eve of the New Year to protect their houses against the invasion of ghosts.

[12]The "parties" here refers to Communist parties.

[13]"Success" refers to the victory of the Cultural Revolution.

But don't the anti-Party elements say so? I feel that some methods of their presentation are not very appropriate; I mean the effect on me. What they want to do is overthrow our Party and myself. This is the difference between me and the black gang. These words cannot be made public at the present time since all the leftists say so now. Publication of these words will mean pouring cold water on them, which helps the rightists. Our current task is to overthrow a part of (it is not possible to overthrow all of) the rightists in all the Party and throughout the country. We shall launch another movement for sweeping up the ghosts and monsters after seven or eight years, and will launch more of this movement later.

I cannot determine when we should publish these words, for the leftists and the broad masses of people do not welcome my saying so. Maybe we should wait until I die when the rightists come to power, and let them do the publication. The rightists may attempt to use my words to hold high the black banner. By so doing, they would get behind the eight ball. In China, after the emperor was overthrown in 1911, reactionaries could not hold power long. If there arises an anti-Communist rightist political coup in China, I am certain that it will not be peaceful, and very probably would be short-lived. For all revolutionaries who represent the interest of 95 percent of the people would not tolerate it. At that time, the rightists may prevail for some time by using my words, but the leftists may also organize some of my other words to overthrow the rightists. The Cultural Revolution this time is a large-scale and serious maneuver. In some areas (such as Peking Municipality), the revolutionaries resurrected overnight. Some units (such as Peking University and Tsing Hua University) collapsed quickly because of their involved and complicated ingredients. As a rule, where the rightists are more rampant, the worse they will be defeated and more vigorous the leftists will be. This is a nation-wide maneuver, in which the leftists, rightists and the staggering fence-sitters will absorb useful lessons. The conclusion is, and still is: our future is bright, but the road before us is twisted.

MAO TSE-TUNG
July 8, 1968

B. Lin Piao's "Outline of the Five-Seven-One Project" (1971)*

We must use a radical change in the form of a revolution by violence to stop any counterrevolutionary evolution which takes the form of peaceful transition. If we should fail to stop the peaceful transition with the "Five-Seven-One Project" and let the other side have its way, there is no prediction how many heads would roll on the ground. Therefore, a new power-seizure struggle seems unavoidable. If we do not seize the revolutionary leadership, the leadership would fall into the hands of others. After several years of preparation, our strength has been considerably enhanced ideologically, organizationally and militarily. Now we have certain ideological and material foundations. Compared with armed uprisings in foreign countries, our preparations and strength are far better. Even if compared with the October Revolution, our strength cannot be said to be weak. Furthermore, geographically we have much room for maneuvering, and we have the mobility of the air force. It would be comparatively easy for us to get hold of the national political power with the "Five-Seven-One Project."

B-52,[1] sensing that his days are numbered, is anxiously arranging things after his demise. He is suspicious of us. So, instead of waiting passively for our fate, it would be better for us to take the great gamble. Politically, the one who waits until everyone else has moved has the best advantage, but militarily the one who acts before everyone else does gain the most. Because of the Sino-Soviet conflict, we have reasons to expect Soviet support to our action. Factors in our favor include: the Chief's prestige and power, and the strength of the United Fleet.[2] We have basic strength and outside help (for launching an armed coup). Basic strength includes: the United Fleet and branch fleets (at Shanghai, Peking and Canton), The Fourth and Fifth Armies

*From *China Report* (Taipei), R.N. 26, pp. 4–7 (abridged).

[1] Code name for Mao Tse-tung.

[2] Code name for the coup forces.

under the control of Wang Wei-Kuo,[3] Chen Li-yun and Chiang Teng-chiao,[4] the Ninth and 18th Divisions, the 21st Tank Regiment, Civil Aviation, the 34th Division. Outside help includes: In the country, the 20th Army Corps, the 38th Army Corps, the Administrative Office of the Military Affairs Committee of Huang (Yung-sheng), the National Defense Science and Technology Commission, (forces in) Canton, Chengtu, Wuhan, Kiangsu, Foochow, Sinkiang, etc. Outside the country, the Soviet Union (through secret negotiation); use the Soviet force to control various forces inside and outside the country; temporary nuclear protection umbrella provided by the Soviets.

At present, our strength and preparations are not yet adequate. The masses' worship of B-52 is still deep-rooted. As a result of B-52's divisive tactics, there is a serious contradiction within the army ranks, and it would be rather difficult for us to form a usable unified strength. Furthermore, B-52 seldom appears in public and his residence is heavily guarded. All his movements are shrouded in secrecy. All these are difficulties we must face in launching our action. As of now, both the enemy and we are on the tiger's back and there is no way to get off. This should be a life-and-death struggle. Strategically, there should be two opportunities for us: One is when we have completed our preparations and are able to engulf the enemy; another is when we find the enemy ready to engulf us. In the latter case, no matter how our preparations are, we'll have to engage in a great gamble. Tactically, the opportunity and measure should be: Getting hold of B-52, getting hold of enemy battleships,[5] which can be achieved by bagging them in one sweep during a high-level meeting. We may first chop off his claws and teeth, create a *fait accompli* and force B-52 to accept our terms. This is in the form of a palace coup. We may also adopt extraordinary measures, such as poisonous gas,

---

[3]Alternate member, CCP Ninth Central Committee and Air Force political commissar.

[4]Political commissar of the Air Force section of the Nanking military region.

[5]Code name for the leading figures of the Maoist camp.

germ weapons, bombing, "five-four-three"[6] car accident, assassination, kidnap, and small urban guerrilla teams.

At no time has B-52 stopped trying to pit one force against another. Today he may try to win over this force to deal with that; but tomorrow he may pit that force against this. Today his words may drip with honey, yet tomorrow he may put you to death on fabricated charges. Today you may be his guest of honor, yet tomorrow you may find yourself in jail. Looking back over the past decades, how many do you see were raised to power and fame by him but later escaped political death? What political force could survive coexistence with him? His former secretaries have either committed suicide, or have been imprisoned. His very few close comrades-in-arms and trusted aides are also mostly behind bars. Even his own son went berserk under his highhandedness. He is a maniac of suspicion and a sadist; whenever he decides to punish a person, he wouldn't stop until that poor person is dead. Besides he is an expert in passing the buck. To put it bluntly, those numerous figures who come to power and then fall into disgrace under him are but his scapegoats. Since the Second Plenary Session of the Ninth Central Committee of the Party, the political situation in the nation has not been stable. The ruling group is exercising a tyrannical rule. The broad mass of peasants is being exploited to the fullest extent. The economy is stagnant.

Because of lowered living standards, discontentment among the mass, the grass-root cadres and the troops is daily worsening, only they dare not speak up. The ruling clique is so corrupt, muddle-headed and incapable that it has alienated the mass and even its own followers. A grave political crisis is in the brewing; a power-seizure struggle is under way; a political coup in the form of gradual peaceful transition is being carried out in China—this form is exactly the favorite tactic of B-52. Now that he has resorted to this form of transition again, the situation is developing toward the direction of the "pen"[7] getting the upper

[6]New secret weapons.

[7]Meaning party theoreticians such as Chang Chun-chiao and Yao Wen-yuan.

hand. Therefore, we must use a radical change in the form of revolution by violence to stop a counterrevolutionary evolution which takes the form of peaceful transition. Trotskyites holding the "pen" are still distorting Marxism-Leninism at will, so as to turn it into the service of their own self-interests. They substitute pseudo-revolutionary rhetoric for Marxism-Leninism, to cheat and swindle the Chinese people. The basic nature of the "continuous revolution" they now advocate is the "constant revolution" of Trotsky. The target of their revolution is in fact the Chinese people, and their first victims are the armed forces and those who differ with them in opinion. The basic nature of their socialism is social-fascism. They have turned China's state machine into a meat-grinder of mutual-killing and mutual-elimination, and the Party's and nation's political life into a life of feudalism and dictatorship.

Of course we cannot deny his historical function of unifying China, and that is why we have given him the rightful place in revolutionary history and the support he deserves. But now he has abused the confidence and status given him by the Chinese people. In fact, he has become a Chin Shih Huang[8] of modern times. To be responsible to the Chinese people, and to China's history, our wait and endurance should have their limits. He is not a genuine Marxist-Leninist, but the worst feudal tyrant in China's history, who practices the preachings of Confucius and Mencius, puts on the cloak of Marxism-Leninism, and exercises the laws of Chin Shih Huang.

Conditions in favor of our armed coup include: Aggravated political contradiction in the country, various crises, and the increasing unpopularity of the dictator; the instability within the ruling clique, and the almost white-hot struggle for power and profits; the armed forces are oppressed; middle-echelon cadres are discontented and disillusioned, and they are the ones who have military power. A handful of "scholars," acting like tyrants, have made numerous enemies. They have swelled heads and over-estimate themselves. Cadres who have been dismissed

[8]First emperor of the Chin Dynasty (221–209 B.C.), first emperor who unified China.

or have fallen victim in protracted intra-party struggles and the Cultural Revolution are indignant but dare not voice their feelings. The peasants are leading a life of inadequate food and clothing. Young intellectuals are being sent to mountainous areas or to the countryside, which is another form of reform through labor. Red Guards were first cheated, utilized and made cannon-fodder, but in the latter stage are forced to become scapegoats. Under the "simplification program," cadres of government organizations are being sent to "May 7 Schools," which is another form of unemployment; workers, especially young ones, have their salaries frozen, which is another form of exploitation. Internationally, contradictions are aggravated. China and the Soviet Union stand against each other. China treats the Soviet Union as an enemy. Our action will have Soviet support.

C. Chairman Mao's Talks with Responsible Comrades (August–September, 1971).*

TOP SECRET

DOCUMENT OF THE CENTRAL COMMITTEE OF THE CHINESE COMMUNIST PARTY
CHUNG-FA (1972) No. 12

Chairman Mao's Instruction: Approved Circular of the Central Committee of the Chinese Communist Party

Leading Groups and Party's Nucleus Groups of the Party Committees of All Provinces, Municipalities and Autonomous Regions, All Military Regions, All Provincial Military Districts,

*From Issues and Studies (September, 1972), pp. 64–71.

All Field Armies, All Headquarters of the Military Commission, All Military Services and Branches of Arms, and All Departments, Ministers and Commissions of the Party Central Committee and the State Council:

From mid-August to September 12, 1971, our great leader Chairman Mao made an inspection tour outside [Peking], having many important talks with responsible comrades in various places on his way. Many units have requested that Chairman Mao's talks be collated for printing and distribution. On the basis of the minutes of Chairman Mao's talks in various places, the Party Central did some editing and produced a summary, which is now being distributed to you. Please immediately transmit it to the whole Party, the whole country and the whole people, in accordance with the prescriptions of the *Chung-fa* (1972) Document No. 3.

In his talks Chairman Mao, with line struggle as the key link, summarized the experience of our Party in waging ten line struggles during the past 50 years. He raised three basic questions: "It is necessary to engage in Marxist activities but not in revisionist activities; to unite but not to split; and to be upright but not conspiratory." He clearly pointed out that the struggle of the Lushan Meeting of 1970 was one between two lines and between two headquarters and repeatedly stressed the need to implement the policy of "learning from past mistakes to avoid future ones, and curing the sickness to save the patient" toward erring cadres.

Chairman Mao's talks are documents of guidance for administering ideological and line education and for strengthening Party and army building and a powerful weapon for smashing the Lin-ch'en anti-Party clique. The whole Party, the whole country and the whole people must seriously study Chairman Mao's talks, go one step further in criticizing and repudiating the Lin-ch'en anti-Party clique and carry the struggle against the Lin-Ch'en anti-Party clique through to the end.

Central Committee of the Chinese
Communist Party

March 17, 1972

A SUMMARY OF CHAIRMAN MAO'S TALKS WITH RESPONSIBLE COMRADES OF VARIOUS PLACES DURING HIS INSPECTION TOUR

(MID-AUGUST–SEPTEMBER 12, 1971)

Chairman Mao has said, it is hoped that you engage in Marxist activities but not revisionist activities; unite but not divide; be upright but not conspiratory.

Whether one is correct or not in the ideological and political line determines everything. With a correct Party line, we will have everything. If we do not have people, we will get them; if we do not have guns, we will get them; if we do not have political power, we will get it. However, if the political line is not correct, we will lose everything we have. The line is the key link; once the key link is grasped, every problem will be solved.

Our Party has a history of 50 years marked by ten major line struggles. During these ten struggles, there have been people who wanted to split our Party but were unsuccessful. This question deserves study. It is such a big country with so many people, but it has not been divided. We can only point out that this is because the people and the Party members do not want to split. From a historical point of view, our Party is hopeful.

In the beginning Ch'en Tu-hsiu engaged in Left opportunist activities. Following the "August 7" meeting in 1927 he and people like Liu Jen-ching and P'eng Shu started organizing the "Left-wing opposition of the Leninists." Eighty-one persons issued statements in an attempt to split our Party. They failed and defected to the Trotskyites.

Next came Ch'ü Ch'iu-pai who committed mistakes in line. They got hold of a pamphlet in Hunan which contained one of my statements saying that "political power grows out of the barrel of a gun." Extremely angered, they asked how could political power grow out of the barrel of a gun? Consequently, I was dismissed as an alternate member of the Political Bureau. Afterwards, Ch'ü was arrested by the Kuomintang and, after writing *The Superfluous Words,* he surrendered himself and defected.

After the Party's Sixth Congress in 1928, Li Li-san became a rising star. From June to September 1930 he pushed the Li-san line for three months. He advocated attacking big cities and seeking victories in one or several provinces. I did not agree to what he had done. Li Li-san fell at the 3rd Plenary Session of the Sixth Central Committee.

In 1930-31 the Rightists led by Lo Lung-chang engaged in divisive activities by
setting up another Central Committee but again failed.

The Wang Ming line lasted the longest time. He [Want Ming] engaged in factionalism when he was in Moscow and organized "28 and one-half Bolsheviks," who, with the support of the Third International, seized Party power for four years. After convening the Fourth Plenary Session of the Sixth Central Committee in Shanghai, Wang published a pamphlet entitled "Struggle for the further Bolshevizing of the Chinese Communist Party." He criticized Li Li-san for not being far enough to the "Left" and was determined to destroy all the base areas. He succeeded in the main. During the four years from 1931 to 1934 I had no right to speak at the Central Committee. The Tsunyi meeting in January 1935 rectified Wang Ming's mistaken line and Wang was overthrown.

During the course of the Long March, after the First and Fourth Armies joined forces, Chang Kuo-t'ao engaged in division by setting up another Central Committee but he did not succeed. The Red Army totaled 300,000 men before the Long March but only 25,000 of them arrived in northern Shensi. The Central Soviet Area had 80,000 men but only 8,000 reached northern Shensi. Engaging in splitism, Chang Kuo-t'ao did not want to go to northern Shensi. However, at that time there was no way out except to go to northern Shensi; it was a question of political line. At that time our political line was correct. Had we not gone to northern Shensi, how could we have gone to North China, East China, Central China and Northeast China? How could we have created so many base areas during the War of Resistance Against Japan? Chang Kuo-t'ao escaped from northern Shensi.

After a nation-wide victory, Kao Kang and Jao Shu-shih formed an anti-Party alliance in an attempt to seize power but without success.

At the Lushan meeting in 1959 P'eng Teh-huai maintained illicit relations with foreign countries and attempted to seize power. Huang K'e-ch'eng, Chang Wen-t'ien and Chou Hsiao-chou also jumped out in opposition to the Party. They organized a military club but they did not talk about military affairs; instead, they charged that "the people's commune had appeared too early," which meant "more loss than gain," etc. P'eng Teh-huai, moreover, wrote a letter, flinging an open challenge and attempting to seize power but without success.

Liu Shao-ch'i and company were also splitting the Party, but they did not succeed either.

Then came the struggle of the Lushan meeting of 1970.

At the Lushan meeting of 1970 they engaged in surprise attacks and underground activities. Why were they afraid of coming out in the open? Apparently, they were plotting against someone. They first engaged in deception and then in surprise attacks. Three of the five standing members were not informed, neither were the majority of the comrades in the Political Bureau, except those several big fighters, including Huang Yung-sheng, Wu Fa-hsien, Yeh Ch'ün, Li Tso-p'eng and Ch'iu Hui-tso as well as Li Hsüeh-feng and Cheng Wei-shan. They did not allow one word to leak out and then launched a surprise attack. Their action did not last only half-a-day or so, but continued for two and one-half days from August 23 and 24 to noon on the 25th. Their action must have had a purpose. When P'eng was organizing the military club, he delivered a challenge. However, they were even worse than P'eng's. How contemptible was their way of doing things!

In my opinion, their surprise attack and underground activities were organized and had a program. Their program was nothing but a creation of a state chairmanship, the advocating of the theory of "talent," opposition to the line of the "Ninth Congress" and the overthrow of the three-point agenda of the Second Plenary Session of the Ninth Central Committee. A certain person was anxious to become state chairman, to split the Party and to seize power. The question of genius was a theoretical question; they advocated idealist empiricism, contending that whoever opposed the theory of genius opposed me. I have never been a genius. I have read Confucius for six years and capitalist literature for seven years. I began studying Marxism-Leninism only in 1918. How can I be a genius? Those adverbs[1] have been deleted several times by me. The Party Constitution had been finalized by the Ninth Congress; why didn't they open it for a look? "Some Opinions of Mine" was written after I talked with a few people and made some investigation and study; it was intended to criticize the theory of genius. I do not mean we should drop the term genius; a genius is merely a person who is a little smarter than others. A genius can not succeed by himself, but only with the help of several persons. A genius must rely on the Party, which is the vanguard of the proletariat. A genius must rely on the mass line and collective wisdom.

The talk by Comrade Lin Piao[2] was made without consulting me, nor was it checked by me. They did not disclose their opinions in advance, presumably because they were sure about their views. It seemed that they would succeed. However, when they realized it wouldn't work, they were upset and did not know what to do. Their courage in the beginning seemed to be able to level Lushan (or Lu Mountain) to the ground and have the momentum of stopping the movement of the earth. However, several days later, the record[3] was quickly recalled. If it was justified, why should it be recalled? It indicated that they were afraid and panicky.

The struggle with P'eng Teh-huai at the Lushan meeting in 1959 was one between two headquarters. The struggle with Liu Shao-ch'i was also one between two headquarters; so is the present Lushan meeting.

This struggle at the Lushan meeting is different from the previous nine. A summing up was made for each of the previous struggles, but no personal summing up has been made this time for the sake of protecting Vice Chairman Lin. Of course, he [referring to Lin] must share part of the responsibility. What should be done to those people? It is necessary to adopt the

---

[1] Refers to "ingeniously," "comprehensively," and "creatively."

[2] Lin's talk at the 2nd Plenary Session of the CCP 9th Central Committee on August 23, 1970.

[3] Yeh Ch'ün privately asked for the recalling of the minutes of her speech at the meeting of Chung-nan Group during the 2nd Plenary Session of the CCP 9th Central Committee.

policy of education, namely "learning from past mistakes to avoid future ones and curing the sickness to save the patient." It is still necessary to protect Lin. No matter who committed the mistake, not to talk about unity and line is not good. After returning to Peking I will again send for them for talks. They do not want to see me but I want to see them. Some of them may be saved but some may not. All depends on their practice. There are two possibilities: one is that they may rectify their mistakes and the other is that they may not. Those who have committed mistakes in principle and in line and orientation and are the leading culprits will find rectifying difficult. In history, did Ch'en Tu-hsiu rectify his mistakes? Did Ch'ü Chiu-pai, Li Li-san, Lo Lung-chang, Wang Ming, Chang Kuo-t'ao, Kao Kang, Jao Shu-shih, P'eng Teh-huai and Liu Shao-ch'i rectify theirs? No, they did not.

I have talked with Comrade Lin Piao telling him that some of his statements were not appropriate. For example, he said there has only been one genius in the world in the last several hundred years and only one in China during the last several thousand years, which does not comply with fact. Marx and Engels were contemporaries and there were less than one hundred years between them and Lenin and Stalin. Thus, how can we say only one has appeared in the last several hundred years? There were Ch'en Sheng, Wu Kuang, Hung Hsiu-ch'üan and Sun Yat-sen in China; thus, how can we say that there has only been one in several thousand years? You over-did it when you talked about "apex" and "one sentence worth ten thousand sentences." One sentence is one sentence. How can it be worth ten thousand sentences! No provision shall be made for state chairmanship and I will not serve as state chairman. I have said so six times. If each time I had made one sentence, there should have been sixty thousand sentences. But, they have never listened to me. Therefore, my words are not even worth half a sentence; they equal zero. Only when Ch'en Po-ta talked to them, was each sentence worth ten thousand sentences. On the surface they were talking about enhancing my prestige, but who knows what was really in their minds. To make it clear, it was actually an attempt to enhance one's own reputation. It is also said that I am the founder and leader of the People's Liberation Army but Lin is the personal commander. Why can't the founder be the commander? I am not the only founder either.

I have always made a point to grasp the question of line and principle. I will not make concessions on major questions of principle. After the Lushan meeting I adopted three measures: one was to cast stones, one to blend with sand and one to dig up the corner stone. After criticizing and repudiating plenty of materials gathered by Ch'en Po-ta, which had deceived lots of people, I approved for distribution the report by the 38th Army and report by the Tsinan Military Region opposing arrogance and conceit. I also gave instruction on one document concerning a long discussion meeting which had done nothing to criticize Ch'en. My method is to get hold of these stones and write down instructions for the public to discuss. This is what I call the method of casting the stone. When clay is too concrete, no air will pass through; however, blending it with a little sand will allow air to pass. The Military Commission needs to be blended with a few more people. Reorganization of the Peking Military Region is digging up the corner stone.

What do you think about the Lushan meeting? For example, what on earth was the No. 6 briefing of the North China Section? Was it revolutionary, semi-revolutionary or counterrevolutionary? Personally, I think it was a counterrevolutionary briefing. All of you attended the 99-man meeting;[4] the Premier made a summing-up talk and handed down the criticisms of five big fighters[5] as well as the criticisms of Li Hsueh-feng and Cheng Wei-shan. Everyone believed that the problem had been solved. In fact, the matter concerning the Lushan meeting has not yet been finished. They wanted to black it out, even so far as to not let the directors of the two departments of the General Staff Department know about it. How can it be tolerated?

These opinions of mine are made only as personal views; they are only casual remarks. Don't draw any conclusions now; let the Central Committee do it.

---

[4]The CCP Central Committe convened a briefing meeting in April 1971 to criticize Ch'en Po-ta and rectify the working style. Ninty-nine responsible persons from the central, local and military units attended the meeting.

[5]Criticisms of Huang Yung-sheng, Wu Fa-hsien, Yeh Ch'ün, Li Tso-p'eng and Ch'iu Hui-tso.

Chairman Mao has said that we must be careful. First of all, the army must be careful, and secondly, local authorities must also be careful. Don't be conceited. If conceited, one will commit mistakes. The army must be united and streamlined. I don't think our army will rebel, nor do I believe that you, Huang Yung-sheng, can command the Liberation Army to rebel. There are divisions and regiments under the army; there are also Commanding headquarters, political and logistic departments. Will they all listen to you?

You must have a hand in military affairs; you must not only work like a civilian official but also like a military officer. The work of controlling the army is nothing but the learning of the line, rectification of inappropriate styles, refraining from forming mountain strongholds and factions, and emphasizing unity. The army has always been stressing discipline and effectiveness; I agree. However, to solve the ideological problem, we cannot use this method; we must stress fact and reasoning.

I put my approval on the document on three supports and two militaries written by the Kwangchow Military Region.[6] In the space for official reply by central authorities, I added four words "Jen-cheng Hsüeh-hsi" (study conscientiously) so as to arouse the attention. Now that local Party committees have been established, they should be allowed to practice unified leadership. If decisions have already been made by local party committees on certain matters, is it not justified to ask military units for further discussion?

In the past we have had the course of basic drilling for our military training. It took about five to six months to proceed from individual training to the training of a battalion. Now, they are engaged in cultural and not in purely military activities. Hence, our army has become a cultural army.

One good brings about four-goods; however, the leadership of the one good may be correct or may not. Moreover, how about

[6] "The Minutes of the Symposium of the Kwangchow Military Region Concerning Ideological Work in Undertaking Three Supports and Two Militaries" approved for distribution by the CCP Central Committee on August 20, 1971. (Editor's Note: "Three supports and two militaries" refers to The PLA assignment of supporting the Left, assisting industry and agriculture, exercising military control and giving military training.)

the effect of those conferences of activists? It, too, deserves study. Some of the conferences are good but some are not. The major problem is that of line. If the line is not correct, the conference will not proceed well.

Learn from Taching in industry and from Tachai in agriculture and the whole country should learn from the People's Liberation Army. This is not perfect. It is necessary to add one item, the Liberation Army must learn from the people of the whole country.

Chairman Mao has said that we must study the article written by Lenin in commemoration of the 25th anniversary of the death of E. Pottier; we must learn to sing the song of "Internationale" and "Three Main Rules of Discipline and Eight Points for Attention." We should not only sing but also explain and Practice accordingly. Both the song of "Internationale" and Lenin's article are devoted completely to the Marxist stand and viewpoints. They urge the slaves to rise for the struggle of truth. The savior has never existed nor should we rely on fairies and emperors. All depends on ourselves. Who creates the world of mankind? It is our laboring masses. I wrote a 700-word document[7] at the Lushan meeting, which raised the question of who creates history, the hero or the slave? The "Internationale" urges us to unite now for tomorrow and teaches that Communism must be realized. In our study of Marxism, we must emphasize unity; we should not talk about splitting. We have sung the song of "Internationale" for fifty years; there are people who have attempted to split our Party ten times. We think there will be ten, twenty or thirty more attempts. Don't you believe it? Even if you don't, I, at least, do. Will there be no struggle once we reach the stage of Communism? I do not believe it. There will still be struggles when we get to Communism. The struggle will be one between the old and new and between the correct and the wrong. Even after tens of thousands of years the wrong will not work and will not stand up either.

As to the Three Main Rules of Discipline and Eight Points for Attention, they "must be remembered item by item." They "are supported and welcomed by the people of the whole country."

[7]"Some Opinions of My Own" by Mao Tse-tung.

Several items have already been forgotten, particularly the first item of the Three Main Rules of Discipline and the first and fifth items of the Eight Points for Attention. If all of them can be remembered and can be carried out, how wonderful it will be. The first item of the Three Main Rules of Discipline teaches that all actions must obey the command and all steps must be taken in unity; that only by doing so can victory be obtained. If the steps cannot be coordinated, we cannot achieve victory. Next are the first and fifth items of the Eight Points for Attention which call for courtesy toward the people, soldiers and all subordinates, and warns against arrogance and assuming the style of the warlord. These are the major points. There will be no policy without major points. I hope that the Three Main Rules of Discipline and Eight Points for Attention will be used to educate the soldier, the cadre, the masses and the Party member and the people.

Chairman Mao has said that he pointed out at the Lushan meeting that we must read Marxist-Leninist books. I hope that you will read more books from now on. High-ranking cadres do not even know what is materialism nor what is idealism. How can this be tolerated? What should we do if we do not understand the Marxist-Leninist books we are reading? We ask for help from teachers. You are all secretaries, but you should continue to act like students. Now I act like a student by reading two volumes of reference materials each day. Therefore, I am familiar with some international affairs.

I have always objected to having one's wife serve as director of one's own office. In Lin Piao's office, it is Yeh Ch'ün who serves as the office director. The four persons[8] must first see her in order to ask for instructions from Lin. All work must be done personally, read personally and replied personally. We should not rely on secretaries and give them too much power. My secretary only handles reception work; all papers are selected and checked by me. We must do our own work lest some mistakes should occur.

Chairman Mao has said, the Great Cultural Revolution dragged out Liu Shao-ch'i, P'eng, Lo, Lu and Yang, which was a great achievement. But there were losses. Some good cadres have not

[8]The four persons were: Hüang Yung-sheng, Wu Fa-hsien, Li Tso-p'eng and Ch'iu Hui-tso.

yet been rehabilitated. Most of the cadres are good; the bad ones are in the majority. Those who have been liquidated amount to no more than one per cent and the figure will not exceed three per cent when taking all questionable persons into consideration. Those who are not good must be given appropriate criticism and those who are good must be recognized. However, there should be no flattery. A person in his 20's should not be praised as a "super-genius," which can do no good. At this Lushan meeting some of the comrades were deceived and misled. It is not your problem but one in Peking. Mistakes themselves are not important. It is the tradition of our Party that when a person makes a mistake, he must conduct self-criticism and be criticized; mistakes are allowed to be corrected.

It is necessary to grasp education in ideological and political lines. The policy remains one of learning from past mistakes to avoid future ones, curing sickness to avoid future ones and uniting for achieving even greater victories.

D. Evidence of the Lin Piao Anti-Party Clique's Attempt to Launch a Counterrevolutionary Coup, 1971.*

TOP SECRET

DOCUMENT OF THE CENTRAL COMMITTEE OF
THE CHINESE COMMUNIST PARTY
CHUNG-FA (1972) No. 24

Chairman Mao's Instruction: Have It Published as Recommended
Circular of the CCP Central Committee

Party Committees of various provinces, municipalities, autonomous regions, large military regions, provincial military

*From Issues and Studies (December, 1972) pp. 92–96 (abridged).

districts, field armies, general headquarters of various armed forces, and various branches of arms and services under the Military Commission; leadership groups and nucleus groups of the Party committees in various departments of ministries under the Central Committee or the State Council:

Enclosed herewith is a copy of the "Struggle for Smashing the Lin Piao Anti-Party Clique's Counterrevolutionary Coup (Material No. 3)" which is "Criminal Evidences of the Lin Piao Anti-Party Clique's Counterrevolutionary Coup" selected and published by the Ad Hoc Team of the Central Committee. You are expected to immediately organize and transmit it for reading and discussion in accordance with the spirit of Document *Chung-Fa* (1972) No. 3. When transmitting or discussing this Material No. 3, you should take the "Summary of Chairman Mao's Talks with Responsible Comrades of Various Places During His Inspection Tour" as a weapon to engage in penetrating rectification movement for criticizing Lin Piao, further expose the transgressions of the Lin Piao anti-Party clique, and unfold a revolutionary mass criticism and repudiation campaign against the Lin Piao anti-Party clique. In transmitting Chairman Mao's important talks and instructions and Central Committee's documents concerning the tenth struggle between [ideological] lines to the masses, [our comrades in] various areas adopted the measures of summarizing experiences at experimental points, opening study classes, and cultivating cadres for key posts. After all these were done, they then transmitted the contents of the messages to the masses at large. These are effective measures for transmitting the Material No. 3. Various areas may adopt them in accordance with their own experience and the actual situation in their own areas. The translation problems encountered in transmitting Central Committee documents to minority nationalities such as Mongolian, Tibetan and Uighur, can be solved by nationality press organizations.

Central Committee of the
Chinese Communist Party
July 2, 1972

Introduction

The sinister purpose of the Lin Piao anti-Party clique's counterrevolutionary coup was to split our Party, usurp the supreme power of the Party and the state, and betray the line of the "Ninth Congress" by treacherous means so as to basically alter the Party's basic line and policy at all socialist historical stages, overthrow the dictatorship of the proletariat and restore capitalism. They wanted to resurrect the landlords and the bourgeoisie which had been overthrown by our Party, our Army and people throughout the nation under the leadership of Chairman Mao. To do this, on the home front, they wanted to unite with the landlords, rich peasants, counterrevolutionaries, bad elements and rightists to practice Fascist dictatorship by landlords, comprador class and the bourgeoisie. And on the international front, they wanted to surrender to the Soviet social revisionism, unite with the Soviet Union and the United States, and oppose China and Communism.

The counterrevolutionary Lin Piao anti-Party clique is the proxy of the landlords, bourgeoisie, imperialists, revisionists and reactionaries, which have been overthrown, in our Party. Their line concentrates on and reflects the aspirations of class enemies at home and abroad for, practicing counterrevolutionary restoration in our country. However, the Lin Piao anti-Party clique's conspiracy of counterrevolutionary restoration can never succeed. Our Party, Army and people, under the leadership of Chairman Mao and Party's Central, have achieved a great victory in smashing the Lin Piao anti-Party clique's counterrevolutionary coup. It is a great victory of the proletarian great Cultural Revolution. It is also a great victory of Mao Tse-tung's thought and Chairman Mao's proletarian revolutionary line. In pursuance of Chairman Mao's instructions "Stress should be placed on evidence, investigation and research; it is strictly forbidden to extort confessions and accept such confessions" and "We should lay stress on evidence but not accept confessions without considerations," we have made repeated investigations and confirmations on the multitude of criminal evidences. On January 13, 1972, we disseminated the program of the counterrevolutionary coup entitled "571 Kung-Ch'eng Chi-Yao." And now, we publish a part of the criminal evidences that have been confirmed.

The Ad Hoc Team of
the Central Committee
June 26, 1972

Part I: Evidences of the Lin Piao anti-Party clique's attempt to launch a counterrevolutionary coup during the Second Plenary Session of the Ninth Central Committee

During the Second Plenary Session of the Ninth Central Committee, the Lin Piao anti-Party clique engaged in underground activities, played their treacherous tricks in a big way and launched a planned and organized attack against the Party under a program by surprise action, igniting and fanning up the fire, fabricating rumors, cheating comrades and other evil means. Their anti-Party program was to "establish a chairman of the state," the "genius," oppose the line of the Ninth Congress, and overthrow the three agenda of the Second Plenary Session of the Ninth Central Committee. Their sinister purpose was to split our Party and Army and seize power from Chairman Mao and the Party Central. The nature of their attempt was exactly that of a smashed counterrevolutionary coup:

(1) Lin Piao's mobilization order for starting the counterrevolutionary coup and the anti-Party program he brought up;

(2) The Lin Piao anti-Party clique's frenzied attack against the Party at the Second Plenary Session of the Ninth Central Committee: and

(3) The Lin Piao anti-Party clique's treacherous underground activities during the Second Plenary Session of the Ninth Central Committee.

Part II: Evidences of the Lin Piao anti-Party clique's preparation starting a counterrevolutionary armed coup

As early as before the Second Plenary Session of the Ninth Central Committee, the Lin Piao anti-Party clique already engaged in treacherous activities for seizing the Party and the power in an attempt to overthrow the Party Central headed by Chairman Mao. After the Second Plenary Session of the Ninth Central Committee, the Lin Piao anti-Party clique, upset with their failure, refused to accept the education and rescue of Chairman Mao and the Party Central. Moreover, they hid themselves in a dark corner, prepared the program of counterrevolutionary coup "571 Kung-Ch'eng Chi-Yao," established clandestine Fascist secret service organizations, created false public opinion, trained secret agents, hired cadres, imported a large number of secret service tools from foreign countries, established an underground activity base and made preparations for the counterrevolutionary armed coup in all aspects:

(1) The so-called "Order No. 1" issued by Lin Piao without permission;

(2) The allied anti-Party activities of Lin Piao, Hüang Yung-sheng, Wu Fa-hsien, Yeh Chün, Li Tso-p'eng and Chiu Hui-tso;

(3) Lin Piao's personally-written letters to Chou Yü-ch'ih and Liu Pei-feng;

(4) Wu Fa-hsien's appointment orders for Lin Li-kuo, Chou Yü-ch'ih and others;

(5) Lin Piao's reactionary theory of "going up to Chingkang Mountain again" and the music and songs for the theory;

(6) An account of Lin Piao and Yeh Chün's play of counterrevolutionary fence-sitters;

(7) Lin Piao's "July 23 Inspection Tour" carried out under the name of "war preparation," but in fact designed to seize the Party and the power;

(8) The black materials fabricated by the Lin Piao anti-Party clique for starting their counterrevolutionary coup and betraying comrades of the Central Politburo, and the relevant information collected;

(9) The materials collected by Lin Piao and Yeh Chün for studying the techniques of the counterrevolutionary coup;

(10) Chou Yü-ch'ih's speech at a meeting of the counterrevolutionary partisan force small "Joint Fleet" manipulated by Lin Piao (abstracts);

(11) The draft of the "Instructions for Membership" of the Shanghai Group;

(12) The intelligence activities of the secret service of the counterrevolutionary partisan force small "Joint Fleet";

(13) The so-called three-nation four-party conference covertly convened by Lin Li-kuo in Shanghai;

(14) Yü Hsin-yeh's plan for "preparing and expediting" the "571" counterrevolutionary coup program (abstracts);

(15) Chou Chi-p'ing's flattering of Lin Piao;

(16) The counterrevolutionary public opinion fabricated by the Lin Piao anti-Party clique for seizing the Party and the power; (abstracts of Liu Ching-p'ing's anti-Party speeches)

(17) The minutes of a black meeting of the counterrevolutionary partisan force small "Joint Fleet" (abstracts);

(18) The counterrevolutionary clandestine base built by Lin Li-kuo and other diehard followers of Lin Piao;

(19) A large quantity of equipment for the counterrevolutionary coup activities engaged by the Lin Piao anti-Party clique, which was seized at the clandestine base;

(20) Flight training in piloting helicopters secretly conducted by Chou Yü-ch'ih; and

(21) The training in driving amphibious vehicles secretly conducted by Lin Li-kuo.

Part III: Evidences of the Lin Piao anti-Party clique's attempt to assassinate great leader Chairman Mao, establish another Central Committee and start the counterrevolutionary armed coup against the Party Central and their attempt to defect the nation and surrender to the enemy after their failure

In September 1971, the Lin Piao anti-Party clique launched a "desperate" counterrevolutionary armed coup in accordance with the counterrevolutionary program "571 Kung-Ch'eng Chi-Yao." Under the direct command of Lin Piao, they ignobly attempted to assassinate Chairman Mao while on an inspection tour in the south and, in the meantime, planned to assassinate comrades in the Central Politburo in Peking to usurp the Party and the supreme power of the state. After this counterrevolutionary plan fizzled out Lin took Hüang Yung-sheng, Wu Fa-hsien, Yeh Chün, Li Tso-p'eng, Chiu Hui-tso and others to Canton to make plans for establishing another Central Committee. Chairman Mao's actions disrupted the disposition of the Lin Piao anti-Party clique, rendering their long-contemplated extremely vicious counterrevolutionary scheme thoroughly powerless. Seeing that his scheme had been exposed and that his last day was coming, Lin Piao hurriedly took his wife and son and a few diehard cohorts to escape to the enemy, betraying the Party and the state. In the early morning hour of 2:30, September 13, 1971, the Trident jet No. 256 carrying them crashed in the vicinity of Ondor Han in Mongolia. Lin Piao, Yeh Chün, Lin Li-kuo and all other renegades and traitors aboard were burned to death. Their death, however, could not expiate all their crimes. After Lin Piao's unsuccessful betrayal and defection, Huang Yung-sheng, Wu Fa-hsien, Li Tso-p'eng, and Chiu Hui-tso destroyed many of the evidences to cover up their own criminal acts.

(1) Lin Piao's order for the counterrevolutionary coup—Lin Piao's order for the counterrevolutionary coup and Lin Piao's personally-written letter to Hüang Yung-sheng were carried by Chou Yü-ch'ih, Yü Hsin-yeh and others escaping by helicopter. After the helicopter was forced to land, Chou Yü-ch'ih tore the two counterrevolutionary documents into small pieces in order to destroy the evidence of their crimes. However, these pieces were collected at the location and reconstructed by our units concerned. According to Chiang Teng-chiao, Hu P'ing, Li Wei-hsin and more than ten others who participated in the counterrevolutionary coup and personally read the order, the original copy of the order for counterrevolutionary coup reads, you are expected to "follow the order transmitted by Comrades Li-kuo and Yü-ch'ih—Lin Piao";

(2) Lin Piao's personally-written letter to Huang Yung-sheng—The letter reads: "Comrade Yung-sheng, I miss you very much and hope that you will be optimistic all the time so as to take care of your health. You may contact Comrade Wang Fei personally when necessary. Salute—Lin Piao";

(3) Confessions made and written personally by Wang Fei;

(4) Frequent telephone contact between Yeh Chün, Huang

Yung-sheng, Wu Fa-hsien, Li Tso-p'eng, and Chiu Hui-tso on the eve of the counterrevolutionary armed coup of the Lin Piao anti-Party clique;

(5) Code names personally written by Yeh Chün for skeleton members of the counterrevolutionary coup: Chin-Chung Tung-Ling (Golden Clock Copper Bell) for Chou Yü-ch'ih; Huang Hsiang Ho Fei for Wang Fei; Awl Hammer for Liu P'ei-feng;

(6) Intelligence information submitted by Huang Yung-sheng, Wu Fa-hsien, Li Tso-p'eng and Chiu Hui-tso to Lin Piao and Yeh Chün;

(7) Ch'eng Hung-chen's diary about the Lin Piao anti-Party clique's treacherous activities for assassinating Chairman Mao and Central Politburo comrades (photo copy of the original), "Map of Tiao Yu Island," "Sun Yung-sheng Chemical Weapon," "Explosives, Liu Shih-ying, September 9, the morning of the day after tomorrow, Express Train No. 10," "Chieh Kuan Cheng Wei Szu Hao Men," and "Express Train No. 16 for Changsha-Peking tomorrow morning";

(8) The IR-10 powerful weapon that the Lin Piao anti-Party clique prepared to use for assassinating Chairman Mao;

(9) Confessions made and written personally by Lu Min;

(10) Confessions made and written personally by Chiang T'eng-chiao;

(11) The "Topographic Map of Tiao Yu Island" secretly drawn by the Lin Piao anti-Party clique for assassinating Central Politburo comrades;

(12) The personnel roster prepared by Wang Fei's who followed Lin Piao, Huang Yung-sheng, Wu Fa-hsien, Yeh Chün, Li Tso-p'eng and Chiu Hui-tso in the escape to Canton;

(13) Confessions made and written personally by Liu Shih-ying;

(14) The flight schedule of the aircraft prepared for Lin Piao and others for escape to Canton;

(15) Lin Wei-hsin's account of the telephone message to Wang Wei-kuo transmitted in the skies over Shanghai on the escape to Canton (based on Li Wei-hsin's diary);

(16) Confessions made and written personally by Hu P'ing;

(17) Li Tso-p'eng's scheme for altering the order from the

Central; records of duties with explanations of the duty officer of Shanhaikuan Airport;

(18) The large number of top-secret documents of our Party and Army which Lin Piao and Yeh Chün prepared to take with them but left behind in their hurried flight;

(19) A description of Lin Piao and Yeh Chün's distress in their hurried flight for betraying the state and defection to the enemy;

(20) An eyewitness' account of Lin Piao and Yeh Chün's hurried flight for saving their lives;

(21) The top of the fuel tank damaged by the Trident jet No. 256 carrying Lin Piao and Yeh Chün at its take-off and the fragments from the right wing of the jet at the time of collision;

(22) The scene of the crash of the Trident jet that Lin Piao, Yeh Chün and others took when betraying the state and defecting to the enemy;

(23) The forced-down helicopter carrying Yü-ch'ih and others in the escape.

(24) A part of the evidences of Lin Piao's crimes for betraying the Party and the state which was captured from the downed helicopter; and

(25) Confessions made and written personally by Li Wei-hsin.

APPENDIX 4: THE "NEW" CONSTITUTION OF THE COMMUNIST PARTY OF CHINA
(August, 1973)*

[The new constitution adopted by the Tenth Party Congress is essentially the same as the 1969 constitution except that it deleted any reference to Lin Piao. There is more rewording of the "General Program" from the 1969 model because of the identification of Lin Piao in that chapter than in any other section throughout the new constitution. However, the party members, instead of being urged to simply "study and apply Marxism-Leninism-Mao Tse-tung Thought in a living way" as provided in the 1969 constitution (Article 3), are now exhorted to "conscientiously study Marxism-Leninism-Mao Tse-tung Thought and *criticize revisionism*" (Article 3) (see Appendix I). Furthermore, the leading bodies of the party at all levels are no longer just elected "through democratic consultation" (Article 5, 1969 constitution), they must now be elected "in accordance with the requirements for successors to the cause of the proletarian revolution and the principle of combining the old, the middle-aged and the young" as provided in Article 5 of the new constitution. Readers are advised to compare the two constitutions.]

CHAPTER I

GENERAL PROGRAMME

The Communist Party of China is the political party of the proletariat, the vanguard of the proletariat.

*From *Peking Review*, 35 and 36 (September 7, 1973), pp. 26–29.

The Communist Party of China takes Marxism-Leninism-Mao Tsetung Thought as the theoretical basis guiding its thinking.

The basic programme of the Communist Party of China is the complete overthrow of the bourgeoisie and all other exploiting classes, the establishment of the dictatorship of the proletariat in place of the dictatorship of the bourgeoisie and the triumph of socialism over capitalism. The ultimate aim of the Party is the realization of communism.

Through more than fifty years of arduous struggle, the Communist Party of China has led the Chinese people in winning complete victory in the new-democratic revolution, great victories in socialist revolution and socialist construction and great victories in the Great Proletarian Cultural Revolution.

Socialist society covers a considerably long historical period. Throughout this historical period, there are classes, class contradictions and class struggle, there is the struggle between the socialist road and the capitalist road, there is the danger of capitalist restoration and there is the threat of subversion and aggression by imperialism and social-imperialism. These contradictions can be resolved only by depending on the theory of continued revolution under the dictatorship of the proletariat and on practice under its guidance.

Such is China's Great Proletarian Cultural Revolution, a great political revolution carried out under the conditions of socialism by the proletariat against the bourgeoisie and all other exploiting classes to consolidate the dictatorship of the proletariat and prevent capitalist restoration. Revolutions like this will have to be carried out many times in the future.

The Party must rely on the working class, strengthen the worker-peasant alliance and lead the people of all the nationalities of our country in carrying on the three great revolutionary movements of class struggle, the struggle for production and scientific experiment; lead the people in building socialism independently and with the initiative in our own hands, through self-reliance, hard struggle, diligence and thrift and by going all out, aiming high and achieving greater, faster, better and more economical results; and lead them in preparing against war and natural disasters and doing everything for the people.

The Communist Party of China upholds proletarian

THE SEARCH FOR A NEW CHINA

internationalism and opposes great-power chauvinism; it firmly unites with the genuine Marxist-Leninist Parties and organizations the world over, unites with the proletariat, the oppressed people and nations of the whole world and fights together with them to oppose the hegemonism of the two superpowers—the United States and the Soviet Union—to overthrow imperialism, modern revisionism and all reaction, and to abolish the system of exploitation of man by man over the globe, so that all mankind will be emancipated.

The Communist Party of China has strengthened itself and grown in the course of the struggle against both Right and "Left" opportunist lines. Comrades throughout the Party must have the revolutionary spirit of daring to go against the tide, must adhere to the principles of practising Marxism and not revisionism, working for unity and not for splits, and being open and aboveboard and not engaging in intrigues and conspiracy, must be good at correctly distinguishing contradictions among the people from those between ourselves and the enemy and correctly handling them, must develop the style of integrating theory with practice, maintaining close ties with the masses and practising criticism and self-criticism, and must train millions of successors for the cause of proletarian revolution, so as to ensure that the Party's cause will advance for ever along the Marxist line.

The future is bright, the road is tortuous. Members of the Communist Party of China, who dedicate their lives to the struggle for communism, must be resolute, fear no sacrifice and surmount every difficulty to win victory!

CHAPTER II

MEMBERSHIP

Article 1: Any Chinese worker, poor peasant, lower-middle peasant, revolutionary armyman or any other revolutionary element who has reached the age of eighteen and who accepts the Constitution of the Party, joins a Party organization and works actively in it, carries out the Party's decisions, observes Party discipline and pays membership dues may become a member of the Communist Party of China.

Article 2: Applicants for Party membership must go through the procedure for admission individually. An applicant must be recommended by two Party members, fill out an application form for Party membership and be examined by a Party branch, which must seek the opinions of the broad masses inside and outside the Party. Application is subject to acceptance by the general membership meeting of the Party branch and approval by the next higher Party committee.

Article 3: Members of the Communist Party of China must:

(1) Conscientiously study Marxism-Leninism-Mao Tsetung Thought and criticize revisionism;

(2) Work for the interests of the vast majority of people of China and the world;

(3) Be able at uniting with the great majority, including those who have wrongly opposed them but are sincerely correcting their mistakes; however, special vigilance must be maintained against careerists, conspirators and double-dealers so as to prevent such bad elements from usurping the leadership of the Party and the state at any level and guarantee that the leadership of the Party and the state always remains in the hands of Marxist revolutionaries;

(4) Consult with the masses when matters arise;

(5) Be bold in making criticism and self-criticism.

Article 4: When Party members violate Party discipline, the Party organizations at the levels concerned shall, within their functions and powers and on the merits of each case, take appropriate disciplinary measures—warning, serious warning, removal from posts in the Party, placing on probation within the Party, or expulsion from the Party.

The period for which a Party member is placed on probation shall not exceed two years. During this period, he has no right to vote or elect or be elected.

A Party member whose revolutionary will has degenerated and who does not change despite repeated education may be persuaded to withdraw from the Party.

When a Party member asks to withdraw from the Party, the Party branch concerned shall, with the approval of its general membership meeting, remove his name from the Party rolls and report the matter to the next higher Party committee for the record.

Proven renegades, enemy agents, absolutely unrepentant persons in power taking the capitalist road, degenerates and alien-class elements must be cleared out of the Party and not be re-admitted.

Chapter III

ORGANIZATIONAL PRINCIPLE OF THE PARTY

Article 5: The organizational principle of the Party is democratic centralism.

The leading bodies of the Party at all levels shall be elected through democratic consultation in accordance with the requirements for successors to the cause of the proletarian revolution and the principle of combining the old, the middle-aged and the young.

The whole Party must observe unified discipline: The individual is subordinate to the organization, the minority is subordinate to the majority, the lower level is subordinate to the higher level, and the entire Party is subordinate to the Central Committee.

Leading bodies of the Party at all levels shall regularly report on their work to congresses or general membership meetings, constantly listen to the opinions of the masses both inside and outside the Party and accept their supervision. Party members have the right to criticize organizations and leading members of the Party at all levels and make proposals to them. If a Party member holds different views with regard to the decisions or directives of the Party organizations, he is allowed to reserve his views and has the right to bypass the immediate leadership and report directly to higher levels, up to and including the Central Committee and the Chairman of the Central Committee. It is absolutely impermissible to suppress criticism and to retaliate. It is essential to create a political situation in which there are both centralism and democracy, both discipline and freedom, both unity of will and personal ease of mind and liveliness.

Article 6: The highest leading body of the Party is the National Party Congress and, when it is not in session, the Central Committee elected by it. The leading bodies of Party organizations in the localities, in army units and in various departments are the Party congresses or general membership meetings at their respective levels and the Party committees elected by them. Party congresses at all levels are convened by Party committees at their respective levels. The convening of Party congresses in the localities, in army units and in various departments and their elected Party committee members are subject to approval by the higher Party organizations.

Party committees at all levels shall set up their working bodies or dispatch their representative organs in accordance with the principles of close ties with the masses and simple and efficient structure.

Article 7: State organs, the People's Liberation Army and the militia, labour unions, poor and lower-middle peasant associations, women's federations, the Communist Youth League, the Red Guards, the Little Red Guards and other revolutionary mass organizations must all accept the centralized leadership of the Party.

Party committees or leading Party groups may be set up in state organs and popular organizations.

Chapter IV

CENTRAL ORGANIZATIONS OF THE PARTY

Article 8: The National Party Congress shall be convened every five years. Under special circumstances, it may be convened before its due date or postponed.

Article 9: The plenary session of the Central Committee of the Party elects the Political Bureau of the Central Committee, the Standing Committee of the Political Bureau of the Central Committee and Chairman and Vice-Chairmen of the Central Committee.

The plenary session of the Central Committee of the Party is convened by the Political Bureau of the Central Committee.

When the Central Committee is not in plenary session, the

Political Bureau of the Central Committee and its Standing Committee exercise the functions and powers of the Central Committee.

Under the leadership of the Chairman, Vice-Chairmen and the Standing Committee of the Political Bureau of the Central Committee, a number of necessary organs, which are compact and efficient, shall be set up to attend to the day-to-day work of the Party, the government and the Army in a centralized way.

CHAPTER V

PARTY ORGANIZATIONS IN THE LOCALITIES AND THE ARMY UNITS

Article 10: Local Party congresses at the county level and upwards and Party congresses in the People's Liberation Army at the regimental level and upwards shall be convened every three years. Under special circumstances, they may be convened before their due date or postponed.

Party committees at all levels in the localities and the army units elect their standing committees, secretaries and deputy secretaries.

CHAPTER VI

PRIMARY ORGANIZATIONS OF THE PARTY

Article 11: Party branches, general Party branches or primary Party committees shall be set up in factories, mines and other enterprises, people's communes, offices, schools, shops, neighbourhoods, companies of the People's Liberation Army and other primary units in accordance with the requirements of the revolutionary struggle and the size of the Party membership.

Party branches and general Party branches shall hold elections once a year and primary Party committees shall hold elections every two years. Under special circumstances, the election may take place before its due date or be postponed.

Article 12: The main tasks of the primary organizations of the Party are:

(1) To lead the Party members and non-Party members in studying Marxism-Leninism-Mao Tsetung Thought conscientiously and criticizing revisionism;

(2) To give constant education to the Party members and non-Party members concerning the ideological and political line and lead them in fighting resolutely against the class enemy;

(3) To propagate and carry out the policies of the Party, implement its decisions and fulfil every task assigned by the Party and the state;

(4) To maintain close ties with the masses, constantly listen to their opinions and demands and wage an active ideological struggle so as to keep Party life vigorous;

(5) To take in new Party members, enforce Party discipline and constantly consolidate the Party organizations, getting rid of the stale and taking in the fresh, so as to maintain the purity of the Party ranks.

APPENDIX 5: CHOU EN-LAI: REPORT TO THE TENTH NATIONAL CONGRESS OF THE COMMUNIST PARTY OF CHINA (August, 1973)*

[This is probably one of the last major reports presented by Premier Chou En-lai in view of his advanced age, seventy-five. After the Cultural Revolution, Chou En-lai emerged to play a dominant role in China's factional politics. However, during the 1973–1974 Anti-Lin Piao and Anti-Confucius campaign, he has encountered increasing criticism from the Leftist-Radicals in the party. His health also deteriorated.

Although considerable space is devoted to critizing Lin Piao in this report, the essence of the report centers on the domestic and international situation which Chou characterized as "great disorder on the earth." He argued for the continuation of "Chairman Mao's proletarian policies" and "to further strengthen the centralized leadership of the Party."]

Comrades!

The Tenth National Congress of the Communist Party of China is convened at a time when the Lin Piao anti-Party clique has been smashed, the line of the Party's Ninth National Congress has won great victories and the situation both at home and abroad is excellent.

On behalf of the Central Committee, I am making this report to the Tenth National Congress. The main subjects are: On the line of the Ninth National Congress, on the victory of smashing the Lin Piao anti-Party clique and on the situation and our tasks.

*From *Peking Review*, 35 and 36 (September 7, 1973), pp. 17–25.

On the Line of the Ninth National Congress

The Party's Ninth Congress was held when great victories had been won in the Great Proletarian Cultural Revolution personally initiated and led by Chairman Mao.

In accordance with the theory of Marxism-Leninism-Mao Tse-tung Thought on continuing the revolution under the dictatorship of the proletariat, the Ninth Congress summed up the experience of the Great Proletarian Cultural Revolution, criticized Liu Shao-chi's revisionist line and reaffirmed the basic line and policies of the Party for the entire historical period of socialism. As comrades may recall, when the Ninth Congress opened on April 1, 1969, Chairman Mao issued the great call, "Unite to win still greater victories," At the First Plenary Session of the Ninth Central Committee on April 28 of the same year, Chairman Mao once again clearly stated: "Unite for one purpose, that is, the consolidation of the dictatorship of the proletariat." "We must ensure that the people throughout the country are united to win victory under the leadership of the proletariat." In addition he predicted: "Probably another revolution will have to be carried out after several years." Chairman Mao's speeches and the political report of the Central Committee adopted at the congress formulated a Marxist-Leninist line for our Party.

As we all know, the political report to the Ninth Congress was drawn up under Chairman Mao's personal guidance. Prior to the congress, Lin Piao had produced a draft political report in collaboration with Chen Po-ta. They were opposed to continuing the revolution under the dictatorship of the proletariat, contending that the main task after the Ninth Congress was to develop production. This was a refurbished version under new conditions of the same revisionist trash that Liu Shao-chi and Chen Po-ta had smuggled into the resolution of the Eighth Congress, which alleged that the major contradiction in our country was not the contradiction between the proletariat and the bourgeoisie, but that "between the advanced socialist system and the backward productive forces of society." Naturally, this draft by Lin Piao and Chen Po-ta was rejected by the Central

Committee. Lin Piao secretly supported Chen Po-ta in the latter's open opposition to the political report drawn up under Chairman Mao's guidance, and it was only after his attempts were frustrated that Lin Piao grudgingly accepted the political line of the Central Committee and read its political report to the congress. However, during and after the Ninth Congress, Lin Piao continued with his conspiracy and sabotage in spite of the admonishments, rebuffs and efforts to save him by Chairman Mao and the Party's Central Committee. He went further to start a counter-revolutionary coup d'etat, which was aborted, at the Second Plenary Session of the Ninth Central Committee in August 1970, then in March 1971 he drew up the plan for an armed counterrevolutionary coup d'etat entitled *Outline of Project "571"*, and on September 8, he launched the coup in a wild attempt to assassinate our great leader Chairman Mao and set up a rival central committee. On September 13, after his conspiracy had collapsed, Lin Piao surreptitiously boarded a plane, fled as a defector to the Soviet revisionists in betrayal of the Party and country and died in a crash at Undur Khan in the People's Republic of Mongolia.

The shattering of the Lin Piao anti-Party clique is our Party's greatest victory since the Ninth Congress and a heavy blow dealt to enemies at home and abroad. After the September 13th incident, the whole Party, the whole Army and the hundreds of millions of people of all nationalities in our country seriously discussed the matter and expressed their intense proletarian indignation at the bourgeois careerist, conspirator, double-dealer, renegade and traitor Lin Piao and his sworn followers, and pledged resolute support for our great leader Chairman Mao and the Party's Central Committee which he headed. A movement to criticize Lin Piao and rectify style of work has been launched throughout the country. The whole Party, Army and people have been conscientiously studying Marxism-Leninism-Mao Tse-tung Thought, conducting revolutionary mass criticism of Lin Piao and other swindlers like him, and settling accounts with the counter-revolutionary crimes of these swindlers ideologically, politically and organizationally, and have raised their own ability to distinguish genuine from sham Marxism. As facts showed, the Lin Piao anti-Party clique was only a tiny group which was extremely isolated in the midst of the whole party, Army and people and could not affect the situation as a whole. The Lin Piao anti-Party clique has not stemmed, nor could it possibly have stemmed the rolling torrent of the Chinese people's revolution. On the contrary, what it did further aroused the whole Party, Army and people to "unite to win still greater victories."

Thanks to the movement to criticize Lin Piao and rectify style of work, the line of the Ninth Congress is more deeply rooted among the people. The line of the Ninth Congress and the proletarian policies of the Party have been implemented better than before. New achievements have been made in struggle-criticism-transformation in all realms of the superstructure. The working style of seeking truth from facts and following the mass line and the glorious tradition of modesty, prudence and hard work, which were for a time impaired by Lin Piao, have been further developed. The Chinese People's Liberation Army, which won fresh merit in the Great Proletarian Cultural Revolution, has made new contributions in strengthening the preparations against war and in taking part in revolution and construction together with the people. The great revolutionary unity of the people of all nationalities led by the proletariat and based on the worker-peasant alliance is stronger than ever. Having rid itself of the stale and taken in the fresh, our Party, with a membership of twenty-eight million, is now an even more vigorous vanguard of the proletariat.

Spurred by the movement to criticize Lin Piao and rectify style of work, the people of our country overcame the sabotage by the Lin Piao anti-Party clique, surmounted serious natural disasters and scored new victories in socialist construction. Our country's industry, agriculture, transportation, finance and trade are doing well. We have neither external nor internal debts. Prices are stable and the market is flourishing. There are many new achievements in culture, education, public health, science and technology.

In the international sphere, our Party and Government have firmly implemented the foreign policy laid down by the Ninth Congress. Our revolutionary friendship with fraternal socialist countries and with the genuine Marxist-Leninist Parties and organizations of various countries have been further strengthened. Our country has established diplomatic relations with an increasing number of countries on the basis of the Five Principles of Peaceful Coexistence. The legitimate status of our country in the United Nations has been restored. The policy of isolating China has gone bankrupt; Sino-U.S. relations have been improved to some extent. China and Japan have normalized their relations. Friendly contacts between our people and the people of other countries are more extensive than ever; we assist and support each other, impelling the world situation to continue to develop in the direction favourable to the people of all countries.

Revolutionary practice since the Ninth Congress and chiefly the practice of the struggle against the Lin Piao anti-Party clique have proved that the political and organizational lines of the Ninth Congress are both correct and that the leadership given by the Party's Central Committee headed by Chairman Mao is correct.

On the Victory of Smashing the Lin Piao Anti-Party Clique

The course of the struggle to smash the Lin Piao anti-Party clique and the crimes of the clique are already known to the whole Party, Army and people. So, there is no need to dwell on it here.

Marxism-Leninism holds that inner-Party struggle is the reflection within the Party of class struggle in society. The Liu Shao-chi renegade clique collapsed and the Lin Piao anti-Party clique sprang out to continue the trial of strength with the proletariat. This was an acute expression of the intense domestic and international class struggles.

As early as January 13, 1967, when the Great Proletarian Cultural Revolution was at high tide, Brezhnev, the chief of the Soviet revisionist renegade clique, frantically attacked China's Great Proletarian Cultural Revolution in his speech at a mass rally in Gorky Region and openly declared that they stood on the side of the Liu Shao-chi renegade clique, saying that the downfall of this clique was "a big tragedy for all real communists in China, and we express our deep sympathy to them." At the same time, Brezhnev publicly announced continuation of the policy of subverting the leadership of the Chinese Communist Party, and ranted about "struggling . . . for bringing it back to the road of internationalism." (*Pravda*, January 14, 1967) In March 1967 another chief of the Soviet revisionists said even more brazenly at mass rallies in Moscow that "sooner or later the healthy forces expressing the true interests of China will have their decisive say," "and achieve the victory of Marxist-Leninist ideas in their great country." (*Pravda*, March 4 and 10, 1967) What they called "healthy forces" are nothing but the decadent forces representing the interests of social-imperialism and all the exploiting classes; what they meant by "their decisive say" is the usurpation of the supreme power of the Party and the state; what they meant by "victory of ideas" is the reign of sham Marxism-Leninism and real revisionism over China; and what they meant by the "road of internationalism" is the road of reducing China to a colony of Soviet revisionist social-imperialism. The Brezhnev renegade clique has impetuously voiced the common wish of the reactionaries and blurted out the ultra-Rightist nature of the Lin Piao anti-Party clique.

Lin Piao and his handful of sworn followers were a counter-revolutionary conspiratorial clique "who never showed up without a copy of *Quotations* in hand and never opened their mouths without shouting 'Long Live' and who spoke nice things to your face but stabbed you in the back." The essence of the counter-revolutionary revisionist line they pursued and the criminal aim of the counter-revolutionary armed coup d'etat they launched were to usurp the supreme power of the Party and the state, thoroughly betray the line of the Ninth Congress, radically change the Party's basic line and policies for the entire historical period of socialism, turn the Marxist-Leninist Chinese Communist Party into a revisionist, fascist party, subvert the dictatorship of the proletariat and restore capitalism. Inside China, they wanted to reinstate the landlord and bourgeois classes, which our Party, Army and people had overthrown with their own hands under the leadership of Chairman Mao, and to institute a feudal-comprador-fascist dictatorship. Internationally, they wanted to capitulate to Soviet revisionist social-imperialism, and ally themselves with imperialism, revisionism and reaction to oppose China, communism and revolution.

Lin Piao, this bourgeois careerist, conspirator and double-dealer, engaged in machinations within our Party not just for one decade but for several decades. On his part there was a process of development and self-exposure, and on our part there was also a process of getting to know him. Marx and Engels said in the *Manifesto of the Communist Party* that "all previous historical movements were movements of minorities, or in the interest of minorities. The proletarian movement is the self-conscious, independent movement of the immense majority, in the interest of the immense majority." Chairman Mao has made "working for the interests of the vast majority of people of China and the world" one of the principal requirements for successors to the cause of the proletarian revolution, and it has been written into our Party Constitution. To build a party for the interests of the vast majority or for the interests of the minority? This is the watershed between proletarian and bourgeois political parties and the touchstone for distinguishing true Communists from false. Lin Piao joined the Communist Party in the early days of China's new-democratic revolution. Even at that time he was pessimistic about the future of the Chinese Revolution. Right after the Kutien Meeting [December 1929—*Tr.*], Chairman Mao wrote a long letter "A Single Spark Can Start a Prairie Fire" to Lin Piao, trying seriously and patiently to educate him. But, as the facts proved, Lin Piao's bourgeois idealist world outlook was not at all remoulded. At important junctures of the Revolution he invariably committed Right opportunist errors and invariably played double-faced tricks, putting up a false front to deceive the Party and the people. However, as the Chinese revolution developed further and especially when it turned socialist in nature and became more and more thoroughgoing, aiming at the complete overthrow of the bourgeoisie and all other exploiting classes, the establishment of the dictatorship of the proletariat in place of the dictatorship of the bourgeoisie and the triumph of socialism over capitalism, Lin Piao and his like, who were capitalist-roaders in power working only for the interests of the minority and whose ambition grew with the rise of their positions, overestimating their own strength and underestimating the strength of the people, could no longer remain under cover and therefore sprang out for a trial of strength with the proletariat. When under the baton of Soviet revisionism he attempted to have his "decisive say" in order to serve the needs of domestic and foreign class enemies, his exposure and bankruptcy became complete.

Engels rightly said, "The development of the proletariat proceeds everywhere amidst internal struggles. . . . And when, like Marx and myself, one has fought harder all one's life long against the alleged socialists than against anyone else (for we only regarded the bourgeoisie as a *class* and hardly ever involved ourselves in conflicts with individual bourgeois), one cannot greatly grieve that the inevitable struggle has broken out. . . ." (Frederick Engels' letter to August Bebel, October 28, 1882)

Comrades!

In the last fifty years our Party has gone through ten major struggles between the two lines. The collapse of the Lin Piao anti-Party clique does not mean the end of the two-line struggle within the Party. Enemies at home and abroad all understand that the easiest way to capture a fortress is from within. It is much more convenient to have the capitalist-roaders in power who have sneaked into the Party do the job of subverting the dictatorship of the proletariat than for the landlords and capitalists to come to the fore themselves; this is especially true when the landlords and capitalists are already quite odious in society. In the future, even after classes have disappeared, there will still be contradictions between the superstructure and the economic base and between the relations of production and the productive forces. And there will still be two-line struggles reflecting these contradictions, i.e., struggles between the advanced and the backward and between the correct and the erroneous. Moreover, socialist society covers a considerably long historical period. Throughout this historical period, there are classes, class contradictions and class struggle, there is the struggle between the socialist road and the capitalist road, there is the danger of capitalist restoration and there is the threat of subversion and aggression by imperialism and social-imperialism. For a long time to come, there will still be two-line struggles within the Party, reflecting these contradictions, and such struggles will occur ten, twenty or thirty times. Lin Piao will appear again and so will persons like Wang Ming, Liu Shao-chi

Peng Teh-huai and Kao Kang. This is something independent of man's will. Therefore, all comrades in our Party must be fully prepared mentally for the struggles in the long years to come and be able to make the best use of the situation and guide the struggle to victory for the proletariat, no matter how the class enemy may change his tactics.

Chairman Mao teaches us that "the correctness or incorrectness of the ideological and political line decides everything." If one's line is incorrect, one's downfall is inevitable, even with the control of the central, local and army leadership. If one's line is correct, even if one has not a single soldier at first, there will be soldiers, and even if there is no political power, political power will be gained. This is borne out by the historical experience of our Party and by that of the international communist movement since the time of Marx. Lin Piao wanted to "have everything under his command and everything at his disposal," but he ended up having nothing under his command and nothing at his disposal. The crux of the matter is line. This is an irrefutable truth.

Chairman Mao has laid down for our Party the basic line and policies for the entire historical period of socialism and also specific lines and policies for specific work. We should attach importance not only to the Party's lines and policies for specific work but, in particular, to its basic line and policies. This is the fundamental guarantee of greater victories for our Party.

Having summed up the experience gained in the ten struggles between the two lines within the Party and particularly the experience acquired in the struggle to smash the Lin Piao anti-Party clique, Chairman Mao calls on the whole Party: "Practice Marxism, and not revisionism; unite, and don't split; be open and aboveboard, and don't intrigue and conspire." He thus puts forward the criterion for distinguishing the correct line from the erroneous line, and gives the three basic principles every Party member must observe. Every one of our comrades must keep these three principles firmly in mind, uphold them and energetically and correctly carry on the two-line struggle within the Party.

Chairman Mao has constantly taught us: It is imperative to note that one tendency covers another. The opposition to Chen

Tu-hsiu's Right opportunism which advocated "all alliance, no struggle" covered Wang Ming's "Left" opportunism which advocated "all struggle, no alliance." The rectification of Wang Ming's "Left" deviation covered Wang Ming's Right deviation. The struggle against Liu Shao-chi's revisionism covered Lin Piao's revisionism. There were many instances in the past where one tendency covered another and when a tide came, the majority went along with it, while only a few withstood it. Today, in both international and domestic struggles, tendencies may still occur similar to those of the past, namely, when there was an alliance with the bourgeoisie, the necessary struggles were forgotten and when there was a split with the bourgeoisie, the possibility of an alliance under given conditions was forgotten. It is required of us to do our best to discern and rectify such tendencies in time. And when a wrong tendency surges towards us like a rising tide, we must not fear isolation and must dare to go against the tide and brave it through. Chairman Mao states, "Going against the tide is a Marxist-Leninist principle." In daring to go against the tide and adhere to the correct line in the ten struggles between the two lines within the Party, Chairman Mao is our example and teacher. Every one of our comrades should learn well from Chairman Mao and hold to this principle.

Under the guidance of the correct line represented by Chairman Mao, the great, glorious and correct Communist Party has had prolonged trials of strength with the class enemies both inside and outside the Party, at home and abroad, armed and unarmed, overt and covert. Our Party has not been divided or crushed. On the contrary, Chairman Mao's Marxist-Leninist line has further developed and our Party grown ever stronger. Historical experience convinces us that "this Party of ours has a bright future." Just as Chairman Mao predicted in 1966, "If the Right stage an anti-Communist coup d'etat in China, I am sure they will know no peace either and their rule will most probably be short-lived, because it will not be tolerated by the revolutionaries, who represent the interests of the people making up more than 90 per cent of the population." So long as our whole Party bears in mind historical experience, and upholds Chairman Mao's correct line, all the schemes of the bourgeoisie for restoration are bound to fail. No matter how many more major struggles between the two lines may occur, the laws of history will not change, and the revolution in China and the world will eventually triumph.

On The Situation and Our Tasks

Chairman Mao has often taught us: We are still in the era of imperialism and the proletarian revolution. On the basis of fundamental Marxist principle, Lenin made a scientific analysis of imperialism and defined "imperialism as the highest stage of capitalism." Lenin pointed out that imperialism is monopolistic capitalism, parasitic or decaying capitalism, moribund capitalism. He also said that imperialism intensifies all the contradictions of capitalism to the extreme. He therefore concluded that "imperialism is the eve of the social revolution of the proletariat," and put forward theories and tactics of the proletarian revolution in the era of imperialism. Stalin said, "Leninism is Marxism of the era of imperialism and the proletarian revolution." This is entirely correct. Since Lenin's death, the world situation has undergone great changes. But the era has not changed. The fundamental principles of Leninism are not outdated; they remain the theoretical basis guiding our thinking today.

The present international situation is one characterized by great disorder on the earth. "The wind sweeping through the tower heralds a rising storm in the mountains." This aptly depicts how the basic world contradictions as analysed by Lenin show themselves today. Relaxation is a temporary and superficial phenomenon, and great disorder will continue. Such great disorder is a good thing for the people, not a bad thing. It throws the enemies into confusion and causes division among them, while it arouses and tempers the people, thus helping the international situation develop further in the direction favourable to the people and unfavourable to imperialism, modern revisionism and all reaction.

The awakening and growth of the Third World is a major event in contemporary international relations. The Third World has strengthened its unity in the struggle against hegemonism and power politics of the superpowers and is playing an ever more significant role in international affairs. The great victories won by the people of Viet Nam, Laos and Cambodia in their war against U.S. aggression and for national salvation have strongly encouraged the people of the world in their revolutionary struggles against imperialism and colonialism. A new situation has emerged in the Korean people's struggle for the independent and peaceful reunification of their fatherland. The struggles of the Palestinian and other Arab peoples against aggression by Israeli Zionism, the African peoples' struggles against colonialism and racial discrimination and the Latin American peoples' struggles for maintaining 200-nautical-mile territorial waters or economic zones all continue to forge ahead. The struggles of the Asian, African and Latin American peoples to win and defend national independence and safeguard state sovereignty and national resources have further deepened and broadened. The just struggles of the Third World as well as of the people of Europe, North America and Oceania support and encourage each other. Countries want independence, nations want liberation, and the people want revolution—this has become an irresistible historical trend.

Lenin said that "an essential feature of imperialism is the rivalry between several Great Powers in the striving for hegemony." Today, it is mainly the two nuclear superpowers—the U.S. and the U.S.S.R.—that are contending for hegemony. While hawking disarmament, they are actually expanding their armaments every day. Their purpose is to contend for world hegemony. They contend as well as collude with each other. Their collusion serves the purpose of more intensified contention. Contention is absolute and protracted, whereas collusion is relative and temporary. The declaration of this year as the "year of Europe" and the convocation of the European Security Conference indicate that strategically the key point of their contention is Europe. The West always wants to urge the Soviet revisionists eastward to divert the peril towards China, and it would be fine so long as all is quiet in the West. China is an attractive piece of meat coveted by all. But this piece of meat is very tough, and for years no one has been able to bite into it. It is even more difficult now that Lin Piao the "super-spy" has fallen. At present, the Soviet revisionists are "making a feint to the east while attacking in the west," and stepping up their contention in Europe and their expansion in the Mediterranean, the Indian Ocean and every place their hands can reach. The U.S.-Soviet contention for hegemony is the cause of world intranquillity. It cannot be covered up by any false appearances they create and is already perceived by an increasing number of people and countries. It has met with strong resistance from the Third World and has caused resentment on the part of Japan and West European countries. Beset with troubles internally and externally, the two hegemonic powers—the U.S. and the U.S.S.R—find the going tougher and tougher. As the verse goes, "Flowers fall off, do what one may," they are in a sorry plight indeed. This has been further proved by the U.S.-Soviet talks last June and the subsequent course of events.

"The people, and the people alone, are the motive force in the making of world history." The ambitions of the two hegemonic powers—the U.S. and the U.S.S.R.—are one thing, but whether they can achieve them is quite another. They want to devour China, but find it too tough even to bite. Europe and Japan are also hard to bite, not to speak of the vast Third World. U.S. imperialism started to go downhill after its defeat in the war of aggression against Korea. It has openly admitted that it is increasingly on the decline; it could not but pull out of Viet Nam. Over the last two decades, the Soviet revisionist ruling clique, from Khrushchov to Brezhnev, has made a socialist country degenerate into a social-imperialism country. Internally, it has restored capitalism, enforced a fascist dictatorship and enslaved the people of all nationalities, thus deepening the political and economic contradictions as well as contradictions among nationalities. Externally, it has invaded and occupied Czechoslovakia, massed its troops along the Chinese border, sent troops into the People's Republic of Mongolia, supported the traitorous Lon Nol clique, suppressed the Polish workers' rebellion, intervened in Egypt, causing the expulsion of the Soviet experts, dismembered Pakistan and carried out subversive activities in many Asian and African countries. This series of facts has profoundly exposed its ugly features as the new Czar and its reactionary nature, namely, "socialism in words, imperialism in deeds." The more evil and foul things it does, the sooner the time when Soviet revisionism will be relegated to the historical museum by the people of the Soviet Union and the rest of the world.

Recently, the Brezhnev renegade clique has talked a lot of nonsense on Sino-Soviet relations. It alleges that China is against relaxation of world tension and unwilling to improve Sino-Soviet relations, etc. These words are directed to the Soviet people and the people of other countries in a vain attempt to alienate their friendly feelings for the Chinese people and disguise the true features of the new Czar. These words are above all meant for the monopoly capitalists in the hope of getting more money in reward for services in opposing China and communism. This was an old trick of Hitler's, only Brezhnev is playing it more clumsily. If you are so anxious to relax world tension, why don't you show your good faith by doing a thing or two—for instance, withdraw your armed forces from Czechoslovakia or the People's Republic of Mongolia and return the four northern islands to Japan? China has not occupied any foreign countries' territory. Must China give away all the territory north of the Great Wall to the Soviet revisionists in order to show that we favour relaxation of world tension and are willing to improve Sino-Soviet relations? The Chinese people are not to be deceived or cowed. The Sino-Soviet controversy on matters of principle should not hinder the normalization of relations between the two states on the basis of the Five Principles of Peaceful Coexistence. The Sino-Soviet boundary question should be settled peacefully through negotiations free from any threat. "We will not attack unless we are attacked; if we are attacked, we will certainly counter-attack"—this is our consistent principle. And we mean what we say.

We should point out here that necessary compromises between revolutionary countries and imperialist countries must be distinguished from collusion and compromise between Soviet revisionism and U.S. imperialism. Lenin put it well: "There are compromises and compromises. One must be able to analyse the situation and the concrete conditions of each compromise, or of each variety of compromise. One must learn to distinguish between a man who gave the bandits money and firearms in order to lessen the damage they can do and facilitate their capture and execution, and a man who gives bandits money and firearms in order to share in the loot." (*"Left-Wing" Communism, an Infantile Disorder*) The Brest-Litovsk Treaty concluded by Lenin with German imperialism comes under the former category; and the doings of Khrushchov and Brezhnev, both betrayers of Lenin, fall under the latter.

Lenin pointed out repeatedly that imperialism means aggression and war. Chairman Mao pointed out in his statement of May 20, 1970: "The danger of a new world war still exists, and the people of all countries must get prepared. But revolution is the main trend in the world today." It will be possible to prevent such a war, so long as the peoples, who are becoming more and more awakened, keep the orientation clearly in sight, heighten their vigilance, strengthen unity and persevere in struggle. Should the imperialists be bent on unleashing such a war, it will inevitably give rise to greater revolutions on a worldwide scale and hasten their doom.

In the excellent situation now prevailing at home and abroad, it is most important for us to run China's affairs well. Therefore, on the international front, our Party must uphold proletarian internationalism, uphold the Party's consistent policies, strengthen our unity with the proletariat and the oppressed people and nations of the whole world and with all countries subjected to imperialist aggression, subversion, interference, control or bullying and form the broadest united front against imperialism, colonialism and neo-colonialism, and in particular, against the hegemonism of the two superpowers—the U.S. and the U.S.S.R. We must unite with all genuine Marxist-Leninist Parties and organizations the world over, and carry the struggle against modern revisionism through to the end. On the domestic front, we must pursue our Party's basic line and policies for the entire historical period of socialism, persevere in continuing the revolution under the dictatorship of the proletariat, unite with all the forces that can be united and work hard to build our country into a powerful socialist state, so as to make a greater contribution to mankind.

We must uphold Chairman Mao's teachings that we should "be prepared against war, be prepared against natural disasters, and do everything for the people" and should "dig tunnels deep, store grain everywhere, and never seek hegemony," maintain high vigilance and be fully prepared against any war of aggression that imperialism may launch and particularly against suprise attack on our country by Soviet revisionist social-imperialism. Our heroic People's Liberation Army and our vast militia must be prepared at all times to wipe out any enemy that may invade.

Taiwan Province is our motherland's sacred territory, and the people in Taiwan are our kith and kin. We have infinite concern for our compatriots in Taiwan, who love and long for the motherland. Our compatriots in Taiwan can have a bright future only by returning to the embrace of the motherland. Taiwan must be liberated. Our great motherland must be unified. This is the common aspiration and sacred duty of the people of all nationalities of the country, including our compatriots in Taiwan. Let us strive together to attain this goal.

Comrades!

We must be aware that although we have achieved great successes in socialist revolution and socialist construction, we are always lagging behind the needs of the objective situation. We still face very heavy tasks in our socialist revolution. The tasks of struggle-criticism-transformation in the Great Proletarian Cultural Revolution need to be carried on in a thoroughgoing way on all fronts. More efforts are required to overcome the shortcomings, mistakes and certain unhealthy tendencies in our work. Our whole Party must make good use of the present opportune time to consolidate and carry forward the achievements of the Great Proletarian Cultural Revolution and work well in all fields.

First of all, we should continue to do a good job of criticizing Lin Piao and rectifying style of work. We should make full use of that teacher by negative example, the Lin Piao anti-Party clique, to educate the whole Party, Army and the people of all nationalities of our country in class struggle and two-line struggle, and criticize revisionism and the bourgeois world outlook so that the masses will be able to draw on the historical experience of the ten struggles between the two lines in our Party, acquire a deeper understanding of the characteristics and laws of class struggle and two-line struggle in the period of socialist revolution in our country and raise their ability to distinguish genuine from sham Marxism.

All Party members should conscientiously study works by Marx, Engels, Lenin and Stalin and by Chairman Mao, adhere to dialectical materialism and historical materialism, combat idealism and metaphysics and remould their world outlook. Senior cadres, in particular, should make greater efforts to "read and study conscientiously and have a good grasp of Marxism," try their best to master the basic theories of Marxism, learn the history of the struggles of Marxism against old and new revisionism and opportunism of all descriptions, and understand how Chairman Mao has inherited, defended and developed Marxist-Leninism in the course of integrating the universal truth of Marxist-Leninism with the concrete practice of revolution. We hope that through sustained efforts "the vast numbers of our cadres and the people will be able to arm themselves with the basic theories of Marxism."

We should attach importance to the class struggle in the superstructure, including all spheres of culture, transform all parts of the superstructure which do not conform to the economic base. We should handle correctly the two types of contradictions of different nature. We should continue to carry out in earnest all of Chairman Mao's proletarian policies. We should continue to carry out well the revolution in literature and art, the revolution in public health, and the work with regard to the educated youth who go to mountainous and other rural areas, run the May 7 cadres schools well and support all the newly emerging things of socialism.

Economically ours is still a poor and developing country. We should thoroughly carry out the general line of going all out, aiming high and achieving greater, faster, better and more economical results in building socialism, grasp revolution, and promote production. We should continue to implement the principle of "taking agriculture as the foundation and industry as the leading factor" and the series of policies of walking on two legs, and build our country independently and with the initiative in our own hands, through self-reliance, hard struggle, diligence and frugality. Marx pointed out that "the greatest productive power is the revolutionary class itself." One basic experience from our socialist construction over more than two decades is to rely on the masses. In order to learn from Taching in industry and to learn from Tachai in agriculture, we must persist in putting proletarian politics in command, vigorously launch mass movements and give full scope to the enthusiasms, wisdom and creativeness of the masses. On this basis, planning and co-ordination must be strengthened, rational rules and regulations improved and both central and local initiative further brought into full play. Party organizations should pay close attention to questions of economic policy, concern themselves with the well-being of the masses, do a good job of investigation and study, and strive effectively to fulfil or overfulfil the state plans for developing the national economy so that our socialist economy will make still greater progress.

We should further strengthen the centralized leadership of the Party. Of the seven sectors—industry, agriculture, commerce, culture and education, the Army, the government and the Party—it is the Party that exercises overall leadership. Party committees at all levels should study "On Strengthening the Party Committee System," "Methods of Work of Party Committees" and other writings by Chairman Mao, sum up their experience and further strengthen the centralized leadership of the Party ideologically, organizationally as well as through rules and regulations. At the same time the role of revolutionary committees and mass organizations should be brought into full play. We should strengthen the leadership given to primary organizations in order to ensure that leadership there is truly in the hands of Marxists and in the hands of workers, poor and lower-middle peasants and other working people, and that the task of consolidating the dictatorship of the proletariat is fulfilled in every primary organization. Party committees at all levels should apply democratic centralism better and improve their art of leadership. It should be emphatically pointed out that quite a few Party committees are engrossed in daily routines and minor matters, paying no attention to major issues. This is very dangerous. If they do not change, they will inevitably step on to the road of revisionism. It is hoped that comrades throughout the Party, leading comrades in particular, will guard against such a tendency and earnestly change such a style of work.

The experience with regard to combining the old, the middle-aged and the young in the leadership, which the masses created during the Great Proletarian Cultural Revolution, has provided us with favourable conditions for training millions of successors to the revolutionary cause of the proletariat in accordance with the five requirements put forward by Chairman Mao. Party organizations at all levels should keep on the agenda this fundamental task which is crucial for generations to come. Chairman Mao says: "Revolutionary successors of the proletariat are invariably brought up in great storms." They must be tempered in class struggle and two-line struggle and educated by both positive and negative experience. Therefore, a genuine Communist must be ready to accept a higher or lower post and be able to stand the test of going up or stepping down many times. All cadres, veteran and new alike, must maintain close ties with the masses, be modest and prudent, guard against arrogance and impetuosity, go to any post as required by the Party and the people and firmly carry out Chairman Mao's revolutionary line and policies under every circumstance.

Comrades! The Tenth National Congress of the Party will have a far-reaching influence on the course of our Party's development. We will soon convene the Fourth National People's Congress. Our people and the revolutionary people of all countries place great hopes on our Party and our country. We are confident that our Party, under the leadership of Chairman Mao, will uphold his proletarian revolutionary line, do our work well and live up to the expectations of our people and the people throughout the world!

The future is bright, the road is tortuous. Let our whole Party unite, let our people of all nationalities unite, be resolute, fear no sacrifice and surmount every difficulty to win victory!

Long live the great, glorious and correct Communist Party of China!

Long live Marxism-Leninism-Mao Tse-tung Thought!

Long live Chairman Mao! A long, long life to Chairman Mao!

APPENDIX 6: WANG HUNG-WEN: REPORT ON THE REVISION OF THE PARTY CONSTITUTION
(August, 1973)*

[This is essentially a "Leftist manifesto" delivered by the newly elected Vice-Chairman and a former Shanghai worker, Wang Hung-wen, at the Tenth Party Congress on August 24, 1973, and adopted on August 28. It is in this report that Wang issued a rallying cry for the Leftists, a minority in the congress, when he quoted Chairman Mao and stated "Going against the tide is a Marxist-Leninist principle . . . and most important in the two-line struggle within the party."]

Comrades!

As entrusted by the Central Committee of the Party, I will now give a brief explanation of the revision of our Party's Constitution.

In accordance with the instructions of Chairman Mao and the Party's Central Committee concerning the revision of the Party Constitution, a working conference of the Central Committee which was convened last May discussed the question of revising the Party Constitution adopted at the Ninth National Congress. After that conference, the Party committees of the provinces, the municipalities directly under the central authority, and the autonomous regions, the Party committees of the greater military commands and the Party organizations directly under the Central Committee all set up groups for the revision of the Party Constitution, extensively consulted the masses inside and outside the Party and formally submitted 41 drafts to the Central Committee. At the same time, the masses inside and outside the

*From *Peking Review*, 35 and 36 (September 7, 1973), pp. 29–33.

Party in various places directly mailed in many suggestions for revision. The draft of the revised Constitution now submitted to the congress for discussion was drawn up according to Chairman Mao's specific proposals for the revision and on the basis of serious study of all the drafts and suggestions sent in.

In the discussion on the revision, all Party comrades were of the view that since the Party's Ninth National Congress, the whole Party, Army and people, guided by the line of that congress, which was formulated under the personal direction of Chairman Mao, have done the work of struggle-criticism-transformation in the Great Proletarian Cultural Revolution in a deep-going way, smashed the Lin Piao anti-Party clique and won great victories in all aspects of the domestic and international struggles. Practice over the past four years and more has fully proved that both the political line and organizational line of the Ninth Congress are correct. The Party Constitution adopted by the Ninth Congress upholds our Party's consistent and fundamental principles, reflects the new experience of the Great Proletarian Cultural Revolution and has played a positive part in the political life of our whole Party, Army and people. The stipulations in the Party Constitution adopted by the Ninth Congress regarding the nature, guiding ideology, basic programme and basic line of our Party have been retained in the general programme of the present draft. Some adjustments have been made in the structure and content. There are not many changes in the articles. The number of words has been slightly reduced. The paragraph concerning Lin Piao in the general programme of the Party Constitution adopted by the Ninth Congress was completely deleted. This was the unanimous demand of the whole Party, Army and people. It was also the inevitable result of Lin Piao's betrayal of the Party and the country and his own final rejection of the Party and people.

Compared with the Party Constitution adopted by the Ninth Congress, the present draft is mainly characterized by its richer content with regard to the experience of the struggle between the two lines. This was a common feature of all the drafts sent in. Under the leadership of Chairman Mao, our Party has been victorious in the ten major struggles between the two lines and accumulated rich experience of defeating Right and "Left" opportunist lines, which is most valuable to the whole Party. Chairman Mao says, "To lead the revolution to victory, a political party must depend on the correctness of its own political line and the solidity of its own organization." All the comrades of our Party must pay close attention to the question of line, persist in continuing the revolution under the dictatorship of the proletariat, strengthen our Party building and ensure that the Party's basic line for the historical period of socialism is carried through.

What has been added in the draft in this respect?

One. Concerning the Great Proletarian Cultural Revolution. The Great Proletarian Cultural Revolution is a great political revolution carried out under the conditions of socialism by the proletariat against the bourgeoisie and all other exploiting classes, and it is also a deep-going Party consolidation movement. During the Great Proletarian Cultural Revolution the whole Party, Army and people, under the leadership of Chairman Mao, have smashed the two bourgeois headquarters, the one headed by Liu Shao-chi and the other by Lin Piao, thus striking a hard blow at all domestic and international reactionary forces. The current Great Proletarian Cultural Revolution is absolutely necessary and most timely for consolidating the dictatorship of the proletariat, preventing capitalist restoration and building socialism. The draft fully affirms the great victories and the tremendous significance of this revolution and has the following statement explicitly written into it: "Revolutions like this will have to be carried out many times in the future." Historical experience tells us that not only will the struggle between the two classes and the two roads in society at home inevitably find expression in our Party, but imperialism and social-imperialism abroad will inevitably recruit agents from within our Party in order to carry out aggression and subversion against us. In 1966 when the Great Proletarian Cultural Revolution was just rising, Chairman Mao already pointed out: "Great disorder across the land leads to great order. And so once again every seven or eight years. Monsters and demons will jump out themselves. Determined by their own class nature, they are bound to jump out." The living reality of class struggle has confirmed and will continue to confirm this objective law as revealed by Chairman

Mao. We must heighten our vigilance and understand the protractedness and complexity of this struggle. In order to constantly consolidate the dicatorship of the proletariat and seize new victories for the socialist cause, it is necessary to deepen the socialist revolution in the ideological, political and economic spheres, to transform all those parts of the superstructure that do not conform to the socialist economic base and carry out many great political revolutions such as the Great Proletarian Cultural Revolution.

Two. Adherence to the principles: "Practise Marxism, and not revisionism; unite, and don't split; be open and aboveboard, and don't intrigue and conspire." Of these three principles—"the three dos and three don'ts"—put forward by Chairman Mao, the most fundamental is to practise Marxism and not revisionism. If one practises Marxism and wholeheartedly serves the interests of the vast majority of the people of China and the world, one is obliged to work for unity and be open and aboveboard; if one practises revisionism and exclusively serves the small number of exploiting class elements, one will inevitably go in for splits, intrigues and conspiracy. Revisionism is an international bourgeois ideological trend. Revisionists are agents whom the bourgeoisie, and imperialism, revisionism and reaction plant in our Party by means of sending them in or recruiting them from our ranks. Liu Shao-chi, Lin Piao and similar careerists, conspirators, double-dealers and absolutely unrepentant capitalist-roaders, though they manifested themselves in somewhat different ways, were all essentially the same; they were all chieftains in practising revisionism and thoroughly turned bourgeois ideologically, politically and in their way of life. They were rotten to the core! Chairman Mao says, "The rise to power of revisionism means the rise to power of the bourgeoisie." This is absolutely true. The principles of "the three dos and three don'ts" have been entered into the general programme of the draft in accordance with suggestions sent in. In Point (1) under Article 3 concerning the requirements for Party members and in Point (1) under Article 12 concerning the tasks of the primary Party organizations, the words "criticize revisionism" have been added in accordance with the views expressed by the worker, peasant and soldier comrades at the forum held by the Peking Municipal Party Committee on the revision of the Party Constitution as well as suggestions from some provinces and municipalities. Revisionism remains the main danger today. To study Marxism and criticize revisionism is our long-term task for strengthening the building of our Party ideologically.

Three. We must have the revolutionary spirit of daring to go against the tide. Chairman Mao pointed out: Going against the tide is a Marxist-Leninist principle. During the discussions on the revision of the Party Constitution, many comrades, reviewing the Party's history and their own experiences, held that this was most important in the two-line struggle within the Party. In the early period of the democratic revolution, there were several occasions when wrong lines held sway in our Party. In the later period of the democratic revolution and in the period of socialist revolution, when the correct line represented by Chairman Mao has been predominant, there have also been lessons in that certain wrong lines or wrong views were taken as correct for a time by many people and supported as such. The correct line represented by Chairman Mao has waged resolute struggles against those errors and won out. When confronted with issues that concern the line and the overall situation, a true Communist must act without any selfish considerations and dare to go against the tide, fearing neither removal from his post, expulsion from the Party, imprisonment, divorce nor guillotine.

Of course, in the face of an erroneous trend there is not only the question of whether one dares go against it but also that of whether one is able to distinguish it. Class struggle and the two-line struggle in the historical period of socialism are extremely complex. When one tendency is covered by another, many comrades often fail to note it. Moreover, those who intrigue and conspire deliberately put up false fronts, which makes it all the more difficult to discern. Through discussion, many comrades have come to realize that according to the dialectic materialist point of view, all objective things are knowable. "The naked eye is not enough, we must have the aid of the telescope and the microscope. The Marxist method is our telescope and microscope in political and military matters." So long as one diligently studies the works of Marx, Engels, Lenin and Stalin and those of Chairman Mao, takes an active part in the actual struggle and works hard to remould one's world outlook, one can constantly raise the ability to distinguish genuine from sham Marxism and differentiate between correct and wrong lines and views.

In waging struggle, we must study Chairman Mao's theory concerning the struggle between the two lines and learn from his practice; we must not only be firm in principle, but also carry out correct policies, draw a clear distinction between the two types of contradictions of different nature, make sure to unite with the vast majority and observe Party discipline.

Four. We must train millions of successors for the cause of the proletarian revolution in the course of mass struggles. Chairman Mao said, "In order to guarantee that our Party and country do not change their colour, we must not only have a correct line and correct policies but must train and bring up millions of successors who will carry on the cause of proletarian revolution." As stated above, those to be trained are not just one or two persons, but millions. Such a task cannot be fulfilled unless the whole Party attaches importance to it. In discussing the revision of the Party Constitution, many elder comrades expressed the strong desire that we must further improve the work of training successors, so that the cause of our proletarian revolution initiated by the Party under the leadership of Chairman Mao will be carried forward by an endless flow of successors. Many young comrades on their part warmly pledged to learn modestly from the strong points of veteran cadres who have been tempered through long years of revolutionary war and revolutionary struggle and have rich experience, to be strict with themselves and to do their best to carry on the revolution. Both veteran and new cadres expressed their determination to learn each other's strong points and overcome their own shortcomings. In the light of the views expressed, a sentence about the necessity of training successors has been added to the general programme of the draft, and another sentence about the application of the principle of combining the old, the middle-aged and the young in leading bodies at all levels has been added to the articles. We must, in accordance with the five requirements Chairman Mao has laid down for successors to the cause of the proletarian revolution, lay stress on selecting outstanding persons from among the workers and poor and lower-middle peasants and placing them in leading posts at all levels. Attention must also be paid to training women cadres and minority nationality cadres.

Five. We must strengthen the Party's centralized leadership and promote the Party's traditional style of work. The political party of the proletariat is the highest form of the organization of the proletariat, and the Party must exercise leadership in everything; this is an important Marxist principle. The draft has incorporated suggestions from various units on strengthening the Party's centralized leadership. It is laid down in the articles that state organs, the People's Liberation Army and revolutionary mass organizations "must all accept the Party's centralized leadership." Organizationally, the Party's centralized leadership should be given expression in two respects: First, as regards the relationship between various organizations at the same level, of the seven sectors—industry, agriculture, commerce, culture and education, the Army, the government and the Party—it is the Party that exercises overall leadership; the Party is not parallel to the others and still less is it under the leadership of any other. Second, as regards the relationship between higher and lower levels, the lower level is subordinate to the higher level, and the entire Party is subordinate to the Central Committee. This has long been a rule in our Party and it must be adhered to. We must strengthen the Party's centralized leadership, and a Party committee's leadership must not be replaced by a "joint conference" of several sectors. But at the same time, it is necessary to give full play to the role of the revolutionary committees, the other sectors and organizations at all levels. The Party committee must practise democratic centralism and strengthen its collective leadership. It must unite people "from all corners of the country" and not practise mountain-stronghold sectionalism. It must "let all people have their say" and not "let one person alone have the say." The most essential thing about the Party's centralized leadership is leadership through a correct ideological and political line. Party committees at all levels must, on the basis of Chairman Mao's revolutionary line, achieve unity in thinking, policy, plan, command and action.

The style of integrating theory with practice, maintaining close ties with the masses and practising criticism and self-criticism has been written into the general programme of the draft. Communists of the older generations are familiar with this fine tradition of our Party as cultivated by Chairman Mao; however, they still face the question of how to carry it forward under new historical conditions, whereas for the many new Party members, there is the question of learning, inheriting and carrying it forward. Chairman Mao often educates us with accounts of the Party's activities in its years of bitter struggle, asking us to share the same lot, rough or smooth, with the broad masses. We must beware of the inroads of bourgeois ideology and the attacks by sugar-coated bullets; we must be modest and prudent, work hard and lead a plain life, resolutely oppose privilege and earnestly overcome all such unhealthy tendencies as "going in by the back door."

Now, I would like to discuss with special emphasis the question of accepting criticism and supervision from the masses. Ours is a socialist country under the dictatorship of the proletariat. The working class, the poor and lower-middle peasants and the masses of working people are the masters of our country. They have the right to exercise revolutionary supervision over cadres of all ranks of our Party and state organs. This concept has taken deeper root throughout the Party, thanks to the Great Proletarian Cultural Revolution. However, there are still a small number of cadres, especially some leading cadres, who will not tolerate differing views of the masses inside or outside the Party. They even suppress criticism and retaliate, and it is quite serious in some individual cases. In handling problems among the people, Party discipline absolutely forbids such wrong practices as resorting to "suppression if unable to persuade, and arrest if unable to suppress." In the draft, the sentence that "it is absolutely impermissible to suppress criticism and to retaliate" has been added to the articles. We should approach this question from the high plane of two-line struggle to understand it, and resolutely fight against such violations of Party discipline. We must have faith in the masses, rely on them, constantly use the weapons of arousing the masses to air their views freely, write big-character posters and hold great debates and strive "to create a political situation in which there are both centralism and democracy, both discipline and freedom, both unity of will and personal ease of mind and liveliness, so as to facilitate our socialist revolution and socialist construction, make it easier to overcome difficulties, enable our country to build a modern industry and modern agriculture at a fairly rapid pace, consolidate our Party and state and make them better able to weather storm and stress.''

Six. It is our Party's consistent principle to uphold proletarian internationalism. This time we have further included ''Oppose great-power chauvinsim'' in the draft. We will forever stand together with the proletariat and the revolutionary people of the world to oppose imperialism, modern revisionism and all reaction, and at present to oppose especially the hegemonism of the two superpowers—the U.S. and the U.S.S.R. The danger of a new world war still exists. We must, without fail, prepare well against any war of aggression and guard against surprise attack by imperialism and social-imperialism.

Chairman Mao says: ''In our international relations, we Chinese people should get rid of great-power chauvinism resolutely, thoroughly, wholly and completely.'' Our country has a large population, vast territory and abundant resources. We must make our country prosperous and strong and we are fully capable of doing it. However, we must persist in the principle of ''never seek hegemony'' and must never be a superpower under any circumstances. All Party comrades must firmly bear in mind Chairman Mao's teachings that we must never be conceited, not even after a hundred years, and never be cocky, not even after the twenty-first century. At home, too, we must oppose every manifestation of ''great-power'' chauvinism, and further strengthen the revolutionary unity of the whole Party, the whole Army and the people of all the nationalities of the country to speed up our socialist revolution and socialist construction and strive to fulfil our due internationalist obligations.

Comrades! Ours is a great, glorious and correct Party. We are confident that the whole Party, acting according to the political line defined by the Tenth Congress and the new Party Constitution adopted by it, can surely build our Party into a stronger and more vigorous one. Let us, under the leadership of the Party's Central Committee headed by Chairman Mao, unite to win still greater victories!

APPENDIX 7: YANG JUNG-KUO: CONFUCIUS—A THINKER WHO STUBBORNLY UPHELD THE SLAVE SYSTEM (August, 1973)*

[Yang Jung-kuo, a professor of philosophy at the University of Canton, sounded the trumpet call for a new anti-Confucius campaign as part of the anti-Lin Piao movement in the December, 1972, issue of *Hung Chi* (The Red Flag), the party's theoretical journal. Yang's article was entitled "The Struggle Between Two Ideological Lines During the Spring and Autumn Period and the Warring States Period." Yang condemned Confucius for preaching "idealistic apriorism." Several months later, on August 7, 1973, the *People's Daily* published the following article by Yang, which was translated by *Peking Review* on October 12, 1973. Finally, the *People's Daily* announced on February 2, 1974, that "a mass political struggle to criticize Lin Piao and Confucius, initiated and led by our great leader Chairman Mao, is developing in all spheres of life." It should be noted that historical facts presented here have not necessarily been accepted outside China.]

What manner of man was Confucius, revered by China's reactionary ruling class as the "sage" for more than 2,000 years?

Lenin pointed out: "The categorical requirement of Marxist theory in investigating any social question is that it be examined within *definite* historical limits." (*The Right of Nations to Self-Determination.*) To analyse Confucius from the historical-materialist viewpoint, one must put him in the context of the class struggle of his time and see which class standpoint he took and which class interests his ideology served.

*Translation by *Peking Review*, 41 (October 12, 1973), pp. 5–9.

Confucius' Political Standpoint

Born in the State of Lu, Confucius (551–479 B.C.) was a descendant of the declining slave-owning clan aristocracy of the Yin Dynasty (c. 16th century-11th century B.C.). His times coincided with the late Spring and Autumn Period (770–476 B.C.). Owing to ruthless exploitation and oppression by the slave-owners, the slaves frequently rose in resistance. Instances of such rebellions may be cited. The slaves building city walls in the State of Chen staged an uprising in 550 B.C. The "artisans" (mostly handicraft slaves) of the royal household of Chou rebelled in 520 B.C. The handicraft slaves of the State of Wei encircled and attacked Duke Chuang of Wei in 478 B.C. and eight years later they drove Marquis Cheh out of the country. The slaves' resistance by fleeing and armed uprisings shook the rule of the slave-owning aristocracy to its foundations, with the slave system wobbling and tottering and the burgeoning feudal forces in the ascendant. Therefore, the struggle between slaves and slave-owners and between the rising landlord class and the declining slave-owning aristocracy constituted the main class contradiction and class struggle of that time.

On which side did Confucius stand? The question may be answered by the examples below.

Under the impact of the class struggle waged by the slaves and other sections of the population at that time, changes began to take place in the system of land ownership. In the Yin Dynasty (c. 16th century–11th century B.C.) and Western Chou Dynasty (c. 11th century–770 B.C.) when the slave system prevailed, all land in the country was crown-land, the property of the monarch (the royal household)—the biggest slave-owner and chieftain of the aristocrats. The dukes (the ducal households), *ching* (ministers), *ta fu* (senior officials) and lesser slave-owners had land allotted to or bestowed on them for their use, but did not own it. Such land, therefore, was called "public land." By the middle of the Spring and Autumn Period, some of the new feudal landlords had grown strong enough to reclaim more and more private land which might also be bought and sold. The royal household and the ducal households refused at first to sanction the private land but were later compelled to levy a tax on such land in order to replenish their dwindling purses, and so feudal private ownership of land came to be recognized. The State of Lu where Confucius grew up started collecting a land tax in 594 B.C. As far as land ownership was concerned, this marked the transformation from the slave system to the feudal system. From this emerged new relations of production, and there appeared landlords, tenants and land-holding peasants who came from among the commoners. Individual economy began to develop.

In Lu, representing the newly rising forces were three families, the House of Chisun, the House of Mengsun and the House of Shusun. In 562 B.C. they divided part of the land under the ducal household into three shares and each got one. The Chisuns adopted a new system of collecting land tax. Twenty-five years later, the three families further divided land of the ducal household, this time into four shares. Following the example of the Chisuns, the Mengsuns and Shusuns also switched to the land tax system and thus changed the relations of production. This was an offensive launched by the developing feudal system against the collapsing slave system, and was a progressive change.

What was the attitude of Confucius in this matter?

He took the view that the Chisun, Mengsun and Shusun families, being slave-owners and senior officials, had overstepped their authority and were undermining the traditional slave system that had existed since the Yin-Shang Dynasty. How could this be tolerated? Therefore, he did all in his power to weaken the influence of the three families so as to uphold the rule of the slave-owning ducal household of the State of Lu.

It was Confucius' disciple Jan Chiu who at the time helped the Chisuns carry out the reforms. Greatly enraged, Confucius denounced Jan Chiu as betraying the "code of the Duke of Chou," that is, the rules and regualtions in the slave society. (The 11th year of Duke Ai, *Tso Chuan* or *Tso Commentary*.) He also renounced his disciple Jan Chiu and urged his other disciples to "beat the drum and set upon him," to close in and attack Jan Chiu. ("Hsien Chin," *The Analects of Confucius*, hereafter abbreviated as *Analects*.)

Which system did Confucius uphold and which did he oppose? The answer is very clear.

There were similar cases in the State of Chi. To oppose the

corrupt slave-owning aristocracy that ruled Chi at that time, Tien Cheng-tzu (as Tien and Chen were the same family name in ancient China, he was also called Chen Cheng-tzu), a representative of that state's newly rising forces, won over the people by using a big *dou* (a Chinese unit for dry measure) in lending grain and using a small *dou* in measuring the repaid grain. Eventually, in 485 B.C., he killed Duke Chien, chieftain of the slave-owning aristocrats in Chi. Confucius was dead against this and he pressed Duke Ai of Lu to send a punitive expedition against Tien Cheng-tzu. Duke Ai flinched, knowing that he was no match for Chi.

The third instance: Confucius opposed the casting of tripods with laws inscribed on them.

Owing to the frequent resistance by the slaves and the emergence of the feudal forces at that time, the slave system could no longer be preserved by the rule of "rites." It had to be replaced by the rule of "law." The rites under the slave system in fact stipulated the relative rank or status of slave-owners and slaves. The slave-owners ruled over the slaves and their will was law. They could oppress and exploit the slaves and even kill them at will. Absolute obedience without resistance was expected from the slaves. This was known as the rule of "rites." But the slaves were very disobedient and their resistance was reported everywhere. Some people who saw this trend and were in favour of progress realized the necessity of changing the old method of rule. Some articles of law, they maintained, must be drawn up to govern the relations between aristocrats and slaves and set certain restrictions on slave-owners. These articles were called the "penal code," which was inscribed on tripods at that time for everybody to see. The process was called "casting penal tripods" and the code later developed into law—part of the superstructure in feudal society. Advocates of the rule of law in later times were the "legalists," representing the newly rising feudal forces.

Confucius was firmly opposed to this thing. When word came that the people of the State of Tsin had cast an iron penal tripod in 513 B.C, his reaction was one of furious disapproval. When aristocrats mixed with slaves, he commented, how could the aristocrats display their dignity and greatness? That would remove all difference between the noble and the lower orders, and in that case how could a state under the slave system maintain itself? (The 29th year of Duke Chao, *Tso Commentary*.)

The fourth instance: Confucius killed Shaocheng Mou.

All his life Confucius wanted to be an official to put into practice his reactionary political ideal. But not until 497 B.C. did he become minister of justice and acting prime minister of the State of Lu for only three months. Seven days after coming into office, he arrested and executed Shaocheng Mou, a noted reformer of Lu.

A "hundred schools of thought" contended during the Spring and Autumn Period and the Warring States Period (475–221 B.C.). Thinkers representing different classes founded their own schools of thought and debated with each other. Both Shaocheng Mou and Confucius took in disciples and lectured in the State of Lu but their two schools of thought were diametrically opposed to each other. The killing of Shaocheng Mou by Confucius was, in fact, a manifestation of the class struggle at that time. Let us see how Confucius pronounced the crimes of Shaocheng Mou. ("Tso Yu" in *Hsun Tzu*.)

Confucius said: Anyone found guilty of one of the following crimes should be put to death.

1. He who was bent on taking venturesome actions because he was acquainted with the changes in the ancient and modern times and understood the development of things;

2. He who did not follow the orthodox way prescribed by the slave system, but obdurately took the road of so-called reforms;

3. He who talked glibly about the reasons for such reforms;

4. He who knew a lot of the decadent and unstable phenomena under the rule of the slave sytem;

5. He who used upright and just words to describe why the slave system should be opposed.

Shaocheng Mou, said Confucius, did all these five things and therefore must be executed. Basing himself on these five charges, Confucius pronounced the accused guilty on the following counts:

1. Gathering a crowd to form an association;
2. Propagating heretical views;
3. Confusing right and wrong.

The reforms advocated by Shaocheng Mou conformed to the historical development of the time and went well with the people's aspirations. When Shaocheng Mou was killed by Confucius, even Tzu-kung—one of Confucius' disciples—thought it wrong. Shaocheng Mou was loved and respected by the people of his day who praised him as an outstanding personage.

These instances should suffice to conclude that Confucius obstinately stood on the side of the declining slave system and resolutely opposed reforms advocated by the newly rising feudal system.

In the Spring and Autumn Period, 52 slave states had become extinct and the slave system was steadily collapsing. In these circumstances Confucius put forward his political slogan: "Revive states that have been extinguished, restore families whose line of succession has been broken, and call to office those who have retired to obscurity." ("Yao Yueh," Analects.) What he wanted was to resurrect the slave states that had been destroyed, restore the authority of the slave-owning aristocracy and turn over the reins of government again to the slave-owning aristocrats who had already declined. This was an out-and-out reactionary political slogan for a return to the old. But Confucius took these as "his duty," vowing to work for their realization "until his dying day." The masses found him very annoying and a door-keeper cursed him for not knowing the times. ("One who knows the trends cannot be turned back and still wants to do it." "Hsien Wen," Analects.) He was also cursed for being a reactionary character going against the times. Confucius and his disciples in attendance went canvassing everywhere and were hounded and attacked by the masses in some places, so they had to turn tail like "homeless dogs." It was a fitting punishment for Confucius who sided with reaction.

Confucius' Thought—"Benevolence"

The core of Confucius' thought was "benevolence" whose origin can be traced to the ideology of the slave-owning class of the Yin and Western Chou Dynasties.

Benevolence was advocated by the slave-owning rulers of the Yin and Western Chou Dynasties to consolidate unity within the slave-owning class and the rule of the slave-owning aristocracy. The Chinese character *jen*, which may be rendered into English as "benevolence," was found by archaeologists on oracle bones. The slave-owners promoted benevolence because they wanted to promote affinity and unity among their kind. At the same time, they wanted to hoodwink the enslaved labouring people, make them obedient to their rule and prevent them from staging rebellions. ("The people cherish only him who is benevolent," Part 3 of Tai Chia in "The Books of Shang," *The Book of History*.) Didn't the Duke of Chou—the "sage" whom Confucius most worshipped—pronounce himself that he was benevolent and obedient to his ancestors? (Chin Teng in "The Books of Chou," *The Book of History*.) From their point of view, as long as every member of the slave-owning class loved one another and was obedient to their clan ancestors, the rule of the slave-owning aristocrats could be consolidated. Therefore, their conclusion was that "exercising benevolence among relatives" was "treasure." ("Tan Kung," *The Book of Rites*.) This shows the tremendous importance the slave-owners attached to benevolence.

Confucius made a systematic deduction of this benevolence and elaborated its meaning. According to his interpretation, benevolence included filial piety, brotherly duty (proper behaviour towards elder brothers), loyalty, forbearance, the accurate defining of concepts, virtue and wisdom. An analysis of their contents shows what class interests the Confucian ideology served.

Confucius concluded that filial piety and brotherly duty were the fundamentals of benevolence.

Why? This was because under the slave system ancient society was ruled by the clan aristocracy. The slave-owners as a ruling class belonged to the same clan and had common ancestors. Confucius thought that the sharp contradictions and strife among the slave-owners would lead to the collapse of their rule. Therefore, he pointed out that so long as all the slave-owners showed filial respect to their ancestors and parents, the slave-owners would be united vertically. By brotherly duty he meant mutual affection and love among brothers, which would unite the slave-owners horizontally. With the slave-owners united both vertically and horizontally, there would be no offending against one's superiors and no stirring up of trouble, and the rule of the clan slave-owning aristocracy could thus be made secure. At the same time, the prevalence of filial piety and brotherly duty among the slave-owners would exert such an influence on the slaves as to make them incline to kindness ("The morality of the people inclines them to kindness," "Hsueh Erh," *Analects*) and completely submissive to the rule of the slave-owners.

So-called loyalty and forbearance were meant entirely to serve the slave-owners' interests. By loyalty Confucius meant loyalty of the slaves to their owners, loyalty of the senior officials and vassals to the dukes, and loyalty of the dukes to the monarch of Chou—the aim of which was to consolidate the rule of slave-owners at different levels. In advocating forbearance, he said: "Do not do to others what you do not want others to do to you." ("Yen Yuan," *Analects.*) Forbearance as such was meant to be shown only to the declining slave-owners, but never to the slaves. A descendant of the declining slave-owning aristocracy, Confucius was obliged to take up what were considered mean jobs such as managing granaries and livestock-breeding in his youth. Thus he could be very sympathetic to persons in stations of life like himself. He proposed that one should not be too particular about the declining slave-owners. ("Do not expect one man to be capable of everything," "Wei Tzu," *Analects.*) Nor should one abandon them as long as they had done nothing seriously wrong. "Old friends should not be neglected" within the slave-owners' community, they should be united to prevent the slaves from staging rebellions.

As mentioned above, the Spring and Autumn Period was an era of great changes, an era of the new feudal forces rising to power, like the Chisuns in the State of Lu and the Tiens in the State of Chi. By attacking the reactionary rule of the slave-owning aristocracy, they had changed the original relations of production and destroyed the rule by "rites" under the slave system. These forces, according to Confucius, were not following the benevolent way because they had failed to suppress their desire and restrain their actions. He dished up the method known since the Yin and Western Chou Dynasties—"subdue oneself and return to ritual" ("Confucius declared: The ancient record says that to subdue oneself and return to ritual means benevolence." *Tso Commentary*.) Confucius told his disciple Yen Yuan: "If (a ruler) could subdue himself and return to ritual, all under heaven would submit to his benevolence." As long as the slave-owners could all control their desire and action and return to the rule by rites, their rule would be docilely obeyed by the slaves. And this was called "all under heaven would submit to his (the ruler's) benevolence." The rule of the slave-owners could thus be secured and prolonged.

Therefore, Confucius clamoured for "accurately defining concepts." ("Tzu Lu," *Analects*.)

What did he mean by "accurately defining concepts"? He meant to use subjective concepts to define and delimit objective realities.

That was because, under the savage rule of the slave-owners, the frequent slave uprisings, the rise of the emerging feudal forces and the continuous changes in the relations of production had brought serious disorder to the slave society ("the rites decayed and music ruined"). Political and military orders could not be issued from the supreme ruler of the slave-owners—the monarch of Chou. The power of the dukes of the various states was not stable either, and in some states it fell into the hands of the senior officials and vassals. On the other hand, people like Shaocheng Mou were rallying the people to assemble and form associations freely and criticizing the authorities at will. The situation was such that "the king is not a king, the minister not a minister, the father not a father and the son not a son." If this state of affairs continued, how terrible would be the outcome? So Confucius made up his mind to use the subjective concepts of the slave-owning class since the times of the Yin and Western Chou Dynasties to define and delimit the changing social realities. He hoped to restore by this method the original order—"The king is a king, the minister a minister, the father a father and the son a son"—in a vain attempt to prop up the collapsing rule of the slave-owning aristocracy.

With this in mind, it was said, he wrote a history of his time called *The Spring and Autumn Annals*. According to Mencius, the book gave the "rebellious ministers and villains" the creeps.

Proceeding from the viewpoint of accurately defining concepts and rank, it set out to reverse the realities in a changing society and restore the old order. Mencius extolled Confucius as a man who wrote *The Spring and Autumn Annals* to set right the confused concepts and rank and thereby exercised the supreme authority on behalf of the monarch of Chou, that is, consolidating the rule of the slave system. Therefore, said Mencius, this was a matter of exceptional importance and worth special mention. ("Duke Wen of Teng," Pt. 2, *Meng Tzu* or *Mencius*.)

In fact, this was nothing but another instance of the diehard standpoint of Confucius.

This was also the meaning and purpose of the benevolence advocated by Confucius.

By "virtue" or "exercising government by means of virtue," Confucius did not mean good government for the enslaved labouring people because it was applied only to the slave-owning class. An article entitled "Li Lun" (On Rites) in *Hsun Tzu* said: "Those who live in the town are mainly officials and gentlemen [big and small slave-owners]; the people [slaves] mostly live outside of the town." A statement at the time went like this: "It is by virtue by which those in the middle states are cherished; it is by punishment that the wild tribes around are awed." (The 25th year of the Duke of Hsi, *Tso Commentary*.) Here the middle states meant the towns. In other words, virtue could only be applied to the big and small slave-owners residing in the town; nothing but punishment should be applied to the enslaved labouring people residing outside of the town. Using a whip to deal with the labouring people—this was how the slave-owners "exercised good government"!

For Confucius benevolence also included "wisdom"—that is, knowledge. He spared no effort to spread the notion that "only the wise men of the upper class and the stupidity of the lower orders cannot be changed." ("Yang Huo," *Analects*.) In other words, the "sages" of the slave-owners were the talent of the upper class and the slaves were merely lower-class servants. The former were endowed with absolute wisdom and the latter with crass stupidity; the status of these two classes could never be changed. Where did the knowledge of a genius come from? He said: "Those who are born with the possession of knowledge are the highest class of men." ("Chi Shih," *Analects*.) The knowledge of a "sage," he considered, was endowed by nature and did not come from practice. In this undisguised way Confucius advocated idealist apriorism and the reactionary fallacy that "heroes are the makers of history."

Confucius, therefore, despised productive labour. When his disciple Fan Chih expressed the desire to learn something about farm labour, he flew into a rage. These were things done by slaves, Confucius bellowed, I wouldn't have anything to do with it. He abused Fan Chih as a "mean man." ("Tzu Lu," *Analects*.) But how did the labouring people answer him? An old peasant was weeding his field when Confucius passed by. He described Confucius as a parasite "whose four limbs do not toil and who does not know the difference between the five grains" and who lived on the labour of others. ("Wei Tzu," *Analects*.) This is the most correct appraisal of Confucius.

Confucius babbled about benevolence, but he excluded the slaves and other enslaved labouring people from his benevolence. As he saw it, the slaves were meant to be pushed around and enslaved and they should never be allowed to know the whys and wherefores ("The people can be herded to do things, but cannot be made to have knowledge." "Tai Po," *Analects*). He reviled them by comparing them to "birds and beasts" whom no slave-owning aristocrats cared to associate with. ("Wei Tzu," *Analects*.) He looked down upon women in particular. Both men and women slaves, he believed, were very hard to keep and deal with and therefore should be kept at a distance. ("Yang Huo," *Analects*.) According to Confucius, there might be slave-owners who lacked benevolence; but the slaves and enslaved labouring people could never have benevolence ("The Master said: Gentlemen, and yet not always benevolent, there have been, alas! But there never has been a mean man and, at the same time, benevolent." "Hsien Wen," *Analects*).

It is clearly all rubbish when Confucius said that "benevolence is to love all men." He never meant to love all people (including the slaves); he reserved his love exclusively for the slave-owning class. He talked about "overflowing in love to all" which seemed love for the general public. Owing to social changes, the character *chung* (all) had by that time lost the meaning it once had in the Yin-Shang Dynasty and the earlier years of the Western Chou Dynasty when it embraced the slaves. In Confucius' time this character denoted only "teachers of royal or ducal houses" and "ministers" (Cheng Hsuan's explanatory note in "Chu Li," *The Book of Rites*); therefore, what Confucius loved was the slave-owning class alone.

Chairman Mao has pointed out: "As for the so-called love of humanity, there has been no such all-inclusive love since humanity was divided into classes. All the ruling classes of the past were fond of advocating it, and so were many so-called sages and wise men, but nobody has every really practised it, because it is impossible in class society." (*Talks at the Yenan Forum on Literature and Art.*) We must never be deceived by Confucius. Though he mouthed such high-falutin phrases as "conduct oneself well with relatives," "give credit to the deeds of ministers," "select men of virtue," "employ the capable" and "supervise the beloved," all these "benevolent measures" were enforced only within the slave-owning class and "not applied to the people." ("Ta Chuan," *The Book of Rites.*) The slaves were excluded because they existed only to be enslaved, whipped and slaughtered.

From the simple analysis given above, we may conclude that despite the extravagant talk by Confucius about "benevolence, righteousness and virtue," all his ideas essentially served the interests of the collapsing slave-owning class of aristocracy.

At that time, Hsun Tzu and legalists such as his disciple Han Fei opposed Confucianists and took the progressive stand of the feudal class. The struggle between the Confucian school and the Legalist school before the Chin Dynasty (221–207 B.C.) was an expression of the class struggle on the ideological front at that time.

Taking the standpoint of the collapsing slave-owning aristocracy, Confucius opposed the emerging feudal forces. The essence of his thought was to uphold the rule of the slave-owning class and prove that the labouring people could only be exploited, enslaved and ruled. In other words, what he wanted to prove was "exploitation is justified and rebellion is a crime." Therefore, the latter-day exploiting classes—feudal landlord class or the bourgeoisie—felt quite free to oppose Confucius and shout

"Down with Confucius' shop" before they came to power. But once they had seized political power and turned reactionary ruling classes themselves, they would make use of Confucius' thought to deceive the labouring people and serve the interests of their own reactionary rule. That was why they had praised Confucius as the "most holy sage" for more than 2,000 years. Only by taking the proletarian standpoint and applying the Marxist historical-materialist viewpoint can we expose the reactionary character of Confucius.

Chairman Mao has taught us: "Contemporary China has grown out of the China of the past; we are Marxist in our historical approach and must not lop off our history. We should sum up our history from Confucius to Sun Yat-sen and take over this valuable legacy. This is important for guiding the great movement of today." (*The Role of the Chinese Communist Party in the National War.*)

In appraising a historical figure from the Marxist viewpoint, we must first analyse the class contradictions and the class struggle at his time, and then examine whether, under the conditions of historical development, he stood on the side of the progressive classes and advocated reform or on the side of the reactionary classes and advocated conservatism. The task of Marxists is to constantly propel history forward. What we affirm is only that which has played a progressive role in history; as to things reactionary and conservative we must firmly negate and criticize them. Criticism of Confucius' reactionary thought is therefore helpful to taking part in actual class struggle in the ideological sphere of the superstructure.

APPENDIX 8: DRAFT OF THE REVISED CONSTITUTION OF THE PEOPLE'S REPUBLIC OF CHINA (August, 1973)*

[The following is a secret draft of the revised constitution for China adopted by the First Plenary Session of the Tenth Central Committee of the Chinese Communist Party, which was held from August 25 through 28, 1973. This document was obtained through underground sources and released in Taipei, Nationalist China, on September 22, 1974. The first constitution was adopted in September, 1954, and was modeled after the Soviet constitution of 1936. A revised draft constitution was issued at the Ninth Central Committee meeting from August 23 to September 6, 1970, to legitimize the dramatic institutional, ideological, and personnel changes of the Cultural Revolution. Lin Piao was named as "Chairman Mao's close comrade-in-arms and successor." (Article 2) With the purge of Lin Piao in 1971, a new constitution was needed. The final adoption of this new draft by the National People's Congress with some modification is expected.]

Draft of the Revised Constitution of the People's Republic of China

(Adopted by the First Plenum of the
10th Central Committee of the CCP)

CHAPTER I

GENERAL PRINCIPLES

Article 1: The People's Republic of China is a socialist state of proletarian dictatorship led by the working class (through the

Background on China (September 26, 1974), B. 74–13.

Chinese Communist Party) and based on the alliance of workers and peasants.

Article 2: Chairman Mao Tse-tung is the great leader of the people of all nationalities in the entire country, the Chief of State of the proletarian dictatorship of our country, and the supreme commander of the whole army.

Article 3: All power in the People's Republic of China belongs to the people. The organs through which the people exercise power are the people's congresses at all levels with the deputies of workers, peasants, and soldiers as the main body.

The People's congresses at all levels and other state organs all practice democratic centralism. Deputies to the people's congresses at all levels are elected through democratic consultation.

The original electoral units and the electorate have the power to supervise and, in accordance with the provisions of law, to recall and replace the deputies elected by themselves.

Article 4: The People's Republic of China is a unified multi-national state. All the national autonomous regions are inseparable parts of the People's Republic of China.

All nationalities are equal, and opposed to great national chauvinism and local nationalism. All nationalities have the freedom to use their own spoken and written languages.

Article 5: The ownership of means of production in the People's Republic of China is: The state permits non-agricultural individual laborers, under the central management of urban and township street organizations and production teams of rural people's communes, to engage in individual labor provided it is within the scope permitted by law and does not exploit others. They are in the meantime to be guided gradually onto the road of socialist collectivization.

Article 6: The state sector of the economy is the leading force in the national economy.

All mineral resources, state forests, undeveloped lands, and other resources are the property of the whole people.

The state may requisition by purchase, take over for use, or nationalize both urban and rural land as well as other means of production on the conditions provided by law.

Article 7: The rural people's commune is an organization in which government and commune are combined into one.

At present, the economy of collective ownership in the rural communes generally practices three levels of ownership, namely: ownership by the commune, by the production brigade, and by the production team as the basic accounting unit.

Where the development of the collective economy of people's communes is guaranteed and has absolute superiority, members of people's commune may operate a small amount of self-reserved plots.

Article 8: Socialist public property is inviolable. The state guarantees the consolidation and development of socialist economy, and development of socialist economy, and prohibits anyone from using any tactics to sabotage the interests of socialist economy and public property.

Article 9: The state practices the socialist principles of "no work, no food," "to each according to his ability," and "distribution according to one's labor." The state protects the rights of citizens to own income from labor, savings, houses, and other means of subsistence.

Article 10: Political work is the lifeline of all works. The state acts to grasp revolution, promote production and work, promote preparations for war, and promote the systematic and proportional development of socialist economy, in order that, on the basis of continually raising social productivity, the material and cultural life of the people will be gradually improved and the independence and security of the state will be consolidated.

Article 11: All working personnel of state and other organs must study and apply in a living way the thought of Mao Tse-tung, stress proletarian politics, oppose bureaucratism, align closely with the workers and peasants as well as all laboring masses, and serve the people wholeheartedly.

Working personnel of all organs must participate in collective labor.

All state organs must practice the principle of simplified administration; their leadership organs must practice the revolutionary, three-in-one combination between army personnel, cadres and masses, and between the old, the middle-aged, and the young.

Article 12: The proletariat must exercise total dictatorship over the bourgeoisie in the superstructure, including various spheres of culture.

Culture, education, literature, arts, and scientific research must all serve proletarian politics, serve the workers, peasants, and soldiers, and unite with productive labor.

Article 13: The state safeguards the socialist system, suppresses all treasonable and counter-revolutionary activities, and punishes all traitors and counter-revolutionaries.

The state deprives landlords, rich peasants, reactionary capitalists, counter-revolutionaries, and other undesirable elements of their political rights during a specific period of time and according to law. At the same time, the state gives them the means of earning a living, in order to enable them to reform through labor and become citizens who can subsist by their own labor.

Article 14: Blooming and contending on a big scale, big-character posters, and big debates are new forms of socialist revolution created by the masses. The state protects the use of such forms by the people in mass movements, in order to create an active and lively political situation where there are both democracy and centralism, discipline and freedom, and unified will and individual contentment so as to consolidate proletarian dictatorship.

Article 15: The People's Liberation Army and the militia of China are the children of workers and peasants under the leadership of the Community Party of China and the armed forces of the whole nation.

The duty of the armed forces of the People's Republic of China is to safeguard the socialist revolution and the achievements of socialist construction, to defend sovereignty, territorial integrity and security of the state, and to guard against subversion and aggression by imperialism, social-imperialism, and their lackeys.

CHAPTER II

THE STATE STRUCTURE

SECTION 1: THE NATIONAL PEOPLE'S CONGRESS

Article 16: The National People's Congress is the highest organ of state power under the leadership of the Communist Party of China.

The National People's Congress is composed of deputies elected by provinces, autonomous regions, municipalities, the armed forces, and Chinese who live abroad. Whenever necessary, patriotic personages may be invited to participate.

The National People's Congress is elected for a term of five years, which may be extended under special circumstances.

The National People's Congress holds its session once a year, but under special circumstances the session may be convened before its due date or postponed.

Article 17: The functions and powers of the National People's Congress are: To amend the constitution, to enact the constitution, to appoint and remove the Premier of the State Council upon the recommendation by the Central Committee of the Communist Party of China, to examine and approve the state budget and the final budget and to exercise such other functions and powers as are determined by the National People's Congress

Article 18: The Standing Committee of the National People's Congress is the permanent organ of the National People's Congress. Its functions and powers are: To interpret laws before the National People's Congress, to enact laws and decrees, to appoint and remove plenipotentiary representatives stationed abroad, to receive foreign envoys, and to ratify and abrogate treaties concluded with foreign states.

The Standing Committee of the National People's Congress is composed of the chairman, the vice-chairmen, and other members who are elected or recalled by the National People's Congress.

SECTION 2: THE STATE COUNCIL

Article 19: The State Council of the Central People's Government: The State Council is responsible to the National People's Congress and its Standing Committee and reports its work thereto.

The State Council is composed of the premier, the vice-premiers, the ministers, and the chairmen of various commissions.

Article 20: The functions and powers of the State Council are: To formulate administrative measures and issue decisions and orders in accordance with the constitution, laws, and decrees; to lead centrally the work of the various ministries, commissions, and local state organs throughout the country; to enact and implement the national economic plan and the state budget; to manage the administrative affairs of the state; and to exercise such other functions and powers as are vested by the National People's Congress and its Standing Committee.

SECTION 3: LOCAL PEOPLE'S CONGRESSES AND LOCAL REVOLUTIONARY COMMITTEES AT VARIOUS LEVELS

Article 21: Local People's Congresses at various levels are local organs of state power.

The term of office of the provincial and municipal People's Congresses is five years; that of People's Congresses of special districts, cities, and counties, three years; that of People's Congresses of rural people's communes and townships, two years.

Article 22: Local revolutionary committees at various levels are the standing organs of local People's Congresses and, at the same time, people's governments of the corresponding levels.

A local revolutionary committee is composed of the chairman, the vice-chairmen, and other members, to be elected or recalled by the People's Congress of the corresponding level.

A local revolutionary committee is responsible to the People's Congress of the corresponding level and to the state organ of the next higher level and reports its work thereto.

Article 23: Local People's Congresses at various levels and the local revolutionary committees elected by the local People's Congresses therein ensure the implementation of laws and decrees in their respective areas and under the centralized planning of the state, fully develop the positiveness of local levels, lead local socialist revolution and socialist construction, review and approve local budgets and final budgets, uphold revolutionary order, and safeguard the rights of citizens.

SECTION 4: ORGANS OF SELF-GOVERNMENT OF NATIONAL AUTONOMOUS AREAS

Article 24: The organs of self-government in autonomous regions, autonomous *chou* and autonomous counties, all of which being national autonomous areas, are the People's Congresses and revolutionary committees.

The organs of self-government of national autonomous areas may exercise, in addition to the functions and powers of local state organs as prescribed in Section 3, Chapter II of the Constitution, autonomy as provided by law.

All higher state organs at various levels should fully safeguard the exercise of autonomy by organs of self-government in national autonomous areas, and positively support the various minority nationalities in promoting socialist revolution and socialist construction.

SECTION 5: TRIAL AND PROSECUTING ORGANS

Article 25: The Supreme People's Court, local people's courts at various levels, and special people's courts exercise judicial authority. People's courts at various levels are responsible to the People's Congresses and their standing organs at the corresponding levels, and report their work thereto. The standing organs of the People's Congresses at various levels appoint or remove presidents of the people's courts at the corresponding levels.

In exercising procuratorial and trial authority the mass line should be implemented. In serious counter-revolutionary and criminal cases, mass discussion and criticism should be launched.

CHAPTER III

FUNDAMENTAL RIGHTS AND DUTIES OF CITIZENS

Article 26: The most fundamental rights and duties of citizens are: To support Chairman Mao Tse-tung, to support the leadership of the Communist Party of China, to support the proletarian dictatorship, to support the socialist system, and to abide by the Constitution and laws of the People's Republic of China.

Defence of the motherland and resistance against aggression are the supreme responsibilities of every citizen.

It is the honorable duty of citizens to perform military service according to law.

Article 27: Citizens who have reached the age of 18 have the right to vote and stand for election, except those deprived by law of such rights.

Citizens have the right to work and the right to receive education. Working people have the right to rest and leisure and the right to material assistance in old age and in case of illness and disability.

Women enjoy equal rights with men. The state protects marriage, the family, and the mother and child.

The state protects the just rights and interests of Chinese residents abroad.

Article 28: Citizens enjoy freedom of speech, freedom of correspondence, freedom of publication, freedom of assembly, freedom of association, freedom of procession, freedom of demonstration, and freedom to strike. Citizens enjoy the freedom of religious belief and the freedom of iconoclasm and of propagating atheism. The freedom of person and the homes of citizens are inviolable. No citizen may be arrested except by decision of a people's court or with the approval of public security organs.

Article 29: The People's Republic of China grants asylum to any foreign national persecuted for supporting a just cause, for taking part in revolutionary activities, or for engaging in scientific research.

Chapter IV

NATIONAL FLAG, NATIONAL EMBLEM, CAPITAL

Article 30: The national flag is a red flag with five stars. The national emblem is: in the center, Tien An Men under the light of five stars, and encircled by ears of grain and a cogwheel. The capital of the People's Republic of China is Peking.

INDEX

Adult education, 120

Agriculture: policy of the People's Republic of China, 117–18; collectivization movement, 118; party communes, 118–19

All-China Federation of Literary and Art Circles, 129

American Society of Newspaper Editors, 158

Anfu warlord faction, 17

Anhwei Vernacular Daily (Anhwei-Su-hua-pao), 30

Anti-Confucius, Anti-Lin Piao campaigns, 125, 148–53, 161

Anti-Maoists, 136

Anti-Rightist campaign, 125, 127

Art, 129–31; Mao on, 96–97

Belgium, 39

Bogus, Treaty of, 13

Borodin, Mikhail, 41, 46, 47–48, 49, 50, 53

Bourgeoisie, Chinese, and new democratic culture, 98

Boxer Rebellion (I-ho Tuan), 14–15, 29, 84

Braun, Otto, 79

Canton Commune, 60

Central bureaucrat faction, 162

Central Committee faction, 64–66

Central Work Expansion Conference, 143

Chang Chi, 45

Chang Chun-ch'iao, 144, 160, 162

Chang Fu-k'uei, 58, 60

Chang Hsueh-liang, 53–54, 90

Chang Kuo-t'ao, 28, 33, 35, 36, 42, 43, 62, 74, 76, 94, 139; Long March, 80, 81, 82

Chang Shen-fu, 33

Chang T'ai-lei, 33

Chang Tso-lin, 17, 29, 53

Chang Tsung-hsiang, 19

Chang Wen-t'ien, 63, 67

Chao Shih-yen, 33

Ch'en-chung pao, 26

Ch'en Hsi-lien, 158, 160

Ch'en Kung-po, 33, 35

Ch'en Shao-yu (Wang Ming), 63, 64, 66; and returned students faction, 67–68

Ch'en T'an-ch'iu, 33, 35

Ch'en Tu-hsiu, 20, 24, 26, 35, 36, 37, 43, 50, 52, 58, 60, 64, 65, 68, 139; and early organization of Chinese Communist Party, 29–33

Ch'en Yen-nien, 33, 43

Ch'en Yi, 42, 109, 143

Ch'en Yun, 80

Ch'en Yung-kuei, 161

307

(Cheng-feng), (rectification movement), 95–96, 98, 133, 139, 142, 143, 149; in art and literature, 129–31

Cheng Wei-shan, 157

Chiang Ching (Mao's wife), 135, 142, 144, 160–61; as possible successor to Mao, 161–62

Chiang Kai-shek, 17, 28, 45–49, 67, 77, 149; studies in Russia, 41; founds Whampoa Military Academy, 42; rise to power, 46–47; northern expedition, 49–54; elected Chairman of Nationalist Party, 56; extermination campaigns, 72–73, 77, 90; second united front with Communists, 90–92; war with Japan, 93; civil war with Communists, 104, 105 ff.; accepts Japanese surrender in World War II, 105

Chih-li faction, 17

Ch'in Chi-wei, 158

Ch'in Pang-hsien, 67, 80

Ch'in Shih Huang, 105

China, 39–40; pre-Communist, 13–20; Japanese invasion of, 90–93; administrative regions under People's Republic 111; international isolation, during Cultural Revolution, 138

China National Gazette (Kuo-min jih-pao), 30

China Regeneration Society (Hsing-chung Hui), 15

Chinese characters, written, reforms of, 120–21

Chinese Communist Party, 20, 40; formation of, 23–38, 104; Marxist influence on, 24–29, 43; early organization, 29–35; membership, 34, 89; early programs, 35–38; First National Congress, 35–38; first united front with Nationalists, 39–44; Second National Congress, 41; Third National Congress, 42; Fourth National Congress, 42–43; schism, 44–49; Chiang's northern expedition, 49–54; Fifth National Congress, 52; putschism, 56–60; Sixth National Congress, 56–57, 60–62, 67; policies, 58–59; strategies, 59; factions, 64–71; soviet bases, growth of, 73–77; land policy, 74–75; Seventh National Congress, 89; second united front with Nationalists, 90–92; Yenan period, 93–97; civil war with Nationalists, 105–10; party leadership and government power, 114; communes, 118–19; ideological campaigns, 125–32; personality and factional conflicts, 138–45; purges, 147 ff., 155; Ninth National Congress, 148, 155; Tenth National Congress, 148, 157, 160; and military, 153–58; political succession, 158–63

Chinese Liberation Army, 142

Chinese National People's Congress, 112–13

Chinese Revolution of 1911, 30

Chinese Revolutionary Party, 25

Chinese Soviet Republic, 74, 75

Chinese Volunteer Army, 150

Chinese Writers Union, 130

Ch'iu Hui-tso, 153

Chou En-lai, 28, 33, 42, 43, 62, 64, 69–70, 87, 139, 140, 143, 149, 152; and Shanghai Communist movement, 50–52; as chief of military affairs committee, 60;

and returned students faction, 63; Long March, 79, 80; and Cultural Revolution, 135, 136; as successor to Mao, 158 ff.

Chou Fu-hai, 33, 35, 36

Chou Yi-ch'un, 62

Ch'ü Ch'iu-pai, 42, 43, 52, 58, 60, 64, 67, 129; assumes party leadership, 58–59; and returned students faction, 63; and Central Committee faction, 64–66

Chu Huai-ping, 92

Chu Pei-lu, 85

Chu Teh, 60, 86, 91, 106, 140, 149, 160; and First Corps of Red Army, 62, 76; Long March, 79, 80, 81, 87; and Red Army leaders faction, 69–71; as commander in chief of Red Army, 109

Civil War (1945–1949), 104, 105–10

Collectivization movement, 118

Comintern. See Communist International

Common Alliance, League of (T'ung-meng Hui), 15–16

Common Program of the People's Political Consultative Conference, 110–11, 112, 116, 119

Communism, as influenced by Mao, 89–101. See also Chinese Communist Party, Lenin, Marx, Marxism-Leninism

Communist International (Comintern), 37, 38, 40, 41, 42, 47, 48, 50, 53, 54, 57, 63, 65, 67, 81

Communist Party. See Chinese Communist Party

Communist Party Monthly, 33

Communist Youth Corps, 68–69, 76

Confucius, 31–32; anti-Confucius campaign, 125, 148, 161

Congress of the Toilers of the Far East, 39, 65

Contradiction, theory of, Mao on, 97–98

County People's Court of the People's Republic of China, 113

Cultural Revolution, 98–101. See also Great Proletarian Cultural Revolution

Democratic centralism, principle of, and PRC, 114

Democracy, and the Chinese Communist party, 31

Dewey, John, 19

Dismissal of Hai Jui, The (Wu), 144

Economy, rehabilitation of, as primary goal of PRC, 114–19

Education, under PRC, 119–21; spare-time, 119–20; adult, 120; work-study approach, 120; science, research and technology, 120; and reforms of written characters, 120–21

Eight Point Compromise, 48

Electoral law of PRC, 111

Engels, Friedrich, 20, 85, 87

Feng Kuo-chang, 17

Feng Ting, 131–32

Feng Tzu-yu, 45

Feng Yu-hsiang, 17, 46, 62

First Five-Year Plan, 117; collectivization movement, 118

First National Congress of the Chinese Communist, Party. See Chinese Communist Party

First National Congress of the Chinese Soviet Republic, 74

First National Congress of PRC, 111–12
First Peasants and Workers Army, 59
Five Antis campaign, 125, 126
Five Power Naval Treaty, 39
"Five Principles of Peaceful Co-existence," 159
Foreign Language Society, 34
Four Clearance movement, 128
Four Good Company, 154
Four Withs, 128
France, 14, 19, 39

Genghis Khan, 105
Germany, 14, 18, 19
Great Britain, 14, 17, 19, 39; Treaty of Bogus, 13
Great Leap Forward period (1958–1960), 117, 127, 131, 140, 141; party communes, 118–19
Great Proletarian Cultural Revolution (1966–1968), 125, 132, 133, 138, 147–48; events of, in chronological order, 134–37; immediate results of, 137; party purges, 147–48; and ascendancy of military, 153–58
Group Friendship, 33
Guerrilla warfare, 93; Mao on, 72–73

Han Hsien-chu, 158
Han Lin-fu, 42
Han Wu Ti, 105
Han Yu, 85
Ho Lung, 57–58, 62, 76, 79, 82, 87, 91; and Red Army leaders faction, 69; civil war, 109
Ho Meng-hsiung, 28, 33, 68
Ho Shu-heng, 33
Hong Kong, 13

Hong Kong-Canton Strike, 44
Hsi Chung-hsun, 109
Hsiang Chin-yu, 33
Hsiang Chung-fa, 60
Hsiang Ying, 74
Hsiao Ching-kuang, 109
Hsieh Ch'ih, 45
Hsu Chung-chih, 46
Hsu Hai-tung, 76
Hsu Hsiang-ch'ien, 62, 76, 82, 109
Hsu Shih-yu, 158, 160
Hsu Shu-tseng, 17
Hua Kuo-feng, 161
Huang Ko-cheng, 142
Huang Ling-shuang, 33
Huang Yung-sheng, 153
Hunan Report (Mao), 99
Hundred Schools and Hundred Flowers campaigns, 125, 126
Hungarian rebellion (1956), 126
Hurley, Patrick J., 106, 107

Ideological campaigns, 125–32
Issue of the Chinese Revolution (Ch'u), 65
Italy, 39

Jao Shu-shih, 109, 139, 140
Japan, 13, 14, 19, 39; Twenty-one Demands, 18, 30; Mukden incident and Manchurian invasion, 73; Chino-Japanese War, 90 ff., 150; attack on Pearl Harbor, 105
Jen Pi-shih, 68, 82
Joffe, A., 41
Judicial system of PRC, 113–14

K'ang Sheng, 160
K'ang Yu-wei, 14, 84
Kao Chun-man, 31
Kao Kang, 87, 139, 140
Kiangsi soviet, 70, 73, 83

Kirkuppas, 85
Kautsky, Karl, 20, 85
Khrushchev, Nikita, 141
Korean War, 150
Kuang-hsu, Emperor, 14
Kuomintang. *See* Nationalist Party

Labor Circle, 33
Labor International, 43
Labor movement, 34, 37, 43–44, 50, 51, 58, 68, 81
Laborers, 33
Land Law, and policy, Communist, 74–75
League of Common Alliance (T'ung-meng Hui), 15–16
League of Left-Wing Writers, 66
Leftist Radical faction, 161
Lenin, Nikolai, 20, 41, 85, 86, 98
Leninism, contribution of, to Chinese Communism, 124. *See also* Marxism-Leninism
Li Chen, 157
Li Chia-yi, 157
Li Chih-lung, 47
Li Chi-shen, 49, 60
Li Fu-ch'un, 33, 79
Li Han-chun, 35, 36
Li Hou-chi, 17
Li Hsien-nien, 160, 162
Li Li-san, 33, 43, 52, 60–64, 67, 69; censure, 63; line, 60–64, 66; and Central Committee faction, 64, 65–66
Li Ta, 35, 36
Li Ta-chao, 20, 24–29, 33, 35, 42, 43, 45, 68
Li Teh-sheng, 160
Li Tso-p'eng, 153
Li Tsung-jen, 49, 110
Li Wei-han, 64
Liang Ch'i-ch'ao, 84

Liao Mo-sha, 144
Liberation Army Daily, 145
Lifton, Robert J., 101
Lin Piao, 42, 91, 106, 142, 144, 159, 161; Long March, 79, 80, 87; civil war, 109; Little Red Book, 134n.; and Cultural Revolution, 135–37; rise and fall of, 148–53, 155, 157, 163
Lin Po-ch'u, 42, 87
Lin Tsu-han (Lin Po-ch'u), 42
Literature and art, 129–31; Mao on, 96–97
Little Red Book, 133–34
Liu An, 85
Liu Chih-tan, 139
Liu Hsiang, 85
Liu Jen-chin, 28, 33, 35, 36
Liu Pao-ch'eng, 79, 81, 87, 91, 109, 160
Liu Shao-ch'i, 43, 80, 87, 135, 136, 139–40, 159; purge of, 142–45, 155, 157, 161
Liu Tsung-yuan, 85
Lo Chang-lung, 28, 68
Lo Juan-huan, 109
Lo Jui-ch'ing, 142, 144
Lo Mai, 33
Lo Yi-nung, 43
Lominadze, Besso, 54, 57
Long Live the Victory of the People's War (Lin), 150
Long March, 77–83, 89
Lu Hsun, 66, 85
Lu Yun-hsiang, 17

Ma Pu-fang, 82
MacArthur, General Douglas, 105
Malinovsky, Marshal, 106
Manchu dynasty, overthrow of, 16
Mao Tse-tung, 23, 27, 28, 33, 35, 36, 42, 43, 45, 52, 58, 60, 66, 68,

69, 76, 90, 126, 154; with First Corps of Red Army, 62; flight to Chingkang Mountain, 58, 70, 71, 86; and Red Army leaders faction, 69–71; on guerrilla tactics, 72–73; and Kiang-si soviet, 70, 73, 83; and First Congress of Chinese Soviet Republic, 74; Long March, 79–83, 87; rise to power, 83–87; as classical scholar, 85; as Marxist scholar, 85–86; contribution to Marxism-Leninism, 86–87, 97–101; policy toward peasants, 86, 87; Yenan period, 93–97; on art and literature, 96–97, 129–31; on theory of contradiction, 97–98; on Cultural Revolution, 98–101; establishment of People's Republic, 103–5, 110; civil war with Nationalists, 104, 106; collectivization, 118; ideological campaigns, 126 ff.; written works, study of 128–29; and Great Proletarian Cultural Revolution, 133–38, 147; personality conflicts within party, 140 ff.; possible successors to, 148, 158–63; and Lin Piao, 148 ff.; assassination attempt, 152; on political and military power, 158

Maoism, 89, 97–101, 124, 163; analysis of, 100–1

Maring, G., 35

Marshall, General George, 104, 107–8

Marx, Karl, 20, 85, 86, 87

Marxism: and organization of Chinese Communist Party, 24–29, 43; contribution to Chinese Communism, 124. See also Communist International (Comintern)

Marxism-Leninism, Mao's contribution to, 86–87, 97–101

Mass line technique, 94–95

May Fourth Movement, 18–20, 24, 30, 68, 124

May Thirtieth Movement, 44

Meisner, Maurice, 24

Mif, Pavel, 63, 66, 67

Military, ascendancy of, during Cultural Revolution, 138, 153–58. See also People's Liberation Army, Red Army

Nanchang uprising, 57–58

Nanking, 52, 53

National Defense Council of the People's Republic of China, 113

National General Labor Union, 43

Nationalist Party (Kuomintang), 16, 17, 29, 36, 40, 56, 67, 70, 77; First Congress, 42; first united front with Communists, 41–44; schism, 44–49; Second National Congress, 45, 46; northern expedition, 49–54; extermination campaign, 72–73, 77, 80, 86, 90; second united front with Communists, 90–92; civil war, 104, 105–10

Netherlands, 39

Neumann, Heinz, 54

New China Daily, 91

New democratic culture, Mao on, 99–101

New democratic stage of the People's Republic, 111

New Fourth Army Incident, 92

New Youth (Hsin Ch'ing-nien), 26, 30, 32, 33

Ni Ssu-ch'un, 17

Nieh Jung-chen, 33, 42, 109

Nikonsky, 35

Nine Power Open Door Treaty, 39–40

On Contradiction (Mao), 97
On New Democracy (Mao), 98–99, 111
On Practice (Mao), 97
Opium War, 13
Organic Law of the Central Government, 110, 112
Organic Law of the People's Political Consultative Conference, 110

Pai Ch'ung-hsi, 49
Pao Hui-tseng, 33, 35
Paris Peace Conference (1919), 18–19
Party communes, 118–19
Pearl Harbor, Japanese attack on, 105
Peasant struggle, 58, 61; Mao's policy on, 86, 87
Peking Marxist Society, 68
Peking University, 31
P'eng Chen, 135, 144
P'eng Teh-huai, 62, 63, 70, 76, 79, 87, 91, 109, 140–42, 144
People's Commune, 127
People's Daily, 136, 144, 145
People's Liberation Army, 109, 140, 147–48, 154–55
People's Literature, 130
People's Political Consultative Conference, 110
People's Republic of China: establishment of, 103–5, 110–14; important documents, 110–11; new democratic stage, 111; government organization, 110–13; voting privileges, 111; constitution, as different from Soviet constitution, 112–13; state adminis-

tration, 113–14; and principle of democratic centralism, 114; early national priorities, 114–22; economic objectives, 116–17; agriculture, 117–18; education, 119–20; public health, 121
Period of readjustment (1960–65), 117
Period of rehabilitation (1949–52), 117
Personality conflicts, with Chinese Communist Party, 138–46
Pi Ting-chun, 158
Po Yi-po, 109
Polevoy, Sergei A., 28
Polish Communists, 126
Political Consultative Conference, 106, 107. *See also* People's Political Consultative Conference
Portugal, 39
Progressive Party (Chinputang), 25, 26
Provincial People's Court of the People's Republic of China, 113
Public health, PRC policy on, 121
Purges, 147–48, 155

Real work faction, 68–69
Rectification movement (*Chengfeng*), 95–96, 98, 133, 139, 142, 143, 149; in art and literature, 129–31
Red Army, 58, 67, 69, 70–71, 74; organization of, 61–62; expansion of, 76–77, 89; and Long March, 77–83; makeup of, 76–77; as Eighth Route Army, 91–92; field armies in civil war, 109
Red Army leaders faction, 69–71
Red Guards, 133, 135, 137
Reform Movement of 1898, 14–15, 29, 84

Reformative Study, 125

Report on Tactics of Fighting Japanese Imperialism (Mao), 98

Reston, James, 121

Returned students faction, 66–68, 80

Revolutionary committees, organization of, 135, 136, 137, 318

Roy, M. N., 52, 53

Russia, 14, 17, 20, 39, 40. *See also* Soviet Union

Russian Revolution, 26–27

Schurmann, Franz, 163

Science: Communist Party and, 31; under PRC, 120

Selected Writings (Mao), 85

Shanghai, 50–52

Shanghai General Labor Union, 50, 51

Shao Ch'uan-lin, 130–31

Snow, Edgar, 77, 85

"Snow" (Mao), 104–5

Socialist education campaigns, 127–28, 129

Socialist Youth Corps, 33–35, 37

Socialist Youth League, 69

Soong Mei-ling, 53

Soviet governmental structure, of the Chinese Soviet Republic, 75–76

Soviets, 86, 87

Soviet Union, 126; Comintern, 37, 38, 40, 41, 42, 47, 48, 50, 53, 54, 57, 63, 65, 67, 81; advisers to Chinese Communists, 41, 46, 47; in Manchuria, 106; assistance, 108; withdrawal of aid, 127; danger of war with, 138; constitution, compared to Chinese constitution, 112–13

Spare-time education, 120

Spengler, Joseph J., 101

Ssu-ma Ch'ien, 85

Ssu-ma Kuang, 85

Stalin, Joseph, 52–53, 54, 86, 104

"Struggle in the Chingkang Mountains" (Mao), 86

Su Chao-cheng, 50

Su Yu, 109

Sukarno, President, 143

Sun Ch'uan-fang, 17

Sun Yat-sen, Dr., 17, 25, 29, 36, 40, 41, 45, 46, 53; revolution, 15–16, 84; Three People's Principles, 56

Sun Yat-sen, Madame, 53

Sung T'ai Tsu, 105

Superfluous Words (Ch'ü), 66

Supreme People's Court of the People's Republic of China, 113, 137

Supreme People's Procuratorate of People's Republic of China, 113–14

Supreme State Council of the People's Republic of China, 113

Tagore, Rabindranath, 19

Tai Chi-t'ao, 28

T'an Chih-t'ang, 33

T'an P'ing-shan, 33, 42, 50

T'ang Sheng-chih, 17, 49, 52

T'ang T'ai Tsung, 105

Teng Chung-hsia, 28, 33

Teng En-ming, 35

T'eng Hai-ch'ing, 157

Teng Hsiao-p'ing, 109, 135, 139, 144, 160, 162

T'eng Tai-yuan, 62

Teng T'o, 144

Third International, 48

Thought Reform campaign, 125

Three Antis and Five Antis campaigns, 125, 126
Three Fixes and One Substitution, 128
Three-Eight Working-Style campaign, 154–55
Three People's Principles, 15–16
Three Red Flags policy, 127
T'ien Han, 132
Ting Shen, 158
Truman, Harry, 107
Ts'ai Ch'ang, 33
Ts'ai Ho-sen, 33, 43
Ts'ai Yuan-p'ei, 31
Ts'ao Ju-lin, 19
Ts'ao K'un, 17
Tseng Mei, 157
Tseng Ssu-yu, 158
Tso Ch'iu-ming, 85
Tuan Ch'i-jui, 17
Tuan Teh-ch'ang, 62
Tung Chung-shu, 85
Tung Pi-wu, 33, 35, 160
Twenty-eight Bolsheviks faction, 66–68
Twenty-one Demands, 18, 30

United States, 39; aid to Nationalists, 105, 106; hands-off policy toward China, 108; danger of war with China, 138

Violence and Politics (li), 26
Voitinsky, Gregori, 28, 32, 34, 68
Voitinsky, H. N., 50
Von Ketteler, Minister, 15
Von Seeckt, General, 77

Wang Chia-hsiang, 79
Wang Ching-wei, 33, 35, 45, 46, 49, 52, 53, 93
Wang Fu-chih, 84

Wang Hung-wen, 160, 162
Wang Ming. See Ch'en Shao-yu
Wang Jo-fei, 33
Wang Pi-cheng, 158
Wang Tung-hsiang, 157, 160
War of Resistance Against Japanese Aggression, 89
Warlords, 16–17, 25, 30, 40–41, 44, 49, 52
Washington Conference, 39–40
Wei Kuo-ch'ing, 161
Wei Li-Huang, 91
Wen Yu-ch'eng, 157
Whampoa Military Academy, 42, 45, 46
White terror (Anti-Maoists), 136
Women, 33
Work-study programs, 120
World War II, 105
Wu Fa-hsien, 153
Wu Han, 144–45
Wu P'ei-fu, 17
Wu Teh, 160, 161
Wuhan Communists, 49–53, 56, 57

Yang Ch'ang-chi, 84
Yang Cheng-wu, 137
Yang Chun-sheng, 157
Yang Hsien-chen, 129–30
Yang Hu-ch'eng, 90
Yang Ming-chai, 68
Yang Sen, 70
Yang Shan-te, 17
Yang Teh-chih, 158
Yang Yung, 157, 158
Yao Wen-yuan, 144, 160
Yeh Chien-ying, 42, 160
Yeh Chun, 151
Yeh T'ing, 57–58
Yen Hsi-shan, 17, 62
Yenan, 108
Yenan period, 83, 93–97

Yu Fang-chou, 42
Yu Sang, 157
Yu Shu-te, 42
Yuan Ming-hsun, 33

Yuan Shih-k'ai, 16, 18, 25, 30, 69
Yung Tai-ying, 33

Zinoviev, G. E., 40